12 Vows to Stay Married
Forever After

Jerry and Shari Rhoads

12 Vows to Stay Married
Forever After

(A TRUE STORY ABOUT STAYING MARRIED FOR 60+ YEARS AND LIVING FOREVER AFTER)

Jerry and Shari Rhoads

Copyright © 2021 by Jerry and Shari Rhoads

All rights reserved. This book or any portion thereof may not be reproduced or transmitted in any form or manner, electronic or mechanical, including photocopying, recording, or by any information storage or retrieval system, without the express written permission of the copyright owner except for the use of brief quotations in a book review or other noncommercial uses permitted by copyright law.

Printed in the United States of America

Library of Congress Control Number:	2021907852
ISBN: Softcover	978-1-63871-102-5
eBook	978-1-63871-103-2

Republished by: PageTurner Press and Media LLC
Publication Date: 04/22/2021

To order copies of this book, contact:

PageTurner Press and Media
Phone: 1-888-447-9651
order@pageturner.us
www.pageturner.us

CONTENTS

PART ONE 12 VOWS TO STAY MARRIED FOREVER AFTER

Get What They've Got
(A True Story Of Longevity And Ageless Living)   1

PART TWO: MARRIAGE VOWS AND LIFESTYLE HABITS

One: Think And Grow Younger Together	36
Two: Hey Good Looking What You Cooking	79
Three: Sex, Kids And Rock-N-Roll	99
Four: Have A Purpose And Destination	129
Five: My Body Is Agile, My Marriage is Fragile	154
Six: Consumption Is For Living Not Dying	186
Seven: Fun Is A Remedy For Stress and Distressed Marriages	208
Eight: Be Better Soul Mates	228
Nine: Be Satisfied With Your Love Life	247
Ten: Give of Yourself for Staying Married	261
Eleven: Be Smart With Your Money and Honey	285
Twelve: Get And Stay Good With Your Matchmaker	313
Last Chapter & Verse: Love Now and Live Forever After	346
Authors' Bio And List Of The Titles	361

Part One
12 VOWS TO STAY MARRIED FOREVER AFTER

Every year more than 2.4 million marriages that end in divorce, 117 million people struggle with chronic illness and as of 2020, the Covid-19 pandemic has affected more than 26,000,000 people. With death and despair omnipresent, the world needs some hope. Jerry and Shari Rhoads are uniquely qualified to write a book about the secret to a successful marriage. They have been married for more than sixty years, each celebrating their eightieth birthday near their milestone anniversary. It's more than compatibility and good genes that have kept them alive and together for more than three-quarters of their lives. Throughout their decades-long love story, they have built a solid relationship based on trust, friendship and adventure that has resulted in four children, twelve grandchildren and eight great grandchildren.

Jerry and Shari's 12 Marriage Vows and Lifestyle Habits, when followed, allow newlyweds to have a long and loving life together. They also apply to older couples who find themselves in need of a refresher course in love and what they need to do to either stay happy or find their way back to better times. Not only do the Rhoades have a literal lifetime of married experiences and wisdom to share with the reader, they both come from the healthcare and nursing home industry. So, they are professionally trained as well. Unlike other "how-to" marriage books, this one is authored by a couple who has defied the odds and has lived and taught by example.

What are the odds of living forever and a marriage lasting 60+ years? Experts calculate that only 1 in 600,000 marriages will last 60+ years. And .001 per 1,000 will last 70 years. To our knowledge none have lived forever after. However, it's our goal to break the world's record of 90 years or die happy trying. Of course, we will be in our hundreds and can't possibly live forever … or can we? That's another 30 years … how in our world can you live that long, look good and feel good doing it? Our answer is love is eternal and we are living OUR life, married for ever after.

WHAT'S LOVE

It's never saying no to sharing
It's giving up and caring
Our lives and paring

Why then do we love?

It's a disposition to sacrifice
And reasons for another's attention
Without fear and apprehension

Who do you love?

That someone outside your selfish zone
Who finds you and you alone
Alluring to the eye beauty prone

When do you love?

It doesn't matter
For love is the only way
To capture Cupid's play

How do you find love?

Seek and you shall find
The right circumstance
Giving into the lore of romance

Where can you find love?

Of course it could be one event
But more so it's your ability to consent
To a best friend's needs with no dissent

Will Love last forever?

True love is always there
Waiting for you to share
Something you cherish and forebear

How do I know it's a soul mate?

A soul mate becomes your mentor
Sharing life's problems front and center
The maker of one heart from two parts
And a future with no new starts

THAT'S LOVE

READ THIS TRUE STORY OF HOW "JERRY MET SHARI" AND

How To Get What They've Got: Jerry at 81 looks 55, Shari at 80 looks 50 … no way that picture on the cover can be them now … that's not real … or they're photo shopped or air brushed! Well, what's real or not is what we got … if you want what we got listen to the song (Genius version paraphrased) and read and dream on …

I want what they've got

Until the stars disappear
And the sun's coming in my eyes
I want what she's got

I can see her heart

And not the rules we live by I
want what he's got
I feel our hands will catch.
Whatever may come

I want what they've got
She says life is a toy
It's not a game
Don't be afraid to be caught

I wish I felt the same
To be someone I'm not
I want what they've got

We believe we are reality, due to our lifestyle, and everyone we meet wants to know "what's your secret for being married 60 years and how can we get what you've got"? With tongue in cheek, I get a laugh, when I say its 'Sex, Kids and Rock -N-Roll." But in essence, it's a give and take loyal partnership and we have defied the conventional aging wisdom … which is retire at 55, 60 or 65 and start the dying process. We however, in our early seventies, acquired three nursing homes then sold them in our late seventies and started a new career … co-writing this book about how our vows and habits formed a lasting happy lifestyle and relationship, reforming them if needed, to stay married and live together ever after …

Surely no one lives forever
But as the rose dies in the winter
And rises again in the spring
Together with this wedding ring

We vow that our soul and spirit live on
Happily ever After
To another dawn

This phrase borrowed, from fairy tale endings, is used to suggest that everything will work out perfectly in the future. It's often used after a couple has just gotten married. "It was a beautiful wedding, and I just know that Jerry and Shari will live happily ever after from this day forward until death do them part" … however it's not like Jerry and Shari magically lived happily ever after, certainly not forever … it takes a lot of hard work to keep a relationship healthy and happy as long as we live. And to our credit …

Americans are getting married later and later. The average age of first marriage in the United States is 27 for women and 29 for men, up from 23 for women and 26 for men in 1990 and 20 and 22 in 1960. The average age for couples going through their first divorce is 30 years old. According to the most recent U.S. Census Bureau statistics, only about 5 percent of married couples ever achieve even a 50th anniversary. That makes our 60th Diamond Anniversary an exclusive club that we will enter in 2019 and at the age of 80, and we plan to live happily and heathy ever after.

Ironically, research shows that marriage contributes to good health, and people who are healthier tend to live longer. Married men and women appear to be less likely to have or engage in unhealthy behaviors. What is it about marriage that leads to a longer, healthier life? Is marriage a means to achieving better health? If so, why is getting a divorce the new norm afflicting more than 50 percent of the marriages? How does this affect the children left behind?

6 OBSTACLES TO MARRIAGE AND LIFE'S LONGEVITY:

1. Divorce and separation of families
2. Chronic illness causing chronic aging lifestyles
3. Inactivity due to technology and lifestyles
4. Worry about Finances and Hurry as the work hours increase and savings decrease
5. Resistance to change even though it's your desire
6. Job stress, or loss or unemployment destroying self-worth and self-image

Most people already know that around 50 percent of marriages in the United States end in divorce. When you break that down by number of marriages:

- 41 percent of first marriages end in divorce.
- 60 percent of second marriages end in divorce.
- 73 percent of third marriages end in divorce.

SIX STEPS TO A HAPPY MARRIAGE AND LIFE'S LONGEVITY:

1. Unconditional Love – Commitment, Romance, affection, loyalty, passion

2. Regular (often) Sexual encounters - Patience, honesty, satisfaction
3. Work and play - Courtesy, determination, prudence, joy
4. Hope -and faith - Laughing, fun, listening to your heart
5. Family and friends - Fun, loyalty, honesty, listening
6. Regular physical exercise - Commitment, consistency, goals

EMOTIONS

I got a handle on my shovel
I got a job to earn my pay
But my emotions are in upheaval
And keep getting in the way

It seems life is spent chasing
Chasing a job during the day
Then at night we are embracing
So we can share where we lay

Two sided lifestyles in our time
Causing us problems as they betray
The results of getting out of line
If we let our morals decay

God and offspring are the spectators
Letting us feel emotions as we play
Much like the tireless gladiators
They then let obsession get carried away

Dying from a debtor's lifestyle
Dishonor every day
Never knowing all the while
The price we'll have to pay

To test our emotions
To test us of our will to say
Leave me to my devotions
Which are to love and then play

For it's our life's work which must root us
Not pleasure nor in its search should we dismay
To such we must carry shallow lust

And let love rise from our emotional disarray
Stability is the lasting reward
Devotion to emotion is not
Promiscuity will take us downward
Wasting all the good times forgot

Having the good wife
And having a good job yes
But the essence of happiness
Is having a good faithful life

Hopefully with our first wife

Our advice is to "Stay Married and Get What We Got": We believe wedding vows are sacred, a permanent commitment to the sanctity of an eternal bond .... In sickness and health, richer or poorer,

In love and happiness
Till forever after is in our heart
And death as our witness
Fate nor chance shall never do us part

My wife Shari and I have been together 62 years as best friends. From the time I saw her standing there in front of Indianola Junior High in 1953, I've never loved another. She was 13 and I was 14. But she wouldn't date me until 1957. After 4 children, 12 grandchildren and 8 great grandchildren we are still in love and happily married for 60 years. (Not even the Chicago Cubs have that distinction, and I've loved them and divorced them many times since 1947).

Although the skeptics question our obvious longevity ... "oh sure, **you're lucky to have the genes** you inherited from your parents" ... just wait a minute ... my parents died of strokes in despicable nursing homes and Shari's mother of Alzheimer's due to a false diagnosis, her sister of cancer, her brother and her father of heart failure and cancer and a nephew of a stroke at the age of 49. We are living proof that genes aren't our destiny. And please don't think we have an unfair advantage because of luck or circumstances. I'm a skin cancer survivor and Shari is bionic with a pacemaker for a congenital heart condition. Scientists call it transcending the human genome.

THE INSPIRATION: We want to prevent or reverse these trends with our book about the 12 Wedding Vows (habits) principally for brides (and their grooms) past and present. In the book we have defined our personal success, not as a physical diet to lose weight or a makeover to be more attractive, but how to form and retain relationships to be happily married for life. Much like the famous self-help book "Think and Grow Rich" we have coined the phrase "Think and Grow Young, Together". Meaning longevity of a marriage and life itself first requires adherence to a healthy lifestyle. We believe people will live longer once they learn how to live together forever after ...

TILL FATE DO US PART

I saw her standing there
Unaware not seeing me stare
I do believe she could feel me
And not touch me

I do believe she could want me
And not need me
I do believe she could love me
And not notice me

I do believe there's friendship
Without pleasure
That there is worth
Without treasure

I do believe I can feel her
And not touch her
I do believe I can want her
And not have her

I do believe I can love her

And not possess her
I do believe I can be her friend
Without measure

Because I too believe a certain event
Is meant to occur
Certain thoughts are meant
Certain feelings don't deter

The embrace of a loving friendship
The spirit of matrimony
The law of attraction we worship

Life without acrimony

Nor do I believe in chance
When a life is put in motion
By romance
With happiness as the potion

For I didn't have to touch her
To feel her
I didn't want to hold her
To possess her
I didn't need to possess her
To love her

All I must do is take
Her in my heart
For my soul
And as my mate
As I have taken you
You have taken me
Not as a possession
Not as a passing passion
But a vow without end
As my best friend

Surely no one lives forever
But as the rose dies in the winter
And rises again in the spring
Together with this wedding ring

We vow that forever after our soul and spirit live on
To another dawn till fate do us part

According to the most recent U.S. Census Bureau statistics, only about 5 percent of married couples ever achieve even a 50th anniversary. That makes our 60th Diamond Anniversary an exclusive club that we will enter November 29, 2019 and I will be an octogenarian. It seems impossible that Shari and I have been together since 1951 when I first saw her standing there and fell in love with the image and 1956 when she finally said yes to our first date … in 1959 I took her hand and 60 years later I'm still falling in love with her reality …and have never fallen out of love with her congeniality.

FALLING IN LOVE

Falling in love
Is a feeling
Not an event

Falling out of love
Is a concession
To some event

Falling in is easier
Than a falling out
To say the least

At least falling in
Is fun and lasting
If the falling out

Becomes the final event

Such as infidelity
Abuse
Financial disaster
Injury to one or the other
Mental breakdown
Death of the romance

Falling back in love
Is an event
To restore that feeling

Reconciliation
Counseling
Mutual admiration

But 50% of the time
A falling out
Means a falling into

Divorce

The other 50% of the time
A falling out

And a falling in love

Are both avoiding
The ultimate fall
A heartache for all

FALLING TO PIECES
(excerpt 3 the song by the Script)

What am I gonna to do when the best part of me was always you,
And what am I supposed to say when I'm all choked up and you're OK
I'm falling to pieces, yeah
I'm falling to pieces, yeah
I'm falling to pieces

(One still in love while the other ones leaving)
I'm falling to pieces
('Cause when a heart breaks no it don't breakeven)

STATISTICS ON THE LIKELIHOOD OF DIVORCE

- If your parents are happily married, your risk of divorce decreases by 14 percent.
- People who wait to marry until they are over the age of 25 are 24 percent less likely to get divorced.
- Living together prior to getting married can increase the chance of getting divorced by as much as 40 percent.
- If you've attended college, your risk of divorce decreases by 13 percent.
- The divorce rate among couples with children is 40 percent lower than couples without children.
- Forty-three percent of children growing up in America today are being raised without their fathers.
- Seventy-five percent of children with divorced parents live with their mother.
- Twenty-eight percent of children living with a divorced parent live in a household with an income below the poverty line.

- Half of American children will witness the breakup of a parent's marriage. Of these children, close to half will also see the breakup of a parent's second marriage.
- How Much Does a Typical Wedding Cost? For three marriage you've invested over $75,000 with no return if it doesn't last.

AVOID THE SILENT COMEDY
(awaiting thee who are silent)

My air exhaled is your air inhaled
Air is our connection for our life
I exhale You inhale
The same sustenance for man and wife

It's not incidental or free
It's Zen favors
A silent comedy
That oft errors

We exchange vows
Lives are changed
A silent comedy
With no script arranged

By the thought police
I think you dream
You think I scheme
We think we redeem

A silent tragedy

With a silent laugh
No breath is shared
We don't talk with our other half
We don't make like we cared

If I exhale or you inhale
The same sustenance of life
You receive my breath though stale

And then you're not now my wife
If you now reject my hale

I will be your ex-
If you reject my in-
Our lives will be Hell

If we don't make it romance
Silently we unload our resort
A Zen silent game of chance
Before the divorce court

Loudly crying for our identity

Playing poker with our Heart
Your diamonds clubs in your cart
While I hold the Jack of Spades
And all my chips in a stack
And your hope for the Joker fades

Meant to have your back

As the Kings and Queens
Fold their hands
And hold their breath
Playing out the silent comedy

For the silent connection dies
When a breath of love
Could sustain our lives

Without alimony being our fitful glove
The price we pay for the Silent Comedy
Settling up never settles the silence

OKAY LET'S JUST SAY IT'S GENETICS OR THE LUCK OF THE DRAW

And please don't think we have an unfair advantage because of luck or circumstances. It's the fact we've been married 60 years and covet our happiness and good health together. If you've been in a long-term relationship, you know that some romantic relationships, family members, and "friends" can reduce your life expectancy just as easily as they can extend it! The real trick is making the most of what you have and figuring out what's right for you. You only need to change what's turning your Fountain off exposing you to the chronic aging process. Just by reducing the stress of chronic harmful habits extends your life.

That 60-year club becomes even more exclusive with divorce rates exceeding 50% and the BABY BOOMERS exploding our health care costs with chronic aging embracing 125 million Americans with their unhealthy lifestyle habits. Chronic diseases are the biggest threat to longevity. ***Chronic aging is defined as a lifestyle that either creates chronic health problems or accelerates the natural aging process by exposing people to chronic diseases.*** It's estimated that 61 million of aging American have up to five active chronic diseases. And they are being told by researches and medical experts that most are unavoidable and irreversible. Why? Because "Modern Medicine" makes its revenue based on this theory. Pills and treatment are the protocol.

Clearly, 80% of the nation's $3.3 trillion health care costs are attributable to chronic illnesses caused by the chronic aging process.

READ MY LIPS OR MY HIPS … IT'S LIFESTYLE HABITS AND EPIGENETICS

LIFESTYLE HABITS

Only if I had another life to live
Happy birthday would be my time to give

But talk is free
Health isn't granted
Time is taken
Habit isn't planted

Pride is stilted
Death is sudden
Where my vow is jilted
I'm ever too young for heaven

Lifestyles call collect
And expect fulfillment
As we play at life so we can expect
To live and pay by slowing decent

There's no compromise to make it work
Not even work equals time missed

If our personal perspective we shirk
Reality is poor lifestyle habits to resist

To pursue our dreams
Our pleasures over the blues
As illusive treasures it seems
Lifestyles are fruits of "free to choose"

No Bourgeois
No politburo
No Third Reich
No Mafia
No KKK
In our way

No inhibition to live
And let live
To try
And let try

Except the golden rule
"In a lifestyle chosen
We can bluff and free a fool
With inhibitions we thought frozen"

Letting life warm the highs
Before the opportunity dies
By saving lives without demise
Read my lips it's the style not the size

The healthy lifestyle is a second chance at
happiness and longevity in disguise

According to the experts, Epigenetics is the study of changes in an organism's DNA caused by modification of the gene's RNA expression, rather than alteration of the genetic code itself. "Epigenetics has transformed the way we think about genomes." Chronic illnesses and chronic aging syndrome are not genetically programmed into our cells but are the foundation for preventing such an occurrence. That is the DNA Fountain of Youth awaiting our personal turning off of harmful habits and turning on youthful habits. According to Depok Chopra in his book Super Genes we control our own well-being.

Not since Juan Ponce de Leon searched for the literal Fountain of water, that supposedly restores the youth of anyone who drinks or bathes in it and couldn't find it, while others have claimed to have it in a pill or supplement or plastic surgery or in a book. You don't have to be a Tibetan Monk practicing rite of rejuvenation ... you only have to change your lifestyle in 12 easy steps. So, why do we all mentally still chase the fictional Fountain of Youth when, according to researchers, you have in your own DNA genes, those that you may have turned off with harmful habits, that are shortening your life and marriage. By turning them back on, since your DNA and RNA in your cells have memory, you will alter your lifestyle habits and longevity. (*According to research Diseases are caused by a combination of genes working in concert with epigenetic factors that turn those genes on and off ... behaviorally known as habits*).

FOUTAIN OF (YOU)TH
(Ageless is the fountain of you)

I'm thinking of beautiful you
And the way we were
When we were younger
And times they weren't blue

Holding hands that opines
Talking of dreams and plans
Embracing as love entwines
Simple as wedding our hands

It seems we've always been together
You and I are a pull and a boost
Through sunshine and stormy weather
You've helped me to come and roost

Yes, it's beautiful you and I
Never through never to die
And I'm finding the truth
That we're the Fountain of Youth
From out-growing immature plans
The pallor of your beautiful skin
Awaiting the touch of my hands
Your beauty deeper than Botox is thin

With a physical body a wonder land
You're so beautiful as our mantle

To find that fidelity does demand
Love as the Fountain's chattel

So, as I finish this piece
Lie down beside our pew
The rest is to be laid in peace
As I commit love eternal to

The Fountain of you
(As Love and Relationships create and sustain the Sanctity of Marriage)

THE SCIENCE:

Most experts who write books about health and wellness: 1) Don't focus on marriage as a defining factor or reactor, 2) Don't focus specifically avoiding premature aging, 3) Don't propose how to prevent chronic aging as a solution to habitual problems such as mood, diet, exercise or sex drive, 4) Offer just one type of solution, often in the form of a pill that, nine times out of ten, doesn't fix the underlying problem, 5) Don't fully understand the aging audience they're prescribing solutions for, and/or 6) Aren't credible due to lack of tangible evidence that their offerings do work. It's more about the science and theory than the practice of living younger, stronger and longer. And that's exactly what this book was designed to do … give you a template for turning your natural Fountain of Youth back on.

In the book The Biology of Belief: Dr. Bruce Lippton the current expert on the science of Epigenetics sets the scene through his research and other leading-edge scientists, stunning new discoveries have been made about the interaction between your mind and body and the processes by which cells receive information. It shows that genes and DNA do not control our biology, that instead DNA is controlled by signals from outside the cell, including the energetic messages emanating from our thoughts. Using simple language, illustrations, humor, and everyday examples, he demonstrates how the new science of Epigenetics is revolutionizing our understanding of the link between mind and matter and the profound effects it has on our personal lives and the collective life of our species. author of The Biology

This book is Shari and my prescription for overcoming the "Law of Reaction" using our 12 Vows (HABITS) for living a fulfilling and gratifying life of reflection that predetermines longevity, strength of body and mind, prosperity and success, with eternal love for our relationships. It is our experience that this will overcome a life of reaction and prevent the inevitable chronic aging that is afflicting Americans more than ever. Over our 60 years (ongoing and forever) of our relationship and marriage we have discovered the 12 lifestyle habits for living younger-stronger-longer than our peers. This is reflected in our biological Real Age calculation (Dr. Roizen's formula) as twenty years younger and stronger than our chronical birth age. It is the very essence of our relationship when it comes to life's adventures and conquests said best by this poem.

GIVE HER A CHANCE

Give her a chance to be great
Don't ask your mate to sit and wait
On the roost at home
When she also has the urge to fly and roam

The family unit yes, it's divine
And raising children is the woman's incline
But I think us guys have to recognize
That she also is seeking life's full prize

She is asked to set down the roots
While he flies around to bring home the loots
He looks to her to be in her place
And guide him home from the rat race

She on the other hand may have a different idea
To dock the ship and calm the sea
For she wants him to understand priority
That for sure it's her responsibility

To clean the boots and mend the family lace
But she also wants to taste the air of outer space
Up where the sky is clear blue and rainbows start
And things look brand new and far apart

This is only natural and such
For a cinder in the clutch
Shall never be a pearl
Till that woman can still feel like a little girl

With the excitement and sensation
Of having some impact on creation
So you guys must recognize
That to let her fly up into your skies

Is to let her see the benefits of her plan
So diligently and on the other hand
It might not hurt for you to land
And see what it's like to stand

Upon the ground
With the fruits of your labor all around
While she can see how being home bound
Is the thrill of the love you've found

Yes, by giving her a chance
To understand how being me will enhance
That such a flight is about being free
The ultimate romance being her being me

We used these rules of the "Rhoads" in the nursing homes we consulted with, managed or owned. We took despicable nursing homes and either assisted or managed them based on these 12 aspects of our programming to restore functionality and cognition and rehabilitate patients' physical and mental capacity to enable them to return to their families. If they had to remain in our facility their quality of life was ensured by these 12 Vows of life. As a result, we were able to restore and rehabilitate thousands of patients back to their families, homes and communities. These 12 Vows/habits are the 12 chapters implementing the longevity in our lives and in the lives of those in the 141 nursing homes that we were involved in.

THE DNA FOUNTAIN OF YOU(TH)

Do you dread looking in the morning mirror? Was it looking back at you older and weaker? Are you looking wrinkled and tired? Are you sexually inactive and would like to be more attractive to your mate? Is your marriage unstable? Is your weight bothering you and affecting what you eat? Have you consulted your doctor about fatigue and libido? Are your personal finances stressing you out? Do you wish you could sleep longer and better? Do you hate the thought of physical exercise? Do you forget your cocktail of pills at night or in the morning? Have you prayed for a better life?

These are symptoms of chronic aging. I certainly have suffered from them, thought them or done them myself. Of course, many of them apply to us because we are victims of bad habits that dwell in our subconscious. And not all of them are relevant to you or I or my mate or my family. But they exist and are lowering our chance to age naturally and lowering our real age score below our birth age. This, and the need to have some control over longevity, mean these chronic habits must be first acknowledged avoided and if necessary reversed.

We all suffer or thrive on our subconscious habits. This is the Law of Reaction to:

1. Our mate, spouse or significant other (soul or other)
2. Our family (extended or blended)
3. Our sex life (not exciting or regular)
4. Our diet and sleep patterns (can't eat or sleep well)
5. Our physical and mental health (exercise of body and brain)
6. Our relationships (friends and neighbors)
7. Our social beliefs (values, feelings, opinions and attitudes)
8. Our will to change (we become what we think we are)
9. Our stress levels (stressed out due to money and future)
10. Our work and financial condition (career and job)
11. Our spiritual beliefs (we are what we affirm we are)
12. And most importantly … Our longevity (real age is higher than birth age)

Lifestyle is defined as the nature of one's habits, habitat and habitual decisions for life's work, family, happiness, health and career. Since Chronic aging is a lifestyle that either creates chronic health problems or accelerates the natural aging process by exposing people to chronic diseases. True prevention requires making lifestyle choices that keep those diseases from showing up at all. To change ourselves and prevent or reverse Chronic Aging we must adopt lifestyles that either avoid chronic health problems or slow the natural aging process by protecting aging Americans from chronic diseases. Preventing chronic diseases is to treat the cause with a combination of natural diets and physical or psychological exercises in concert with a mapping of the epigenetic factors that turn those genes on and off… behaviorally known as the 12 natural Lifestyle habits.

12 Natural health remedies for changing the outcome of your inherited genes:

1. *Hope and understanding using the power of the mind*
2. *Positive thinking knowing that nothing positive can be attained with negative outcomes*
3. *Believing in something that you cannot control*
4. *Faith and vision to follow the footsteps of a higher being*

5. Sleeping well with restful nights
6. Exercising the body, mind and attitude
7. Diet of moderate but fulfilling consumption that feels right
8. Fun and games with family and friends
9. Relationships based on love and giving of yourself to another
10. Relaxation/meditation for those quiet times with yourself
11. Purpose is to have the energy to get up in the morning and work late at night
12. Success at last not as a destination but a journey = Lifestyle for all the ages

The experts on life styles and behavior have found that the social fitness is connected to that portion of the brain storing subconscious beliefs. First being social is being a friend, while being sociable is being a family. Being married can be sociable without first trying it out to see if it works. Today's society condones living together before marriage. Our children have done it but without our permission. In our day, it just wasn't done so the following poem is just our opinion and our advice to those who believe commitment comes first then the other social events come out better. On the other hand, it has worked out for some members of our family. Take this advice in the context of your personal situation and apply it if possible.

"Next Generation Advice" by Alyson Hudson … I quote: "When you fall in love with someone and decide to move in together, you are essentially picking, the fruit before it's ready to come off the vine. You are acting like a husband and a wife … sharing bills, moments, chores, meals and a bed, but that's just it: You are acting like something you are not. Until you say "I do" in the public arena, you are not an authentic husband or wife, you are pretending. I've seen some pretty good ceramic fruit in my day. It's pretty to look at, but you can't eat fake (or unripe) fruit no matter how attractive it looks". So take the path as you will but remember marriage is a commitment to stay together forever after the love making.

COME LIVE WITH ME

You say you love me
And I know you do
But prove it to your heart
Come live with me too

To dreams so far
Till you know who we are
You say you need me
And I know don't you see

Prove it to your arms
Come hold my charms
To keep us together
Through any stormy weather

You say you want me
I know you don't you see
Come take my hand
But prove it with a wedding band

It's about today and anytime
So want away my doubt
And say you're mine
And I'll know it's about

Proving it to you

Come live with me

And fold your wings
In line with mine
Don't just fly away from rings

To someone else's roost

Granted there's no perfect way
To confirm your commitment
All I'm trying to say
Is take the moment to prevent

Parting as permanent mates
Take the odds 100% chance to stay
While sex awaits
Together forever the old fashion way

Make this our wedding day

(Live in Divorce rates in America exceeds 50%)

On average, researchers concluded that couples who lived together before they tied the knot saw a 33 percent higher rate of divorce than those who waited to live together until after they were married … sex a reason not the means to an end. It seems to be the culture. So, not to judge those that do it successfully please warn your children of the risk they take by not enjoying a wedding cake before living together. If this sounds self-serving Shari and I believe in some old fashion ways and feel it's worth what it pays … 60 years of a happy and healthy marriage

Clearly most people blame circumstances for bad luck and avoidance of being diligent about their personal health. But Shari and I believe we have found the **six steps and twelve Marriage Vows to a happy, healthy and prosperous life:**

FALLING IN LOVE

Falling in love
Is a feeling
Not an event

Falling out of love
Is a concession
To some event

Falling in is easier
Than a falling out
To say the least

At least falling in
Is fun and lasting
If the falling out

Becomes the final event

Such as infidelity
Abuse
Financial disaster
Injury to one or the other
Mental breakdown
Death of the romance

Falling back in love
Is an event
To restore that feeling

Reconciliation
Counseling
Mutual admiration

But 50% of the time
A falling out
Means a falling into

Divorce

The other 50% of the time
A falling out
And a falling in love

Are both avoiding
The ultimate fall
A heartache for all

By turning back on "Your DNA Fountain of Youth", you will find as we did, longevity will be perpetuated by a renewed love for life, each other, and other people (as well as rock-n-roll, but that's optional). Our family of four grown children, twelve grown-up grandchildren and eight great-grandchildren will be the first to tell you our "12 Vows (HABITS) to Stay Healthy and Happily Married" work. It's not about the genes you were born with, or the jeans you can't wear but the jeans you want to wear.

Therefore, when Jerry met Shari we began a lifestyle based on our ingrained habits that emanated from our parents, friends, mentors forming our beliefs, values and life changing decisions. Ever maturing and changing into what we're calling "Finding Our DNA Fountain of Youth". The technical and science aspects of aging of how this happens is presented in each chapter labeled habits one through 12 for the readers' use in changing the pace of their aging process. The most important thing to learn and understand is how life style affects how and at what rate you age. Note to the reader: our hope is to make this an enjoyable journey to help you find your own DNA Fountain of Youth. We will speak to you from a female and male voice to widen our point of view. We have also included poems to give you a more personalized perspective of the reason and results of each lifestyle habit.

Life and marriage aren't the sum of our years, like it or not, it's the sum of our daily habits." This book is based on actual events about how Shari and I successfully applied lifestyle genetics in our lives and in our nursing home patients' restorative care. It's more than self-help for your job, it's self-health for your life. It's 12 Vows (HABITS) that will make or break your marriage and life. Now that this new science of Epigenetics: is re-coding our genes by changing how we live we have the latest and greatest discovery of the 21st century ... "genes are not our destiny". They are our opportunity to live longer and stronger. Read my hips it's about our environment and daily HABITS that determine longevity.

THE OUTCOME:

This means that our weight, appearance, happiness, health, relationships, prosperity, faith, sex life, intelligence, behavior are all dictated by our DNA and genetic response to outside stimuli. That response can be positive or negative depending upon our subconscious mind and its habitual routines. This is where the mind needs to be turning on the right response rather than the wrong reaction to determine the results. In effect you control your own Fountain of Youth. The faucet (RNA), so to speak, is turned on by your reward and off by your negative reaction which means you are in control of how you age and how long you live.

How's that going to work for you if you're too old before your time, divorced, sick, unhappy in a nursing home for the last ten years of a miserable (chronological) chronic aging life. It's about the quality of your entire life not the number on your birthday card. The research shows that harmful habits are a subconscious brain function and a body behavior function (muscle has memory) so the solution is in how you think, act and behave that affects your other genetic brain and body functions for feeling good or bad. So, the change of a harmful habit to a youthful habit will make a genetic change in your body's ability to reverse chronic aging and never stop being the you in Youth.

Researchers have found that on the day one becomes an Octogenarian (80 to 89), nature bestows a mathematical birthday gift: a gradual reprieve from the relentlessly increasing likelihood that he or she will die in the coming year. An analysis of 4,000 very long-lived Italians suggests that the rise in in the risk of imminent death continues to slow until the age of 105. After that researches estimate to making it to another birthday holds steady at 50-50. The mortality rate levels off the data suggests. Or in other words if you haven't already killed yourself with bad habits an 80-year-old stands a better chance of being a centenarian than a 65year old. So maybe life does start at 70 and the chances of 100 get better with each day.

In summary our "12 Vows (HABITS) to Stay Happily Married" have become the healthy habits that contributed to our longevity in sixty years of marriage and our upcoming eighty years of our happy, healthy and prosperous lives… here's hoping that we can help you along the same "Rhoads" to a longer, stronger and younger life avoiding chronic aging and a nursing home.

BREAKING UP

Breaking up is so hard to undo

Love's so easy when I'm thinking of you
Love's the easiest thing I have to do
Times have been good and times have been bad
But being with you is more glad than sad

Yes love's so easy until we have to part
Leaving you a piece of my hear
That way you'll always know
That it's your looks I'm loving so

Love's so easy when it's being you

Love's the easiest thing I have to do
And though it seems a permanent way
For me to say
I need to see you every day

And though that need cannot now be fulfilled
For even the mockingbird has been killed
Trading love for passion must be chilled
For to the heart love must be tilled
Not just romance to which we've thrilled

Yes love's so easy
Loving you

It's the easiest thing
I don't have to do

But breaking up is so hard to undo
(Shari and I let ourselves break-up
Something we could make-up
Into something no one nor event can undo)

Breaking up never breaks even

MAKING UP

Loving you is better than fighting you tonight
Loving you is better than getting uptight
Loving you makes everything all right
I've been down and broken to pieces

Choking on words and desire which never ceases
Loving you is better than anything I've ever done
Loving you puts the brightness in my sun
Loving you I don't know what I would do
If I weren't loving you

They say you stay too busy to be sad
Work and work till you're glad
Glad we'll have times together
Like flocking birds of a feather
There's nothing better than the clearing
After our stormy weather

Yes loving you is better than fighting you
Loving you is better than anything I have to do
Let your defenses down
Put your hair up
Don't give your cares a sound
For this is too good to disrupt

Loving you would be so easy
If you had truly been loving me
So no one could corrupt
That feeling I've had for you

Yes loving you is the easiest thing
I don't have to undo

Because making up is the easiest thing to do
But making do never makes do

HOW LONG DO YOU WANT TO LIVE?

Facts (the challenge for Americans):

- 65% to 70% of Americans are obese or on their way.
- 80% of Americans will die before their time.
- 90% of Americans do not knowingly strive to live for wellness and fitness.
- 100% of Americans eventually die but most due to untimely deaths.

In fact, there is a new study reported by JAMA and AARP that suggests a "public health crisis" … the study done by the National Institute of Alcohol Abuse and Alcoholism found "that Alcohol abuse soars by 106.7% in the last ten years for older Americans. Baby Boomers had higher levels of drinking and drug use said Director George Koob". "Another possible factor: recent economic stresses for older Americans. The 2008 recession had a toll on the most vulnerable, said Bridget Grant, the lead author of the study". "Brenda Iliff, executive director of Hazelden of Florida was "shocked by the study results".

LIFE EXPECTANCY TABLE

YEAR	AVG	MALE	FEMALE
1900	42	40	45
1925	54	50	55
1950	62	55	60
1975	63	60	65
2000	77	76	82
2010	79	77	81
2017	78.6	75	79
2020	77.4	74	78
2025 (estimates) life expectancy	73	73	75
Possible Life Expectancy		100	120

For the second time in three years, life expectancy in the U.S. has ticked downward. In three reports issued Thursday November 29, 2018 the Centers for Disease Control and Prevention laid out a series of statistics that revealed some troubling trend lines — including rapidly increasing rates of death from drug overdoses and suicide. CDC Director Robert Redfield described the data as "troubling." "Life expectancy gives us a snapshot of the Nation's overall health and these sobering statistics are a wakeup call that we are losing too many Americans, too early and too often, to conditions that are preventable," he said in a statement released November 29, 2018. (Updated for 2020 Pandemic 77.4).

Redfield tied the drop in overall life expectancy, which averaged 78.6 years in 2017, a decrease of 0.1 from the year before, to the rise in deaths from overdose and suicide. Read the CDC reports: More than 70,000 people died of drug overdoses last year alone, according to the CDC. That number marks a nearly 10 percent increase from 2016 and the highest ever in the United States for a single year. By comparison, only about 17,000 people died of overdoses in 1999, the earliest year for which the CDC offered data.

THE GOOD NEWS

Scientists once thought an average life expectancy beyond 90 was impossible. Now they are estimating that people in some countries will eventually survive an average of at least 100 to 120 years of age. While most people born in rich countries will live longer by 2030, Americans will have one of the lower life expectancies and highest divorce rates of any developed country.

Dan Buettner, an explorer and researcher for National Geographic, was looking for the reasons why natives in certain areas of the world live longer then the U.S. He deduces that we should live to at least 120 by making a case for certain areas of the world that promote better health and longevity called "blue zones." Examples were from the far reaches of the World include Okinawa, Sardinia, Loma Linda, California, Nicoya Peninsula, Cost Rica. He deduced their type of lifestyle could solve America's environmental problems and lead to a longer and stronger life. This would entail environmental changes in our society that would contribute to longer life.

I for one, as the coauthor of this book, wrote a contradiction to the Blue Zone hypothesis, called "America in the Red Zone", that predicted such an approach would not change one habit or lifestyle. It takes changing a culture of whole communities to do what "Blue Zones" propose. And it hasn't, so far, done what was promised in numerous communities across the country. In my opinion we as individuals will never go back to what Buettner found in Okinawa, Sardinia and Costa Rico which was self-preservation and starvation. America will not change without a reason as presented in this book and America in the Red Zone makes the case that the only long-lasting effective way to improve American cultural longevity and environment is for individuals to break bad habits through thinking and doing the right things. Marriage longevity being the most important for health, happiness and prosperity. That's the underlying benefit or what this book is about.

CAN WE AVOID OR REVERSE CHRONIC AGING?

It obviously depends on who you ask … physicians and pharmacists say no way, nutritionists and fitness gurus say of course. When we mention living longer most people, if truthful, cringe about being old, sick and living unhappily in a failed marriage or in a nursing home. Why? Because our culture doesn't focus on health for longevity but health for self-satisfaction during the journey. "If I have to suffer, I don't want anything to do with it. I would rather live my way now and not worry about later!" How's that going to work for you when you are old before your time, sick, unhappy in a nursing home for the last ten years. It's about the quality of your entire life. Your Real Age versus your Birth Age is a good indicator of whether you should avoid or reverse Chronic Aging … to avoid is to change before Chronic Aging starts and to reverse is to make up for the time you've lost to unhealthy lifestyle habits. Thus, you need to know your Real Age in relation to your birth age. Then decide to either avoid or reverse where you are and how you're aging.

YOUR BIRTH AGE VS. YOUR REAL AGE
(Chronological Age Versus Biological Age) … the true measure of our lifestyle habits

Millions of people have taken Dr. Oz and Dr. Roizen's Real Age® Test. www.realage.com. Find out how old you are. Go to their web site or other biological calculators http://www.biological-age.com/# and get your score. We've used this test more than once to inspire ourselves and our family to live longer, better and together forever. By answering yes or no to the question, "Do I believe my real age is determinable?" you will know where you're going with this book. It takes belief in change to make it happen.

	Birth Age	Real Age	Difference
Beggining Real Age Score	_____	_____	+/- _____

If your Birth age is less than your Real Age calculation and you're honest with yourself, you are aging too fast a rate. More than likely, for 90% who take the test, the Real Age will be more than the birth age. Is it a scientific reality? It's up to you to decide, but that's the experts' opinion and the only way of getting everyone's attention on practicing healthy habits. Look at it as an opportunity to be your own doctor before you get what most Americans have, which is 1 to 4 chronic diseases and a declining life expectancy. Traceable to harmful personal habits.

DNA Genetic Check-up:

Ask yourself the following questions to see the areas where you can improve:

QUESTION	YES	NO
Do you know what your Real Age is vs. your Birth Age?		
Is your Real Age les than your Birth Age?		
Do you ever avoid looking in the mirror?		
Do you feel strong and energetic?		
Does your doctor say you're in good health?		
Are you as sexually active as you'd like to be?		
Do you sleep well?		
Do you have a regular exercise routine?		
Do you have hobbies you enjoy?		
Are you giving back to others?		
Do you have good friends?		
Do you have close relationships with your family?		
Do you laugh a lot every day?		
Are you being smart with your finances?		
Do you have a good relationship with God or Source?		

The No's tell your story about avoiding or reversing Chronic Aging. All though the above might seem like a lot, but if you don't fix those N0's now... Then when will you fix those No's?

- Life is short...
- And you're not getting any younger.
- Take a chance on change!
- Age changes some things, but not everything.
- We might be getting older, but Shari and I are also getting better.
- Join us on our journey to help you do the same.

Part Two

MARRIAGE VOWS AND LIFESTYLE HABITS

HOW THIS BOOK IS ORGANIZED

"Stay Married, Live Longer and Get What We Got" contains one chapter for each of the 12 Ways to Stay healthy and happy together forever after. We present the bad versus the good habits. The Do's versus the Don'ts. We're going to give you an inside look at how we have evolved our current aging profile and our relationship that underlies our Real Age data. When I first started working for Arthur Andersen & Co. in Chicago, I was taught to start every written plan of action with an objective, follow it with goals, benchmarks, procedures and finish it with a conclusion and a follow-up evaluation. To do this, each of the 12 chapters includes:

- Topical anecdote for change
- Values – objectives
- Feelings – goals
- Research and Statistics – benchmarks
- Action Plan – procedures and commitment
- Outcome – conclusion
- Self-Evaluation – measuring progress
- Affirmations – positive reinforcement
- Poems – for additional inspiration and reflection

We also have a Girl Talk and Guy Talk section in each chapter since men and women want and need to hear different things perspectives when it comes to each habit. There is also a short quiz at the end of each chapter to help you determine where you are at any point in your journey to a better Real Age and the underlying habits that take you there, along with a self-rating score of you progress. If you want better scores reread the chapter and work on your exercises enclosed for that purpose.

Read our book, practice the 12 Vows/Habits these chapters propose and practice the steps you score low in. We realize you may be strong in any number of the 12 vows (habits) but we have found that we have to practice them daily until they become second nature and like the .300 hundred hitters in baseball, we must take habit practice every day. We must change our lifestyle to fit our dreams for them to come true and our work habits to finance those dreams and our marriage habits to be happy and healthy forever after. Such as,

WHAT I SHOULD HAVE SAID

Why don't we
Dance anymore
Romance anymore
Talk or whisper low anymore
Let each other know fun anymore
Embrace sex anymore
Look at each other's eyes anymore
Smile in front of the children anymore

Why is it
So hard to get me involved
So hard to get my silence resolved
When it was we that grew apart absolved
Until we aren't in each other's heart
You have just asked for a new start
That you get the kids scot free
And say we can part amicably

Do I
Have any recourse
By the look in your eye
I think you said yes
I guess I don't understand guilt
I am ready to confess
So tell me how we can begin again
Tell me how we can be lovers and a friend
As we did when we first met before this end

You say
We can do it by just talking
You feel we can do this without

Mocking each other
We can embrace and take joy in

Passion once again
Seeing each other's eyes
Each other's face
All these things we haven't been able to do

Oh, Is that what's bothering you
What I should have said
Is it
As simple as just talking out these things
If so I say let's start right now and if need be
You can show me how to say what I haven't done
How we can again have fun
As we heard in our wedding song
So I begin to see what's wrong

Why don't we
"Just close the door when I don't
Talk anymore
And open it with amour"
An illicit love affair together
For the excitement of being newly wed
In our new-found bed
Turned into a licit thrill instead
Overcoming what I should have said

Avoiding divorce and its obstacle course

Poetry is a good way to express our feelings verbally. We have chosen this median to express our feelings about a productive lifestyle as we age and the importance of having love, family and work to fulfill our healthy lives. The poems that appear in this book are also published in our five Wonders of the World poetry books. They are meant to inspire not look to retire; to set a fire not change your attire; to set goals higher not to expire too soon; to forget prior habits not seek hopes too dire. Life is meant to be a high flyer not a high wire. (Here's an idea, Jerry reads poetry to Shari each night in bed, so use our book to recite with your spouse).

SHARI AND I HEREWITH GIVE YOU THE 12 VOWS /HABITS TO GET WHAT WE GOT – A HEALTHY MARRIAGE LOVED AND LIVED HAPPILY EVER AFTER … SO HELP US GOD!

1. How we think and act younger
2. How we strive to look better, feel better, be more attractive
3. How we relate to each other, and others
4. How we plan for the future and solve life's problems
5. How we exercise for feeling fit
6. How we consume a living recipe for wellness
7. How we better ourselves in our work and play
8. How we treat others especially family members
9. How we give of ourselves to others
10. How we continue to learn and experience from love
11. How we budget our time and resources
12. How we honor our spirit and match maker

HOW TO LIVE FOREVER AFTER

Life has no age
It only has you
Love has no limit

It only has us

Feelings have no time
They only show us the way
Memories have no reason

They only pass us by

Birthdays have no certainty
They just count for today
Marriage Vows are our enduring

Legacy for living longer and stronger

Surely no one lives forever
But you've just met Jerry and Shari
We Believe our spirit lives on

Together forever after
As love is eternal

Marriage Vow/Lifestyle Habit Number One:
THINK AND GROW YOUNGER TOGETHER

> *"Your beliefs become your thoughts,*
> *Your thoughts become your words,*
> *Your words become your actions,*
> *Your actions become your habits,*
> *Your habits become your values,*
> *Your values become your destiny."*
>
> — Mahatma Gandhi

THINK AND GROW YOUNGER TOGETHER

Marriage Vows become thoughts and good INTENTIONS become BAD habits. Our marriage vows are our opportunity to stay married so we can live longer and younger. In a life where thoughts are things and happiness is what marriage brings.

WE CAN LIVE FOREVER YOUNG

Birthdays have no certainty
They just count for today

Habits are our enduring
Legacy for living younger longer and stronger

*Surely no one lives forever
But you've just met Jerry and Shari*

*We Believe our spirit lives on
Together forever after
For love is eternal*

As our habits are its kernel

This Marriage Vow and Lifestyle Habit explains how to change your thinking habits that can stress you out and age you prematurely, so you can attain a younger outlook and lifestyle. It's also about how to avoid or reverse the unhealthy life style habits and behaviors that result in poor decisions that lead to chronic aging. Like the famous self-help book "Think and Grow Rich" we have coined the phrase "Think and Grow Young Together". We are what we think we are ... says the author of "The Secret", Rhonda Byrne. What is the formula for changing our "getting old" thinking to "getting young" thinking?

How check out my Real Age?... am I older than I look or younger than I am?

Where should I put my emphasis?... females on their shape the males their fitness

What is my preference for youthful looks? ... choose good taste visual and physical

Who is my best critic?... you yourself and I

When should I be the happiest with myself?... on the scale or mirror with positive self-image

Why is thinking young important to relationships, longevity and a healthy lifestyle:

It's an expression of self-image ... mental wellbeing is a DE stressor

It relieves morbid thoughts of getting older ... youth flows eternal

It slows the aging clock ... happier is the fountain of youth

It prevents chronic aging... a youthful attitude is fearless

It demonstrates a strength in the person ... acting young is reality

It builds permanence and a feeling of security ... a positive codependency

It may make or break your marriage ... your behavior and thinking are your vows

It's making youth your pursuit ... morning, noon or night

It's a trait that shows inner beauty ... your children will inherit your youthful ways

Shari and I are exact opposites: She's a Libra and I'm a Sagittarian. She would rather have fun than work and I would rather work than have fun. We're different in many other ways as well, but we both know the number one habit to stay happy and healthy is thinking and acting young. This Marriage Vow and Lifestyle Habit reveals how to maintain a positive outlook as a key strategy to thinking and acting young. It explains the difference between thinking old and being old, and reveals some of the bad habits and stinkin'-thinkin' that makes people unhealthy and unhappy.

We really are what we think we are. And, if we want to change our thoughts, we must choose to change our thought processes, most of which are learned from childhood and have become subconscious feelings and responses to situations without well thought out consequences. It just happens without restraint, until we take responsibility for changing the outcome.

Changing your thinking about Aging will eventually change your lifestyle to healthy habits just waiting to happen. It's your reward for changing daily routines. Think young, act young and be forever young. The brain has this amazing ability to find happiness even when the memories of it are gone. Much like the famous self-help book "Think and Grow Rich" we have coined the phrase "Think and Grow Young". And that's exactly what this book was designed to do. Give you a template for turning your natural DNA Fountain of Youth back on. This is the organic response to life that we got when Jerry met Shari ... by believing we will always be young. It's the Fountain we were born with and will bless our future generations by helping them to find or regain their natural DNA Fountain of Youth. So, they can avoid the stresses of chronic aging.

- And please don't think there is no such thing as The DNA Fountain of Youth or that we have an unfair advantage because we've been married 60 years and were meant for each other. Our own DNA Fountain of Youth has been turned down by stress, harmful habits and a belief that we can't control our genes. You only need to change what's turning your DN Fountain Of You off.

- And this will subconsciously turn it back on. Not since Juan Ponce de Leon searched for the literal Fountain of water, that supposedly restores the youth of anyone who drinks or bathes in it and couldn't find it, others have claimed to have it in a pill or supplement or plastic surgery. Good luck finding it that way but with a little faith, effort and rock-n-roll you can last 60+ years in a relationship.

- "When Jerry met Shari" we were fortunate to have fallen in love young, married young, had children young, changed our lifestyle young, had grandchildren young, great grandchildren young and have never thought we are old …so our Fountain has never been completely turned off by chronic disease or aging. However, in our "Guy and Girl Talk" sessions we confess how the Fountain has dribbled at times and had to be regained.

THINKING OLD

AARP membership at 55 (assumes you will retire at the age of 55) that becomes an insurance company for financing old age … old? … over 65, drawing social security, past its time, out of stock, rickety, weak, no longer relevant, retired, over the hill, decrepit, out of touch, past your prime, and divorced. Ironically, if you believe you're old you are old at any age. My point is usually to define old as someone else not me. Of course, that is just a mental exercise for ignoring fate.

Let's try another definition: old, little or no exercise, poor eating habits, hateful attitude, decrepit, cynical, low esteem, unworthy, unemployed, divorced, sickly, dull, boring, unhappy, dead before death and an expiring member of AARP. And another: Trans-ager, like teenager, is the aging process where your birth age is lower than your Real Age based on your harmful habits. If you are any of these conscious states you are aging too fast and are not far from disease, chemical use, poverty, lack of friends, spouses, children, relationships…you're old at any age.

Lifestyle habits that contribute to aging too fast:

- Divorces over 50% of those who marry get divorced
- Drug use over 75% of those depressed actively use drugs, alcohol or substances to drop out
- Life expectancy is measuring death not life
    - Females 80
    - *Males 70*
- Retirement is reducing lifestyles not inducing better health
    - Females 62
    - Males 65

Signs and symptoms of true youth that we should pursue at any age:
- Happy
- Healthy
- Prosperous
- Faithful spouse
- Positive Attitude
- Goal Seeking Purpose

What's your emotional and mental age? Have you now determined your real age? If you are emotionally old … the sun is setting on your future. No hope, no job, no marriage, no relationships, no life. If you are mentally old, the moon has eclipsed on your past, no dreams fulfilled, no love gained, no successful events, no joyful memories, no happy bed time stories, no value of life as you know it. This state-of-affairs must be reversed for you to age naturally, happy, healthy, and prosperous. Many will just accept unhappiness as happenstance that one must endure, while in waiting for circumstance to change. Guess what, it does not happen if your stance is on blaming others or just good ole circumstance. The cure is, as always, in your head … you either think young or feel old … why not feel young and forget thinking old. Make it your new routine.

There is a story told in baseball about Yogi Berra when he was the skipper for the New York Yankees…in the ninth inning of game 7 of the World Series the opposition had the tying run on base and two outs … Yogi goes to the mound to direct the relief pitcher on what to do … he proceeded to tell the pitcher "to not walk the hitter, throw the ball over the plate"… walked back to the dugout and watched the pitcher do exactly what was planted in his head … he threw the ball over the plate and the hitter drove it into the seats to win the game.

The power of suggestion is stronger than will power! Yogi was a great catcher but not a successful manager … instead of telling the pitcher what to do; "strike him out by throwing your curve ball outside and low" he planted a seed of failure in the pitcher's head that created a negative outcome.

What to do is be conscious of our decisions and not letting our subconscious control our lives … for it is the subconscious that plays back learned responses based on "what not to do". You can have a choice if you reprogram your routine responses. Use the power of suggestion on yourself and beat the Yogi syndrome. So, to change the way we respond to situations not circumstances, we must change our subconscious. This will take mental exercising our daily routines in advance in a positive manner.

For example, today is Monday and we have just had a miserable weekend due to anger and disappointment. The mental state is one of dread and dislike for our jobs and current circumstances. The mental state is negative and the day will be negative if approached from this perspective. When this happens, awareness must enter your mind, and take a 180 degree turn for the betterment of your day. So, on Monday you will want to forget Saturday and Sunday…knowingly basing the week on better thoughts for better days.

THE LIFESTYLE VOWS FOR AGING …
www.lifestylesforaging.com

What is aging? "Aging is not, according to Dr. Roizen author of the book Real Age, a mysterious metaphysical phenomenon. Aging happens in the particulars of your arteries and body systems. Age is not just a chronological measurement; it's the rate at which the primary internal guardians of health – your cardiovascular and immune systems --- decline". The bigger question is how do we stop the decline and slow our aging process. Read his lips "it's your habits that dictate your aging."

The experts on behavior have found that our attitudes are all connected to the subconscious mind, the brain and heart manager. They function as the habit commander in chief for situations that demand a reaction. Am I hungry? What will I do tonight? Who will I talk to? How will I raise my kids? Attitudes are changeable in an instant with a comment … "I agree with you and I respect your opinion. Have you considered alternatives? Let's talk this out before we make any decisions. Two minds are always better than one ego or bad attitude. I personally have a hard time verbally expressing my feelings so I became a poet with a tape recorder. The outcome was five books of poetry but more importantly it shows my wife, children and grandchildren that I am human and want them to know how much I love them. They now know more about my feelings of a caring human being. It also has improved my spelling and vocabulary.

BEHAVIOR

A man is not what he says
But what he does
No man can judge another
Not even his sister or brother

By what they say
Or what their thoughts are today

There's just no way
To determine what a man was
Unless you look at what he does

Because we mortals
Have only visual portals
We cannot see between
What a man will do
And what he will mean

We also can't know
Where his thinking will go
All we can possibly observe
Is what his behavior will serve

For behavior is the master
The predictor of an impending disaster
For man cannot conceal
What his actions make real

For it is not what a man says
That was
It's what the man does
That is

The act is above intentions
And forever will be beyond pretentions
In spite of feelings for the past
Behavior is the die we cast

Well, you need to be looking or have opportunity take you there because most of us do not have the awareness to recognize our special talents let alone capitalize on them. In my case I went from being a bored auditor to becoming a health care expert because the company I worked for said I could, and would not accept anything less. But my first mentor was a Rabbi who owned nursing homes and he admired my talent…knowledge about the Medicare programs and enlisted my expertise in his businesses … he let me practice on his playground and he paid me for it.

After taking on his facilities and turning them around I worked myself out of a job at the age of 50 and met my next mentor who had responsibilities for 50 long-term care facilities and I was hired as an Administrator to turn-around the worst of the worst. I again worked myself out of a job and at the age of 52 went back into my own business.

Because of the belief two mentors had in me and my talent, inspired me to take on a new business at the age of 70 to practice what I have learned. Which was I can help the elderly and disabled have a quality of life ... extend their lives not just end them. Looking back, I feel I was destined to find good expression of my talents because my first memories of the elderly was a rest home across from my house in Indianola, Iowa ... these poor souls were spending all day in rocking chairs with nothing to do or live for...to me that seemed wrong and it still does. And now I can do something about it.

The D. C. Whitehouse (named after Shari's mother Dorothea Corny White) was our dream house dedicated to changing the lives of aging America through better life actions through planning and pre-forming attitudes about age. We need to become a nation of health preservers not life safety preservers...this all starts in our home with our children and their habits ... ironically their habits are our habits ... like it or not the future of our children is set in motion by our feelings and actions about ourselves. The ripple effect of you becoming happy, healthy and prosperous isn't only for the future of your children but America in general.

Habit formation is the WAYS by which new behaviors become automatic. If you instinctively reach for a cigarette the moment you wake up in the morning, you have a habit. The good news is that, through repetition, it's possible to form—and maintain—new WAYS. First, there is a cue, a trigger that tells your brain to go into automatic mode and which way to go. Then there is the routine, which can be physical or mental or emotional. Finally, there is a reward, which helps your brain figure out if this particular loop is worth remembering for the future. Habits, the way we live, emerge without our permission. Habits are resistive and delicate to change. Replacement of the old way with the new way is a loop of craving, cue, routine and reward repetitively. To change the way you respond, you must keep the old cue and deliver the old reward but insert a new routine. That's the rule: if you use the same cue and provide the same reward you can shift or replace the routine and change the way you live. Almost any behavior can be transformed if the cue and reward stay the same.

According to the experts there are 16 habits of the mind. Persistence, managing impulse, listening, thinking flexibility, cognition, striving for accuracy, question for problem solving, applying knowledge, communicating, gathering information, creating/imagining/innovating, responding in awe, taking risks, finding humor, independent thinking, remaining open to learning. Our 12 mental and physical lifestyle habits implement opportunities for improvement using all 16 categories

Prevention magazine proposes there are 10 ways, practiced by people who happily live to be 100. They mix and mingle, are physically active, use brain training, see the glass half full, chill out, listen to their gut, keep scales in balance, pop pills with caution, work on a schedule, and most importantly, don't skip a beauty rest. Shari and I are using all ten in our lifestyle and this book.

LIFESTYLE HABITS TO AVOID (the way you live your life determines your quality and quantity of life)

"An ounce of prevention is worth a hundred pounds of fat and stress habits causing chronic aging"- Jerry Rhoads

"Nothing so needs reforming as other people's habits." - Mark Twain

A good habit is a behavior that is beneficial to one's physical or mental health, often linked to a high level of discipline and self-control. But never stop being the you in Youth.

A bad habit is, well, the opposite.

Jerry and Shari propose that both good and bad habits are a result of a lifestyle that naturally determines life's longevity. The 12 Vows (a way to live your life) for a happy, healthy and prosperous marriage for longevity are pursuing both quantity and quality of life. The bottom line for our readers isn't to be like Shari and Jerry but to be yourself in light of what will make you happy, healthy and prosperous over your remaining years here and hereafter. We want to be your enablers not just role models. For example…

TWENTY-ONE LIFESTYLE HABITS CAUSING CHRONIC AGING
(It's Your Choice)

1. Smoking
2. Drinking in excess
3. Using mind altering drugs
4. Gaining weight to excess
5. Stressing over fears and anxieties
6. Not eating healthy
7. Ignoring loss of sexual vitality
8. Believing prescription drugs will fix it (popping pills rather than physical and mental activity)

9. Thinking yourself old and homely
10. Never having fun
11. Not having any friends
12. Hating your job
13. Bored with your mate
14. Not having faith in some higher power
15. Wasting money on bad habits
16. Having aberrant sexual relationships
17. Never saying I love you
18. Not believing in being nice is being smart
19. Not being sociable except on Face Book, twitter and Instagram
20. Not sleeping well or long enough
21. And the bigly one:

WORRY

I regret
I spent hours of my life
Worrying and hurrying

A life spent on worry
Is a misspent excuse to hurry
Worry over something simple
Is simply worrisome to others

Scurry here worry there where
Will all this hurry get us
Hurry towards worry for that fifth
Of booze is to scurry until blurry

Then to the bottle in the medicine
Cabinet next to the cigarettes
Then into rehab for 12 steps
Though we have to hurry to get there

Worrying if others know about it
Then burying it in lies that shout it

Worry must be eradicated
For those who hurry to get there

With road rage sleep apnea
And speeding tickets hurrying
To get to a job we hate
Because a better one asked us to wait

And get prepared and slow down
Our temptations to worry about
Taking a new job and its blurry

When it comes to the future

How do we stop worry
Why not stop and think about hope
Hope is the medicine for worry
So why not hurry to get some hope

A natural way to cope

According to the researchers for Men's Health if your lifestyle has any 5 of these consistently you are wasting away your better years at a high rate of metabolism creating an older than you should be in real age terms (defined as your Real Age by renowned physicians Dr. Roizen and Dr. Oz). You'll discover how to prevent chronic aging with the 12 Rhoads lifestyle habits you should be practicing, later in this book. But first let's talk a little more about what habits really are, how they're formed, and how they're changed.

WHERE DO OUR LIFESTYLE HABITS COME FROM?

Are you saying that I will be disease free if I don't do all of the above? No, this is not a medical prediction. What we are practicing and saying is your lifestyle habits will inevitably determine how long and how well you will live your life. And to double down on that we believe it will affect your marriage and how your offspring live their lives and marriage.

According to the experts, lifestyle is influenced most by our past and current environment. Subconscious habits dictate behavior and most everything requiring a response. Do you remember hearing any of the following statements when you were a child? And, do you believe any of the statements below helped form any of your and your children's current ways of behaving?

- Shut the door, were you born in a barn?
- Don't talk like that to your Mother.
- What happened to your allowance?
- Okay, but don't tell your Mother I let you.
- You're grounded.
- That's my chair you're sitting in.
- If you're living in this house, you live by my rules.
- You don't know how good you've got it.
- This is going to hurt me more than it hurts you.
- Who left my tools out?
- Who opened two bottles of milk?
- Don't slam the door.
- If you don't cut that out I'll ground you.
- I'll give you something to cry about.
- Turn that thing down.
- You're not sleeping open your eyes.
- Turn on the lights do you want to ruin your eyes.
- I'm only going to say this one more time.
- I get no respect around here.
- Do as I say not as I do.
- Do you think I'm made of money?
- Who left the bicycle in the driveway?
- Don't slam that door one more time.
- Why didn't you go before we left?
- Because I said so.
- Don't talk back or I will take the car keys.
- Eat your dinner . . . there are people starving in China.
- When you can pay the rent, you can decide who's in charge.
- Old is old anyway you live it.
- Can't wait to be 65 and retire.

Yes, your home life and past environment initially forms your lifestyle habits (cues, routines and rewards) and starts the subconscious storing instinctive responses for your current and later lifestyle decisions. Those are then inherited by your children and theirs. In our experience the mind and the subconscious thinking dictate how the body will age ... so how we personally think about aging will stimulate our behavior and can strengthen our bodies and minds for longevity. In doing this our mind and immune system are the captains of our fate. We don't dread or dispel at the aging numbers but use them to prove how much younger our real age is comparted to our birth age.

Most other books deal with the physical side of growing older but aren't using habits as the basis of a better marriage, daily affirmations and meditation exercises to trigger changing thought processes and physical and mental outcomes. Most of these titles have theory as the foundation of their premise that age is not manageable nor avoidable let alone reversible and if it is, they lack the physical proof that we ourselves provide in person or in our nursing homes. The driving force behind our longevity is not just physical and mental exercises but our relationship (commitment to each other for the sake of our family) in a loving and supportive living environment. Our thinking is dictated by what impact it will have on our children, who in turn, teach the same to their children and so on.

Does this require that you and your spouse have to act alike? No, it's unhealthy to be co-dependent to the extent that you are wedded to each-others habits. That's why we separate our comments into "Guy talk" and "Girl talk" as we discuss implementing our 12 lifestyle habits throughout the 12 proceeding Chapters. On the other-hand finding a partnership that lasts 60 to 80 years takes a commonality of interests, activities and passions. It's certainly give and take, rather than take it or leave it.

If we don't think alike are we going to end up alike with your program? In fact, Shari and I are exact opposites ... she a Sanguine and I a type A Choleric ... she would rather have fun than work and I would rather work than have fun. So, how could we be married 60 years, 35 of which we worked together every day in our businesses? Opposites attract, likes repel. Oh, so true in our case. Like interests, like values, like each other, like children, grandchildren, great grandchildren ... and we look nothing alike unless you see us as soul mates. But, also totally different in feelings and opinions. Politics we agree and religion not so much. However, we have learned to walk away when it gets too heated. I'm told continually how lucky I am to have married Shari and not screwed it up. Well, I have managed to not screw it up. And looking back over the 62 years of our relationship what stands out is our attraction to each other physically and emotionally but more importantly we had and have similar lifestyle habits in our thinking, dressing standards, likes and dislikes for nutrition, friends, beliefs for raising children, home environment, vacations, exercise, hobbies, family events, sports teams, housing, etc.

If, thoughts are things then feelings are things then Habits are things. Habits, a settled or regular tendency or practice, especially one that is hard to give up. Some good some harmful, such as hate and anger that are inward habits while love and kindness are outward habits. Habitat, a derivative of habit, is a person's usual or preferred surroundings reflecting and affecting their attitudes and Lifestyle. Lifestyle is the habitual culmination of values affecting the way in which a person or group lives. The behavioral psychologists stipulate that your action to change any one of these, must be a literal makeover of the way you think, which is a spontaneous reflection of your subconscious feelings, values and decisions on lifestyle.

Therefore, experts on behaviors all agree we are what we think we are. Your current situation is a result of your thinking, not your circumstances. But we are what our thinking habits are. If we want to change our thoughts, we must CHOOSE to change our thought processes ... most of which are learned from childhood and have become subconscious feelings, values and responses to situations and circumstances not well thought out consequences. It just happens without restraint. Until we take responsibility for changing or improving the outcome.

THE YOUTH OF OLD AGE

Don't think of seventy as the old age of youth
But think of it as the youth of old age
What's more important youthful living or loving
Is it the feelings that creates the appetite
Or is it the appetite for loving
That creates the desired essence of a youthful life

Good health is the flight pattern
of the young at heart
And those who don't idle on the runway
Takeoff towards those dreams that start
With visions held in high esteem
A churning stream of life that can't stop
For their work love and life
Are taken down to its very last drop

So, don't think of seventy as the old age of youth
But think of it as the youth of old age

With loving that creates the insight
And aging foresight that creates the flight

To "forever young" land

Rhonda Byrne in her timely and bestselling guide to happiness "The Secret", states: "life isn't happening to you, life is responding to you. Life is your call. You are the creator of your life. You decide what your life will be." Through the Universal Law of Attraction, you attract your own results through your own thoughts and actions.

Depok Chopra in his "7 Spiritual Laws of Success" establishes: that thinking, doing and finding happiness is a mental process from Karma (giving) to Dharma (finding your true talent and place in the Universe).

Earle Nightingale in his teachings stated that "what you can conceive and believe you will achieve". "And worry is not an achievement, it is a wasteful effort."

Dr. Venice Bloodworth, a clinical psychologist, said in her wonderful book The Key to Yourself, "We have so long failed to understand the wonderful power of thought for it is taught by every religion and philosophy in the history of the world." She goes on to say that an affirmation of "I am happy, healthy and prosperous" isn't just words. It's the retraining of the subconscious to be positive which is a principle of Universal law that puts aside the negative as being a result of not following Self-Help Universal law. "Those that help themselves to improve are in turn changing the way we appear to and affect others."

I agree with Dr. Bloodworth, who says most of us fail to think in terms of truth, honesty, justice, purity and loveliness. If we changed the way we think, this world would be transformed from a planet of confusion, sickness and poverty into one of radiant health, happiness, and prosperity.

Decide today to move your thinking in a different path so the future does a mental house cleaning and a new thought conditioning called "I am happy, healthy and prosperous" affirmation enough to replace the subconscious feelings for negativity programmed into all of us by parents, media and life's problems and challenges. You then are what you think you are without concern for aging too fast, too fat, too stressed, too old, too tired ... you then have attained what we, the authors, and their family have ... lifestyles of the healthy, happy and prosperous parents. For us mental and physical exercise has enabled us to overcome a negative self-image, a fear of the unknown, because we can control our thoughts about what we want, then take action to do it, this works for us as it has for many others by preserving our health, preventing chronic illnesses and premature aging. Resulting in and measurable as a positive Real Age score.

Even though most of my life has resulted in positive results I still feel unfulfilled. Why? Because negativity still lurks in my subconscious … I work daily on suppressing the darkness and focusing on the bright lights of tomorrow. Today has already been set in the stone of my past thoughts and actions … no changing that … but the next day (s) are up to me and my ability to think positively in a negative world. Still I love the challenge.

I get mad at the Cubs and the Bears, I rant at the politicians, I wonder about money, I hope for attainment of my goals, I fear the unknown, I am a victim of mood swings … I certainly have my negative moments … but my study continues on how to keep a positive outlook that results in positive outcomes … I read Deepak Chopra, I reread the Secret, I read "The Key to Yourself" as well … I work at it. Still I love the Cubs and Bears. Now when they lose, I state my affirmation "I'm happy, healthy and prosperous" and look forward not backward.

But probably more important, I believe I can change my attitude and future if it becomes negative by saying "remember" … if you start out negative you will finish the day negative so why would you do it that way … and it always works out that the day is dependent on my every morning thinking not just my doing. Just speaking the word "I love" can put you in a positive state of mind. I am now 80 years young and just did one set of 80 pushups, plus 2 to stay young on, to celebrate my birthday. I love being fit, and I love knowing that more often than most of us realize, we can do something if we simply think we can. Have you ever heard an Olympian say I can't … if they did or do they aren't even given the chance because can't never did anything and can does everything? So, I plan to do 85 pushups when I'm 85, 90 when I am 90 and 100 when I reach 100…after that I plan to slow down. In the next life, it is all mental anyway!

NEVER TOO OLD

Listen closely
To what you're told
Don't you see
You're getting old

The story's an old refrain
Doesn't take any effort to get there
Graying hair, a bigger weight gain
Pound for pound I guess I don't care

Isn't poor health self-undone
Told by bodies hanging out
Hidden from the sun
And what this story's about

Despite a fallen mast and no chest
Yes, about the health less
American first class
Who always knows best?

Listen closely
To what you're told
Don't you see
You're finally too old

Fallen down arches
No love affair
Rocking on porches
With a sightless stare

Not me brothers
I got all this desire
I'm really the druthers
In Mister fire

Telling stories anew
After other hands fold
Because they knew
They were too old

A coop they never flew
Downed like a spent flier
For if they only knew
Good Habits' desire

Never Too Old are Mister and Misses Fire

HOW LONG DOES IT TAKE TO GET RID OF A BAD HABIT?

That's an impossible question to answer because it depends on the person and the habit. As psychologists would say, it's always the individual and the situation together. Breaking a habit really means establishing a new way of behaving, a new presence in certain situations. One popular claim is that a habit can be broken in only 21 days, an idea that seems to reference Psycho- Cybernetics, a 1960 self-help book written by cosmetic surgeon Maxwell Maltz. Other vernacular accounts very from 72 hours to two weeks. But, of course, some habits can take six months or more to change. And some harmful habits are never broken.

However long it takes, you're going to need a good strategy (look no further than this book). You'll need commitment. And you'll need to practice, which is typically experienced as two steps forward, one step back. This may sound pessimistic, and we may want to believe that we can break our ways of behaving much more quickly, but you only really know if you've broken the habit when you're challenged somehow. For example, we get very stressed or "off-balance" in our life, because we typically regress to old ways of being (habits) under duress. So, at first you may think you have "changed the habit," but change the circumstances a bit by adding some stress, physical fatigue or emotional exhaustion, and you realize that the new way of living may not be as well established as you think. There must be a concerted effort made to get back on track ... then measure your progress and results.

THE PRINCIPLES OF THE "RHOADS" LIFESTYLE

The images used of Shari and I throughout out this book are examples of why seventy IS the new middle age. Change your thinking and change your life. Shari and I have worked all our lives for a healthy lifestyle and now at our age we are starting businesses to assist the aging American improve their outlook and always practice the pursuit of living forever young by thinking young with the attitude that "I'm too young to die early". Currently this is our Real Age profile:

Shari 79 has a 54 Real Age score (115 pounds, BMI 22, body fat 15%)… she married an older man one year her senior … Jerry 80 has a 55 Real Age score (175 pounds, BMI 27, body fat 10%)… he has a trophy younger looking wife.

It only takes desire—and the right lifestyle habits!

Please for just a little while
Pursue each bad habit's demise
Replace with habits of the wise

WE'LL NEVER BE OLD (a poem written for Shari's 77th birthday)

Our birthright is steady; We're childhood dolls; And we'll never be ready; For we're as ageless as Saul; We've got to play childhood games; Our children are the real dolls of our playhouse; Our home is the backyard of our memories; Our work is the dreams of the past; My thinking is not of myself; I can't stand selfishness; I'm naive in my belief that Life is meant to be simple; Not complicated by emotions; But just simple thoughts of family and work; I love to play yesterday's songs; My words are the grass roots of my ancestors; My fears are the doubt of the unknown; My tears are the sensitivity of a Victorian Jack of Hearts Married as the King of Queens; My hopes are the real roots of home; The softness of our bed; The warmth of our family; The embrace of our eternal love; I'm never to be old Shari nor will you be; If to yourself behold; You're forever a beauty; A Cinderella to me ...

Signed Jerry Lee

IS IT EVER ENOUGH?

When is life enough? Does everything important to you seem out of reach? Following are the top ten scales of a meaningful life:

#1 ... Is it fame and fortune?

#2 ... Is it security?

#3 ... Is it happiness?

#4 ... Is it good health?

#5 ... Is it a great family?

#6 ... Is it your own successful business?

#7 ... Is it a perfect face and body?

#8 ... Is it a happy marriage?

#9 ... Is it a beautiful home?

#10 .. Is it feeling and looking younger than you age?

Go ahead pick your #1___. Mine is #5 with #8 as the reason. Because #5 is a result and #8 is the reason the rest are an endless pursuit of never enough. Life isn't a score but a journey to enough. If you fall short of #5 and #8 all you can do is chase the others to never enough. (In the movie "Brad's Status" Ben Stiller is never having enough until he is told by his son "you have enough" be a pursuer of #5). Ben finally finds enough when his son answers his question "what do you think of your dad." That becomes enough when his son answers "I love you." WHAT'S YOUR ANSWER … DO YOU HAVE ENOUGH? IS LOVE AND FAMIY ENOUGH? ARE YOUR HABITS SUPPORTIVE OF THAT?

SELF SURVEY	YES	NO
1. Do you think your old?	____	____
2. Do you feel old?	____	____
3. Do you act old?	____	____
4. Do you want to be young again?	____	____
5. Do you need to be younger?	____	____
6. Are you unhappy with your lifestyle?	____	____
7. Do you have an unhealthy lifestyle?	____	____

Being honest about your thinking is the first step to living forever younger-stronger- longer. The 12 "Jerry met Shari" habits (vows) for changing your thinking and lifestyle are in the succeeding chapters.

When I read "The Secret" the first of numerous times it didn't sink in that there is a path to our experiencing our dreams. After a number of readings, it occurred to me that my current life story is what I wanted it to be and didn't know it … it was by the Law of Attraction (you are what you think you are) as applied by my wife and family life made everlasting (love) sense … my life, work and fate will be determined by what I commit to and pursue … yeah but, also one must believe until it is conceived, achieved and received.

My life would be entirely different if I had missed out on my attraction to Shari. She is the maiden and maker of me as I am and will always be. Like honey to a honey bee she is the honey in me and the queen of the hive to our family. Did I have a life before her … yes unfocused and looking at her. When I saw her standing there I knew I had found her … she wasn't attracted to the inner me that didn't let go until it was matrimony. Then she claims it was her picking me … oh well I can't fight destiny. But it was the Law of Attraction at work.

For me mental and physical exercise has enabled me to become more attentive to the way I look at hard times. Ben Franklin said, "hard times are inevitable and it is the way you handle them that is important". The positive attitude shows in decisions you make and the outcomes it creates. A negative self-image, a fear of the unknown, and a feeling of not in control compounds thoughts about what I must do to make life work for me not against me.

Mental Fitness with our plan is for exercising your attitude towards improving your self-image and feeling of self-worth from a stronger set of habits. If your goal is to be happier you need to replace negative thoughts about yourself and your current lifestyle with positive and affirmative thoughts. The first Step can be physical fitness by mapping out the cues for when to workout, the routines and the rewards as the necessary requisite to the second Step for your mental attitude towards your other lifestyle habits. If you feel good you will think good thoughts about life in general.

In the Affirmative section of the book we give sayings for daily affirmations to stimulate your thinking in a positive manner. "Mind over matter". Mental fitness like physical fitness takes a commitment and a continuous use of tools and evaluation techniques to see how you're doing. Improvement is the motivator, not just wanting to be better. Quitting can be the biggest obstacle to change and must be battled until the habits are changed by your commitment to feel better, act better, be a better person.

Better thoughts (for practice exercises) (Each chapter has 7 daily affirmations and/or prayers):

- I can be and will be thinking positive today
- I can be and will be healthy today
- I can be and will be a better person today
- I can be and will be successful today
- I can be and will be mentally strong today
- I can be and will be stress free today
- I will rest on the seventh day

For a Better Tomorrow: (repeat the exercises daily or at least weekly and you will be amazed how you improve your stress-free aging results by thinking results not causes)!

ONE NEGATIVE DESTROYS TEN POSITIVES, ONE POSITIVE CURES TEN NEGATIVES

Failure is a figment of human imagination
Dwelling on the negative makes it happen
Given enough time even a monkey can fail

Are you ever sure you're a failure or
Is it just your mother's opinion that becomes yours or
Was it your impression of your father

We all have fears that come from dreams unreached
Time tells us it's too late and we believe it
Even though others have been beseeched with roses

However, life is not a destination but a journey
Meant to be at your direction and fortune
Whether rich or poor, in sickness or health

The avoidance of failure is not wealth
But only a fleeting surge of pride that subsides
And leaves the dreamer in for a nightmare
So this book is not about failure but success
Daily thoughts that propel us forward
Into tomorrow despite doubt and fear of the unknown

I call it the "Prescription for Happiness"
Because it takes the mind off the expectation of failure
And put the words of success into our will (brain) power

Forging a habit and thought process inseparable
From the subconscious not needing a fear of God
Is a belief in self=health

Take this trip with me and you shall never fear
The action and will benefit from the act
Until you have an addiction for the love of self=health

For if you love you can be loved
If you are loved you are connected to happiness
And its mighty pull towards fulfillment

RESEARCH AND STATISTICS

- Dr. Roizen states in his book Real Age that more than 70% of aging can be linked to behavior and other environmental factors leaving 30% related to genetic influences. Those can also be managed using prevention techniques and health altering medications and surgeries (breast removal, Alzheimer's treatment, heart disease medication and surgery, etc.).

- Purpose may even help stave off Alzheimer's

  I watched my father die from emphysema and my mother in law from chronic diseases and if purposeful activity can keep it at bay, bring it on. I provided my father a stationary bicycle that extended his life and we placed my mother-in-law in an assisted living center where she had socialization and was provided with purposeful activities where she lived for twenty years after Shari's father died. She lived to the age of 93, with a life cut short by abuse in a nursing home.

"Scientists have discovered that purposeful activity not only can slow cognitive decline, but also may delay the onset of Alzheimer's and buffer its effects on the brain," according to the report. "These findings emerged when Patricia Boyle and her colleagues at the Rush Alzheimer's Disease Center interviewed older adults about purpose in their lives, conducted cognitive testing and neurological exams, and examined brains postmortem for evidence of Alzheimer's. They found that higher levels of purpose reduced harmful cognitive effects and slowed the rate of decline by about 30 percent, even when the brain already exhibited the disease's genetic damaging plaques and tangles.

A separate longitudinal study spearheaded by Boyle found that people who reported having greater purpose in life were 2.4 times more likely to remain free of Alzheimer's than those with lower self- reported purpose scores. To give these results context, it is important to note that science currently has no way to keep dementia-related pathology from accumulating." But, Dr. Bredesen, an Alzheimer's expert is proving this wrong ... by recoding the ApoE4 gene he has been successful in slowing and/or reversing the impact of Alzheimer's.

- Research has repeatedly shown that changing knowledge and intentions does not translate into changing habits. Habits are formed through doing. And the long-term memory systems involved in habit formation don't shift with new resolutions.

- In our research, we've found that old habit associations endure, and hinder behavior change, even after people adopt new intentions. For example, once you see a text on our cell phone, it's hard to get that out of your head and instead focus on your resolution to call our children. With habits, in essence, we change them not by learning, but by ACTING AND DOING the opposite.

- What is mental exercising? Generally speaking, we learn by repetition ... so by reading and rereading the mental exercises in this book hopefully will start you thinking and acting in a different way. We have been taught, in most instances, what not to do ... not what to do. That flaws our results. Now we must turn the tables and concentrate on what to do.

- The power of positive thinking makes common sense but is uncommon among most Americans. We are buried in negativism ... newspapers, tabloids, television cruelty, movie perversions, gangster rap, violent reality shows, aberrant sexual behaviors as porn, etc. To counteract this social mental break-down practice your own form of liberty using common sense terms and make your own first amendment commitment to your own aging process.

- The world is negative because we tend to see things in a fearful way. We by nature fear the future because of the unknowns. Our own world does not have to be negative but our subconscious has been filled with negativity. To overcome this situation takes acknowledging its existence and a concerted effort to reprogram our subconscious. How is that possible when we continue to respond when we are confronted by crisis, stress, cynical thoughts, fear, anger, sexual insecurity, false hopes, failures, fantasies, lost dreams, etc.? Just do what you do in a positive manner …

THE DO'S

1. Do … Think you "can" be younger and "can't be older" looking and acting. Know your Real Age and make plans.
2. Do … Make it your commitment to stay married and keep your family together.
3. Do … Find something that you're good at and make it your goal to achieve excellence.
4. Do … Spend as much time as possible reading self-help books and articles about current styles and technology.
5. Do … Hold on to old memories for supporting current choices but limit practicing old tendencies and habits.
6. Do … Practice your affirmations about yourself and prayers and absolutions for others.

BREAKING UP

Breaking up is so hard to undo

Love's so easy when I'm thinking of you
Love's the easiest thing I have to do
Times have been good and times have been bad
But being with you is more glad than sad

Yes love's so easy until we have to part

Leaving you a piece of my heart
That way you'll always know
That it's your looks I'm loving so

Love's so easy when it's being you

Love's the easiest thing I have to do
And though it seems a permanent way
For me to say
I need to see you every day

And though that need cannot now be fulfilled
For even the mockingbird has been killed
Trading love for passion must be chilled
For to the heart love must be tilled

Not just romance to which we've thrilled

Yes love's so easy
Loving you
It's the easiest thing
I have to do

But breaking up is so hard to undo
(Shari and I let ourselves break-up
Something we could make-up
Into something no one nor event can undo)

Breaking up never breaks even

MAKING UP

Loving you is better than fighting you tonight
Loving you is better than getting uptight
Loving you makes everything all right
I've been down and broken to pieces

Choking on words and desire which never ceases
Loving you is better than anything I've ever done
Loving you puts the brightness in my sun
Loving you I don't know what I would do

If I weren't loving you

They say you stay too busy to be sad
Work and work till you're glad
Glad we'll have times together
Like flocking birds of a feather

There's nothing better than the clearing
After our stormy weather

Yes loving you is better than fighting you
Loving you is better than anything I have to do
Let your defenses down
Put your hair up
Don't give your cares a sound
For this is too good to disrupt

Loving you would be so easy
If you had truly been loving me
So no one could corrupt
That feeling I've had for you

Yes loving you is the easiest thing
I don't have to undo

Because making up is the easiest thing to do
But making do never makes do

THE DON'TS

1. Don't let life be a rut to stinking thinking about yourself and others.
2. Don't frown when someone make a comment about your age.
3. Don't become what others are unless you respect their intentions.
4. Don't act like you're over the hill.
5. Don't perform activities that make you sad or mad.
6. Don't say don't, won't, can't, when you should do, can and will.

Only you can determine the before and after results. We will assist in the planning and tracking of results. Only you can say you can't. Why not just do what you can do and forget what you can't do.

WHO SAYS?

Who says you can't?
Who says you can?
Are you a plant?
Or are you a
man/woman

For only the plant can't
Only the man can
So why do we have man saying he can't
And a plant sitting in a can

Let's take a plant and tell it can't
And let's take a man and tell him he can
And let's give them both a hand
As they sit rooted in the land
Who says I can't
Who says I can
Well it's I who says I am
So why shouldn't I stand

On a can
Rather than stuck as a plant
In the mire of saying I can't
Or shan't
My healthy habits are the fireman
Agreeably the mind is the fertilizer
And the man that says he can
Is all the wiser

And the fool that says he can't
Facing the trials and tribulations
Is nothing more than a plant
Of bygone habitations

Regretting having been a man
Dying as a forgotten plant
Because he chose to fall off the can
Because he said I can't

And died a didn't

VARIOUS WAYS TO THINK AND ACT YOUNG

For example: have you ever listened to and danced with your partner to Rod Stuart's "Forever Young" in the Bathroom in the AM till you feel young and resilient ... Shari and I have! Try it. Music and Dancing are our number one mental stimulant for thinking and acting young on a daily basis. Even as you get ready for the day in the bathroom.

FOREVER YOUNG

May your hands always be busy
May your feet always be swift
May you have a strong foundation
When the winds of changes shift
May your heart always be joyful
And may your song always be sung
May you stay forever young
Forever young, forever young
May you stay forever young.

(last stanza of lyrics by Bob Dylan and sung by Rod Stewart)

Start a business or create a product for sale

Guy Talk (Jerry)

After starting my own CPA firm in 1977 Shari, Kip and I have also started a software development business (1994), a nursing home consulting and management company (1987), a nursing home ownership company (2009). So, for forty years we have not worked for someone else. The latest venture was to buy three nursing homes in 2009 and sell them six and seven one-half years later. During that time Kip, Shari and I developed expertise in consulting with and operating a nursing home business and did with some alarming results that are well documented in my health care books. I've always had a place in my heart for the elderly and disabled. So, all three of the facilities were renovated, we restored their creditability and quality only to sell them to operators that turned them back into warehouses for the elderly. This breaks our hearts to see what we had changed and improved undone by the new owners acquiescing to the surveyors' pettiness not good business principles.

This is all documented in my books Remedy Eldercide, Restore Elderpride, The Boomers are Coming, Failing Government Taketh Away and The Monopsony Game. We had planned to implement our software and management systems in the first three facilities then set up a franchising approach by purchasing the nursing homes in small towns, renovating them, leasing them to a local investor and putting in a local business person to run them. This way effective management systems and procedures could be implemented for quality control, cost accounting, financial management and government compliance. But the culture is still money and what the regulators decide, not what the elderly really need. Oh well maybe someday.

Girl Talk (Shari)

Since selling the three nursing homes Jerry and I have started a writing venture, I have invented a clothing protector and Kip is working for a software integration company serving nursing home chains. I loved being the Administrator of All-American Care of Washington Iowa, being able to restore our patients so they could have a quality of life. But due to Jerry's exposés on why regulators don't improve care, we were targeted and retaliated against until we were forced to sell. All of this was made possible because of Jerry's expertise in operating skilled nursing facilities and his knowledge of Medicare and Medicaid regulations and payment systems. My parents also had small businesses in Iowa and Jerry's father's family were independent farmers in Iowa. Unfortunately, our good ventures were not suitable for the times.

Read or write blogs, articles or books

Guy Talk (Jerry)

I just released my first novel "2084 Americana" after six self-health care books, five poetry books, three political books and a cost accounting book. My writing career was focused on business for 35 years and after selling the nursing homes I started completing books written over the last twenty-five years. To this I've been a reader so I could be a writer. My goal is to write bestsellers pertaining to American's quality of life and throw in my opinions on health care and politics. If you read you learn, you grow, you get inspired and then can create your own anthology or biography. Using my published book website www.jerryrhoadsauthor.com and www.lifestylesforaging.com I have a blog attached to express my views on health care and aging to promote this book and the others already published.

Girl Talk (Shari)

My favorite author after Jerry, is Hemmingway and many others that have a positive message. I'm not into the serial killers, criminal minds or exposes. I have read and edited most of Jerry's books and now taking part in the writing. My advice on filling your spare time and we have eight hours to make productive use is writing about solutions to problems rather than the fake news, Soaps or the use of Facebook for gossip. I'm concerned about the aging factor for the mind that isn't active ... so I keep mine very active. Reading is an important part of our life so we can also write with some authority.

Well, I avoided it for as long as possible but I'm now on Facebook because I'm involved in planning my next class of '58 reunion. Since there is a Facebook page dedicated to that class I'm using it for communicating with the remaining graduates. Of course, once you touch it you can't leave it alone ... much like potato chips that's probably not that good for you. However, my children and grandchildren are on there so we are linked in daily with texting and email ... Instagram is next. Then Snap Chat. Also, the number of photos we now have of our family is great except Jerry is no longer the family photographer ... everyone is. Who said technology doesn't steal jobs?

Associate with younger friends, neighbors and associates

Guy Talk (Jerry)

Our goal is to associate with people acting and playing "The Younger Games" rather than the "I'm Always Hunger Games". We rarely socially associate with people our own age since they are either in nursing homes or on their way. That may sound heartless but it isn't when you consider we bought nursing homes to teach people how to get out or stay out ... that's where we practiced our view on self-health and restoring our patients functioning so they could go home. There is a positive attitude with the younger crowd that isn't dwelling on their poor health. If they are healthy and active, they have our respect and we would be proud to associate with them ... if we can find them and help them stay that way.

Girl Talk (Shari)

My suggestion is read Jerry's self-health books and practice his methods for physical and mental health. Then you will look younger, act younger and be younger. It works for us. When we go out on Thursday evening to dance at our favorite venue there are two ladies one 85 and the other 80 who look and act in their 60's. the other patrons are in their 40's to 60's ... some seemingly older than Jerry and I and some about our real age. It's fun to sit with them and talk current events, sports and politics. This is our favorite night of the week. Jerry says I love my yah yah time with the girls. Yes, I do. But I also love my dancing time with Jerry.

Keep fit, look fit and participate in sporting events

Guy Talk (Jerry)

In my case, much of my negative thoughts were about the fear of rejection and being incapable to control my emotions. Success was a pursuit not a result of preparation and dedication. However, this condition existed from a childhood of little love, support or encouragement ... because my parents were a product of their fears, habits and rejections and I took them on for myself.

Self-help books have been an important part of our life ... early on I was into Earle Nightingale, then Napoleon Hill, now it is The Secret, Depok Chopra and I'm writing a book on human psychology in business. They all carry the same message: you are what you think you are ... you become what you want to be ... but random conditioning of your subconscious mind relegates you to your past habits.

When I found a love of sports, I found a way to feel good about my talents…I was good at it…not excellent but better than most…however, I was never the star…just the backup or the sixth man. But I had this drive, desire to be the best…which spurred me on to this day. I loved it and love it today. It occurs in the form of daily exercise, tennis, photography, writing another book of fiction, this book and poetry but more importantly reflecting on the life style of our family and enjoying Shari and our daily activities together. As for Shari, she needs to have her yah yah time with her female friends and associates. She and I play doubles tennis, walk together holding hands, hold hands when roller blading, hold hands in bed, touch each other doing Yoga ... she and I thrive on affection and romance. It keeps us feeling fit, young and connected ... our friends and children comment that is the kind of relationship they want and we say just try it and you may also thrive on it.

Girl Talk (Shari)

My first thought was always to look my best for my husband. I never wanted him to wonder why he fell in love with me. My mother always made sure she dressed up with hair done, makeup on and dinner on the table when dad walked in. The first part always stuck with me …not so much the dinner on the table part. My parents always had a loving relationship, and so did moms' parents, which to me is a normal expectation, and always worth working on.

My mom also said, "if you look good, you feel good about yourself, and you don't have to apologize for anything." No matter whether I am wearing jeans, shorts, or workout clothes, I pick pieces that match. This is all part of building your self-esteem. Having confidence in yourself is one of the strongest benefits you will ever have. I'm also a fanatic about having a clean and neat home which is also a self-esteem builder. Your home is definitely a reflection of you, and when it looks good you feel good.

One thing I hear so many women say is, "I have to get my makeup on before I go out." Why? The most important people in my life live with me. I always put my makeup on whether I am going any place or not. It is part of my daily routine ... shower, dry and style hair, put on makeup and pick out an outfit.

As for sports, I also took my mother's lead ... sit with your husband viewing his interests and he will mimic the routine for you ... anything together is better than personal interests alone. And now I can participate in my children's and grandchildren's love of sports and help teach them what that means to a healthy lifestyle.

Be active in some organization for making America better

Guy Talk (Jerry)

I've been active in Rotary (three different communities), CPA associations, licensed nursing home administrator associations, Lyons Club, Methodist church board, leader of the Indian Tribe, coach of Kip's baseball teams in Springfield and Morton Illinois, Chairman of the Long-Term Care Committee for Illinois CPA's, and American CPA's, Chairman and President of the Rhoads companies, President of the Hyde Park Association, Chairman of the Pumpkin Festival Tennis Tournament, New Comer's clubs, various Tennis Associations. I used to be shy and stand offish for social events but having my own business forced me to be more outgoing.

Girl Talk (Shari)

I was the President of the PTA for Christie, Kimber and Kip's grade school. Secretary of the Rhoads companies, Blue Bird leader, Provisional Administrator, Newcomers Club, various Book Clubs, Midtown Tennis and Fitness Club, Republicans for Trump supporter. I love to socialize with new acquaintances ... but never a joiner just for the fun of it. However, after the kids grew up I had more time to read, sew, paint and be involved in community affairs.

Compliment your spouse on a youthful and trendy look

Guy Talk (Jerry)

Shari has always made my heart flutter. It's her youthful personality, figure and beauty. There has never been a day in our 60 years of marriage that I didn't look and marvel at my wife's assets. When I found her, I found a marriage that is very positive and fills the blanks of the lack of love and support from my parents...our children are healthy, happy and thrive on my attitude that "can't never did anything" and dreams are to be pursued not squelched. Feeling and acting young ... I love it.

My wife and son helped me form a better business after an initial set back. We now are building for the future to assist the elderly to be healthier and had facilities where we provided restorative services to overcome the harmful habits of their earlier years. I love it.

Girl Talk (Shari)

Jerry is now listening to my advice on taking care of his skin. The next most important function in his daily routines is to follow my coaching on using a face moisturizer and aftershave, always. When we got married, I got him to wash his hair daily using a recommended shampoo and conditioner ... since I was a cosmetologist he listened. Of course, shaving, cologne and deodorant are staples. Even on the weekends. He is fortunate to have his mother's hair and skin and his father's build. His mother's skin was phenomenal up until she passed at the age of 84 which influenced Jerry to no end. His father never weighed more than 150 pounds and kept a muscular build till he died at the age of 82. Yes, the genetics help. But it takes our effort to repeat it or better it. Since we don't leave our home to work our dress is now what I call home-casual. We still wear outfits that look good and are comfortable. Our motto is "always look your best to do your best." I think too many women just give up, and don't care how they look. I say, "you are not too old to look good and keep a younger than you are look." So, let's use our best look, at all times, right now.

To my distress, Jerry's dressing habits have changed since going into re- hirement. For about 55 years he wore a suit and tie five days a week, 50 weeks a year (two weeks off for vacation). Now, since he works out every day, he dresses for working out first then casual after that unless the occasion calls for the good ole coat and tie. He told me his dad said, "if you look at most peoples' shoes, they don't care how they look" … "You always want your shoes to look good" … so his did. Jerry's dad worked in a factory for 33 years, but still understood even foot ware can dictate how people perceive you. Along with clothing, hair and attitude of course.

Be active with your family and their offspring

Guy Talk (Jerry)

Every holiday we are with family. Easter, Memorial Day, July 4th, Labor Day, Thanksgiving we spend at the Stephens Lake or the Lawrence Lake fishing, boating, swimming, driving four wheelers, playing Frisbee games, whiffle ball, card games, board games, having food and drink to supplement the movies and board games in the evenings.

Girl Talk (Shari)

I can't believe I'm in my late seventies. I don't feel old and I still like to do the fun things we are always doing. So, don't tell yourself you are too old to live. I think your body listens to your mind and your mind makes good things happen if you let it. So, don't continue to send it the wrong messages if you want better results. My mother always commented that she couldn't be 92 … and time passes us by if we don't try.

Jerry is a hopeless romantic with his poetry (author of five poetry books) and gentlemanly habits … such as walking on the street-side with me protected on the inside, opening the car door for me, insisting that he open all doors for me, waiting for me to go through doors first, helping me pick out clothes, sharing his side of the bed, about 50 shades of I love you. I reciprocate in every one of his obsessions and he with mine … I express I love you often, I'm what he calls a gift-a-holic, we have to call all of our 22 family members on their birthdays, give them cards and gifts and sing happy birthday (Jerry has to harmonize due to being tone deaf).

Every day now seems to be another spontaneous venture with impulses for having fun together doing our common interests … exercising, walking, eating out, dancing, traveling to our children's' homes, participating in holidays with them and spending time at their summer homes and attending Kim and Kelli's art fairs or Kip's music shows and Christie's Cabbie clothing sales. Plus, we now have twelve grandchildren and eight great grandchildren where we attend their birthday parties, graduations, sporting events, beauty contests and meeting their girl or boy friends (Jerry is the family photographer so we have thousands of pictures and albums of these events. He also writes and prints the annual Christmas Cards and prepares an annual picture calendar for each family for the New Year). The message here is being active keeps you young by acting young.

Never say no to playing games and having fun with friends and family

Guy Talk (Jerry)

This comes after a business career that was not much more than reactionary. I did very well in school, particularly college but still was not the 4.0 pointer or the magna cum lade. I was rewarded the highest business award in college. I have taught all of our children and grandchildren how to play tennis and provided the balls and rackets. I still play my daughter Kelli, her husband (son-in-law) and boys, and my oldest daughter, Christie's two boys and our son Kip when we can.

Girl Talk (Shari)

I love any type of board games, cards, word games, Yahtzee, Pictionary, Scrabble, etc. Even the younger grandkids participate. What a way to learn to think and have fun. Our children were brought up on board games, tennis, touch football, softball, going to the carnivals, taking fun vacations to San Diego California, Cabo Saint Lucas Mexico, Denver Colorado, Marco Island and Cape Coral Florida, Dallas Texas, Indianola Iowa, Holland Michigan, Branson Missouri, Hilton Head South Carolina, etc.

HOW DO I KNOW … that I've changed my thinking? Look in the mirror every morning and night seeing yourself in a positive light. Letting go of seeing negative thoughts about any wrinkles, blemishes and worries. Do that until you own it. "Your actions follow your thoughts, your habits follow your wants, your wants follow your needs, your reality follow your actions." Mahatma Gandhi … I call this the happy, healthy aging cycle. As Nike says, "just do it and it will happen".

SELF-EVALUATION

After reading this chapter take the following Self=Health quiz … update your Real Age calculation, put a checkmark for your answers and come back later to rate yourself for complying with the actions recommended in this chapter:

	Birth Age	Real Age	YES	NO
Beginning Real Age score	_____	_____		
1. Are you thinking old … wrinkles, blemishes, worries?			____	____
2. Do these harmful habits control your thinking?			____	____
3. Do you feel like letting your thinking taking a different track?			____	____
4. Do you have a plan for implementing habit changes?			____	____
5. Do you now use the real age calculator to measure results?			____	____
6. Do you feel compelled to change your thinking?			____	____
7. Later rate your progress … 1 being low and 10 being the best			____	____

Your rating and answers are your confession booth for judging for yourself where you are with your commitment to change your lifestyle habits at this point. A yes is a positive and says you are working on it and a no is an indicator of more work to start trying to change. The rating, on the other hand, lets you know what you think your progress is and you then are the judge of your own lifestyle status that converts to a better Real Age, and a longer stronger life expectancy.

DAILY AFFIRMATIONS

For us, affirmations are for those senses that need expression to knock down fences. The affirmations in this book will help you live the 12 DNA Fountain of Youth Habits. They will take your thinking in a different path using experience to coach you through a mental house cleaning. By using new thought conditioning called "I am happy, healthy and prosperous" affirmations to replace the subconscious thoughts of negativity programmed into all of us by parents, media and life's problems and challenges … the feelings of inferiority to be replaced by positive reinforcement focusing on changing harmful habits and then lifestyles.

For us mental and physical exercise have enabled us to overcome negative self-images, a fear of the unknown, because we can control our thoughts about what we want and it will eventually appear as it has for many others. We believe that we do in fact create our own reality.

When I started my own business my daughter Kim said I needed to make sure I stayed healthy because who would pay the bills if I got sick. She even advised me on how to stay healthy … jump rope … so I did … but I still felt sick when I contemplated the loneliness of a new venture with no means of support so I wrote an affirmation for each day of the first year to keep my mind positive and my habits in conformance with my philosophy of spiritual life, work, marriage and family. This evolved into my dictating on my hand recorder enough poems to fill five books on the Wonders of the World.

Shari and I feel this is a tool for you to get or stay positive each day and avoid negative feelings that reflect the harmful habits and plant healthful new ones. The routine should be something you can do immediately after getting up each morning.

AFFIRMATIONS

A youthful mind is the impulse

That makes the oldest heart pulse

* * *

Life has given me myself

I feel the need to achieve self-health

* * *

We don't appreciate getting older

Until losing it looks over our shoulder

* * *

I know my goals and seek a destination

My healthy habits will show me the direction

* * *

Sympathy is a judgment with a smile

Faith is a measurement of each mile

* * *

Look and you shall find you'll be more

In eating an apple and strengthening the core

* * *

My flame is hot and my habits are mellow

Played on my field of dreams a happy fellow

* * *

See the My Real Age app, Tool #2, for modifying your thinking to younger behavior for living longer and stronger.

POEMS FOR RECITING OR RAPPING:

(Since I say I was the first rapper, following are poems from my collection that seem fitting for this chapter ... forgive me I'm still pitching feelings as well as analytics)

AGE IS AN ATTITUDE

Think old and pan for mold
Think young and pan for gold
Age is an attitude
Thinking young is no platitude

As soon as you're old enough to think
And your eyes start to focus and blink
Age becomes a factor
Somewhat a hindrance and a detractor
In those younger years
The strain of growing up can be the fears

As each person goes at this own gait
But in many respects tis maturity that can't wait
Days seemed so long
And Daddy only seemed to see what's wrong
Pushed here and going there
At times it's rather hard to care
Then fighting upward to the school days
Still looking for attention and some parental praise

Wondering if that's why we're unsure
Feeling more than somewhat insecure
As having fun is nothing pure
Thinking life must be a cure
And if there isn't a firm hand
Directing traffic with some command

The route can take a rocky course
Ending up in the ring or sing-sing
Or riding the wild white horse to divorce
With Rehab to get clean from remorse
Of course that doesn't necessarily round out squares
Most kids come through with some of these scares

Yes, it's true but all in all
Youth is just stretching to be tall
That will last through life

Like the cutting edge of a knife
Walked on the sharp edge
Then age will be like falling off a ledge
Be it nothing or something dull
To get common sense through that skull

When it's as simple as a positive attitude
At any age for just being alive is gratitude
Unlike the people around you joining their cult
Until thereto emerges as an insult
Accepting chemicals and drugs
Sweeping dreams and goals under the rugs
Either living around pride or
Just another occult
Tying to be a productive adult

With authority setting the path for going places
Or trying to fill in the insecurity and dead spaces
But no matter what
It's true that what you've got
Is an attitude of mind
It's the lifeline you've allowed to unwind
A biological age is an attitude of what when and where
Activated by the cool collected ability to care
So, no matter if you're at the fifty sixty seventy or eighty
And look and feel weighty
Are you happy, healthy, prosperous?
Is this your chorus

Knowing that tomorrow won't cease
And staying young is for the most not the least
That chronological age is a platitude

Fifty sixty seventy eighty ninty-nine
The shape of the body is a sign
All shaped by the mind
It's not your heritage from your past
But what you believe in legacies cast
Positive attitudes enable the body to outlast
Those negative thinkers aging too fast

Just as Oprah and Bob Green proved
That the body moved
And the mind grooved
For the long run
Will pan the gold until a healthy life is done

And your real age is a race won

THE SAME EFFORT

The irony of rolling the dice
Is that it takes the same effort
To succeed as it does to give in to one's vice
Set upon the path of destruction
And trying to stop the process
Before your better self needs resurrection

Ironically the effort is the same
The effort to live a controlled life
Is to establish self-discipline
Through better habits
Bad habits bad results
Good habits good results

Yes truly the irony of the ages
Is the fact that it takes the same effort
To acquire bad habits until it rages
Then suffer and resort
To consequences as its retort

If the effort is the same
And a good score is the game
Let our habits acclaim
Health and happiness are the same

Thankfully it's a heavenly world of self-worth
Without a hell on earth for an obese girth

TOGETHER FOREVER

I spotted you from across the school yard
You were an apple in my eye
I found you off guard
You didn't know me or why

So, I took your picture brand new
From my best friend's billfold as he slept
And while he dreamed of you
I conceived our love as dreams unkept

The law of attraction set in
I envisioned you then
And later stole
You from the grasp
Of his den

To this day you're exceptional to my eyes
Forever young and not all knowing
As we hold onto our age in disguise
Exactly why our love is growing

A look can sometimes deceive
And yours belies the ages
Even if you don't believe
Others astound at your life's stages

As each birthday
That we celebrate
Frozen time can display
Why old age can wait

Forever young
Forever exceptional
Forever is our nuptial
And I must sing along

Hoping I too will belong
To those who don't lose passion
For my body of work
Must be masculine and strong

Then we are physically alluring
Until the very end
Without old age occurring
Before our dust hits the wind

Love birds of a feather
Together forever

YOUTH

Youth is for the mind
And time to unwind
Relative to no age
By the players on the stage

Youth is more what's gone
Than what is certainly true
Under an aging sun
That rises and sets on you

What I'm saying and this is the point
Youth is reserved for everyone
Regardless of how old we anoint
The disability to have fun

And young love that has just begun

With the flipping of the calendar stock
For as you take the page and tear
Just ignore the ticking of the clock
Don't contemplate the timetable as despair

For our heartbeat shall restore
The infinity of youth
The rings upon the tree's core
Is the same as believing in truth

It's the faith held by the human mind
That's truly believing
Leaving fear and apprehension behind
That youth is truly a matter of retrieving

The feeling of desire
Of enthusiasm of internal fire
Led by youth that will never tire
By looking back can inspire

We know this can be you
That what we thought we would lack
Can become what is true
If we live it as the very fact

Youth then can be eternal for all
Regardless of age
It's just another curtain call
Acted upon the aging stage

We are the actors and the future is our page

Marriage Vow/Lifestyle Habit Number Two:
HEY GOOD LOOKING WHAT YOU COOKING

"Hey, good lookin' Whatcha got cookin'?
How's about cookin' somethin' up with me?
Hey, sweet baby
Don't you think maybe
We could find us a brand-new recipe"?

— Jonny Cash

GET THE LOOK GOOD TO FEEL GOOD HABIT

Look your age and you own it, look yourself and you are it. Your looks count for half of your aging because of your mirror and your mate's opinion. Truth is in the eyes of the beholder, is yourself looking in the mirror. You don't like it change it. Then your mate will behold you then hold you then getting old isn't a losing game. Looks aren't everything but may be life changing:

How often should I check out my looks?... often is for acceptance and pride

Where should I put my emphasis?... females the face and both on shape

When am I the happiest with myself?... while not on the scale or in front of the mirror listening to spousal compliments

Why are looks and self-worth important to relationships, longevity and a healthy marriage:

It our expression of self-image ... physical attraction is a love sustainer

It relieves stress and frustrations ... satisfaction triggers pride

It slows the aging clock ... happier you are the younger you look

It treats depression and sadness ... a positive self-worth is a natural high

It displays beauty in the person and the relationship ... in the eyes of the beholder

It builds permanence and a feeling of security ... a positive codependency is longevity's bedfellow

It can make or break marriages ... saving the marriage is the looking good, acting good and being good

It's a sexy bed time pill ... polishing the stone anytime

This Marriage Vow and Lifestyle Habit explains the many ways that you can do things to look better and feel better. It's also about how to avoid or reverse the unhealthy life style habits and behaviors that result in poor decisions regarding chronic aging. We cannot guarantee you will look like us but we can guarantee you will feel like us. Proud of our mate and proud to be happy, healthy and prosperous.

When Shari and I met, it wasn't just our values that attracted us to each other, it was also our appearance (hair, clothes, figure, cleanliness). We dated in high school in the fifties. The days of graffiti, Elvis, Little Richard, Jerry Lee Lewis, and Bill Haley. Rock-and-roll was the new wave. If you remember Grease, that was our look. I found I had as much rhythm as Travolta, but it was better with Shari than with other girls.

That hasn't changed much in 60 years and we exhibit that in our dancing—that youthful look and attitude Thursday night of every week.

Sometimes twice a week, with comments all the time about us not stopping our obvious vitality, regardless of our age, and seeing us as role models. It might not seem important to some people but spending some time on how you look is important. When you look good, you feel good. And when you feel good, you look even better! Look your age and you own it, look yourself and you are it.

LIFE IN MY SUIT

A maker bred me with his hands
A tailor thread me with his hands

A baker fed me with his hands
A preacher wed me with his hands
A teacher led me with his hands

A woman said she loves me with her hands
All bled life into my suit
Now my hands treat that fruit
With excess abuse and misuse
Without regard to its origin its tailor
Its breadwinner its sanctity
Its sustenance its best friend
Which is its longevity considering mortality's brevity

Except with a maker of my coffin
My eulogy
My burial ground
My last will and testament

Yes, it's a restatement of my life

A maker takes me with his hands
A tailor prays for me with his hands
A baker cooks my last supper with his hands
A preacher eulogizes me with his hands
A teacher remembers me with his hands
A woman says she loved me with her hands

All bled life into my suit
Now my hands treat that fruit
Without excuse and no abuse

For I now have heaven or hell as my suitor

FEELINGS AND ACTIONS ARE HABITS OF THE MIND

The song "Memories are Made of This" sung by Dean Martin, written by Gus Kahn and Water Donaldson says it best:

> "Take one fresh and tender kiss
> Add one stolen night of bliss
> One girl, one boy some grief, some joy
> Memories are made of this "

> "Don't forget a small moon beam
> Fold in lightly with a dream
> Your lips and mine, two sips of wine
> Memories are made of this"

Experts, according to Charles Duhigg in his book "The Power of Habit", have linked our feelings to memories to our actions that are all connected to the subconscious mind in the Basil Ganglia portion of the brain so the body can respond without thinking. Basil Ganglia is central to recalling patterns and acting them out. In other words, it stores habits while the rest of the brain goes to sleep, thus forming behavior that we use every day. Basil Ganglia habits are formed by repetitive actions not central to memory or intellect.

The brain, left to its other functions, will try to make almost any routine into a habit. The Basil Ganglia determines which habits to takeover, unless you find new routines, the habit will unfold automatically. Therefore, habits can be ignored, changed or replaced. Simply understanding how habits work makes them easier to control. The problem we face is the brain cannot discern between harmful and helpful habits. This explains why it is so hard to create exercise routines. Without routines our brains would shut down overwhelmed by the minutiae of daily life. That's why habits are often as much a curse as a benefit.

What role does "will power" have on developing habits. Is it a thought process or a muscle designated by the brain to act when cued? Researchers in Australia found that will power isn't a skill it is a Basil Ganglia muscle … like your arms and legs and it gets tired as it works harder. Also, they've found that muscle has memory so working out regularly will change other habits.

Shari and I grew up in a small town in the forties and fifties that wasn't glamorous or Lifestyles of the Rich and Famous. It was somewhat austere because the economy was farm or small business-based subject to weather conditions and right to work laws supporting unions. We now call that a blue-collar culture. My parents were depression babies and were brought up always hungry or going without. Shari's parents were from a closer family background but also not without wants and needs. When we met, it wasn't just our values that originally attracted us to each other. It was also our appearance. It might not seem important to some people, but spending some time on how you look is important. When you look good, you feel good. And when you feel good, you look even better!

Shari and I dated in high school in the fifties. The days of graffiti, Elvis, Little Richard, Jerry Lee Lewis and Bill Haley. Rock and roll was the new wave. We both learned to dance together at the Indianola Youth Center. If you remember Grease that was our look. I found that I had as much rhythm as Travolta but it was better with Shari than with other girls. That hasn't changed much in 60 years and we exhibit that in our dancing skills ... that youthful look and attitude Thursday night of every week. Sometimes twice a week ... with comments all the time about us not stopping our obvious vitality, regardless of our age, and see us as a role model. Even our children are supportive of our Rhoads lifestyle.

Various ways we use to look good and feel good:
- The right clothing for the age group you're with
- Cosmetic products and other enhancements
- Daily hair and skin care
- Amazing makeup and nail finishes
- Teeth and smile
- Good posture and a confident gait
- Jewelry accessories for the occasion
- Dressing for effect and the occasion

Shari and I don't want to die before our time, and our time is under our control ... 75 years of marriage seems probable and 80 is possible. Looking good is just a part of it but a very important part. Our good friend Dee, who we have known for 55 years, gave us a picture she took of us with this poem beneath.

LOOK AT US
(Lyrics by Vince Gill)

Look at us, After all these years together
Look at us, After all that we've been through
Look at us, Still leaning on each other
Look at you, Still pretty as a picture
Look at me, Still crazy over you
Look at us, Still believing in forever

If you want to see how true love should be then just Look at us
In a hundred years from now, I know without a doubt
They'll all look back and wonder how we made it all work out
Chances are we'll go down in history

When they want to see how true love should be they'll just Look at us
When they want to see how true love should be
They'll just Look at us

Our friends at the Chicago Prime Steakhouse in Schaumburg keep telling us that we are so much in love that we don't seem to need anyone else to be with or dance with. We are their inspiration for a better lifestyle and relationships. They indicate they want what we have … and what is our Secret? Well, looking good to feel good is certainly one of our secrets. That's why you should make it one of your habits, to reinforce taking your thinking in a different path to feeling good about yourself.

Decide today to do a mental house cleaning and start making changes in your appearance as an affirmation to replace the subconscious feelings for negativity programmed into all of us by parents, media and life's problems and challenges. There is an old saying "that if you look good, you act good, if you act good, you feel good and there is nothing you cannot achieve, except acting old."

The pictures you are seeing in this book were taken in 2012 when I was 73 and Shari was 72 was by Adventure Photos in Cabo, Mexico. Cabo became our favorite vacation site after we could afford a vacation outside of the United States. We still have a villa time share there and continued to go there along with taking three cruises to the West and East Indies and Alaska. We plan to sell the time share and use book signings for our trips. Cabo is exotic enough to make you feel and act young. Truly a good habit to get into and is affordable if you make it a priority.

What we found is if you wait until you can afford it … it won't happen. We rented someone else's time share, then upgraded over the next eight years by not living our lives in reverse. What if we could live our life in reverse?

LIFE IN REVERSE

What you're thinking
Right now
Makes a difference

Only we humans
Have this volition
To improve our position

Only to realize
That our harmful habits have wasted
Most of our lives

Why couldn't life
Have been in reverse
Rather a future to rehearse

With the hearse being first
And flying at half mast
Before I'm to have passed
With a vision of what
When and why
Each day we have to try

But then it would
Have been a bore
Knowing the final score

Rather than
Hiding our winning hand
With the wonder of our last stand

With risk out of the fray
Why would we want to pray
About not getting old and gray

Most of us don't want the fuss
With life running us
Come hell or bust

But my reason here
Is to get you to steer
Your life and your career

By knowing you're the difference
You're the thinker
And the change maker

For when you're the trend setter
The world will be greater
Because you're better

But why couldn't life
Be reversed
Putting the future first

Because disappointment can't be last
Nor can our death be rehearsed

RESEARCH AND STATISTICS

According to Frank Conaway, president of Prime Life and a mature market expert, "Baby boomers (76.7 million) are not going to 'age gracefully,' nor will they age beautifully. They will go into maturity kicking and screaming all the way, and they will do whatever they can to challenge the stereotypes, and realities, of aging." We agree. Here's what we found.

- Most Americans (85%) admit that they don't always feel good about their appearance. (Gallup Poll)
- At nearly every age level, men are more likely than women to feel good about their appearance, though this margin narrows among older age groups. (Gallup Poll)
- Plastic surgery is booming with a 47 percent increase in procedures requested by 51 to 64 year old's. (American Society for Plastic Surgery)
- The number of seniors getting facelifts and cosmetic eyelid surgeries has more than doubled over the last two decades. (American Society for Aesthetic Plastic Surgery)
- The dental industry has new technologies that allow you to have healthy and good-looking teeth more easily and comfortably than ever before.

Top Quotes About Dress for Success:

1. "Sometimes, she reflected, she dressed for courage, sometimes for success, and sometimes for the consolation of knowing that whatever else went wrong, at least she liked her clothes. "Author: Emma Bull
2. "If my shoes were made of humility; my dress of compassion; my hat of respect, my jewelry of gratitude, and my perfume of determination, I would be dressed for success." Author: Joan Marques
3. "Dressing for success may sound intimidating, expensive, and a bit vain; however, keep in mind that your presentation creates credibility. "Author: Michelle Moore
4. "I am on the stage of life and the life I play needs the best costume made. "Author: Jerry Rhoads

THE DO'S

1. Acknowledge your wishes and plans for a better appearance.
2. Discuss Self=Health with friends and spouse.

3. Use your thinking young habit to put yourself together in good taste.
4. Look at your budget for the amount you have to spend to be more with it.
5. Dress for the occasion.
6. Dress for the right to be seen.
7. Dress for your mirror not your kids' styles.
8. And a little weight can be concealed by avoiding tight clothes.
9. Have a medical and dental checkup every 6 month for preventive Self=Health.
10. Look at the negative but dwell on the positive (such as wrinkles and some sagging that isn't noticeable when you smile).

THE DON'TS

1. Try to compete with the younger, more-trendy, friends.
2. Put on more than the climate will bear.
3. Be intimidated by others.
4. Dress too casual or too formal.
5. Feel depressed if the new look doesn't come off the first time.
6. Let your hair stylist pick the cut or the color … you pick it.
7. Practice poor hygiene assuming it doesn't matter.
8. Blame your genes for poor appearance and a cynical attitude.
9. Expect the worst as you think of aging and the future.
10. Accept that your life is over as you retire and have an empty nest.

VARIOUS WAYS TO LOOK GOOD, FEEL GOOD
CLOTHING – dress for successful relationships

Guy Talk (Jerry)

After college, I took a job in an accounting firm in Chicago that insisted I wear a business shirt, suit and hat. So, for the next 50 some years I wore a suit and tie every day of the week except Saturday and sometimes on Sunday for church. Now Shari loves to see me in a suit and tie because that is the old normal. The new normal is causal to business casual with workout clothes for the morning. But we both dress up if we are going out to shop or meet someone I dress as if we were going out for a social event.

Now as a senior, my approach to how I dress hasn't changed. I still want to be fashionable and dress for taste not age. I do have a flair for the latest look and can handle color combinations so they match the occasion. My advice would be never stop being you but do it with flair, passion and confidence. And I did read and practice "Dress for Success" for my business wear and religiously followed its advice.

Girl Talk (Shari)

You don't need to buy a whole new wardrobe. Fashion goes in cycles with small variations. Look at similarities from your wardrobe and you will find pieces that can be put together that still fit. Just be sure to pick pieces that you know you look good in. You can add three or four new pieces. For example, a couple tops, maybe a dress or skirt and pull out some pieces of jewelry, scarf and/or belts from your current wardrobe, that haven't been worn for a while but are now back in style.

Fashion and wardrobe is such a personal preference but one of the most important aspects of Looking Good to Feel Good.

JEWELRY – dress for good taste

Girl Talk (Shari)

I'm a proponent of selecting jewelry that fits the outfit. If it requires hoop ear rings so be it. I also like to high light a sweater or blouse with a necklace that fits the length and fashion of my overall outfit. I also wear multiple rings and bracelets … all in good taste. My watches are also a conversation piece as is my tennis bracelet. I have some memorabilia charm bracelets commemorating our children and grandchildren. I wear them on holidays. I like some of the longer (two inch) earrings but not with a heavy look and still I like them simple and not past my chin. My preference is sophisticated not gaudy.

Guy Talk (Jerry)

Shari has been my advisor on rings. I do like the bling for the occasion and usually pick leather for bracelets, though Shari bought a beautiful gold bracelet for my thirtieth birthday and I still wear it. I also have a gold necklace with a sea gull (Johnathon) she got me in 1981 for Father's Day. Neither of us have class rings and I lost my Lambda Chi pin long ago. I was tempted to order the Cubbies World Series ring until I heard the $10k price ... just a pipe dream for a fan of 69 years

CLOTHING – dress for the occasion

Girl Talk (Shari)

Jerry and I both stress dressing for the event or purpose and avoid the extremes dictated by the big-name designers. I pride myself on being able to pick out clothing that Jerry likes but that's as far as it goes. He likes to select the designer clothes at the White House Black Market because he knows my size and tastes. Same with him, I know what he likes but I don't have to dress him. We both have good tastes that are somewhat expensive if we give into that emotional buying moment. Probably due to limited resources during our youth. Our mothers made much of our clothes for grade school and Jerry's mother made his shirts when he was in high school because of a lack of money ... but also, she was a terrific seamstress. When our four children were all in school, I needed a challenge more than cleaning and cooking. So, I bought a book and taught myself how to tailor and started making Jerry's three-piece business suits. Anyway, I loved making them, and Jerry was always very particular about his clothes, and he loved the suits, so I kept making them for a number of years. I got so I could make a three-piece suit in five days or about forty hours. We actually didn't save much money since I bought expensive fabrics for the suits but he always got compliments on how good he looked in his tailored suits. His bragging on his tailor made me very proud.

Guy Talk (Jerry)

I have always dressed for the occasion. I could put myself together at a very young age. I attribute that to my mother who always looked well dressed and pretty. High School and college weren't any different except I had to buy my shirts and pants from C-Docs on the square in Indianola. Unfortunately, my mother insisted on buying my shoes too short and narrow so my feet are ugly from being deformed by the wrong shoes. Never could figure that out. Now I suffer from shoes too small so I buy them to fit for the look.

Now, not being wedded to the old standards I conform to our new life style. Since I work out each morning, I wear warmup clothing. But for the afternoons and evenings my dress is dictated by what we are doing. Shopping, visiting family, vacation, doctor and dentist visits, nights eating out or dancing determine how I dress. Shari lets me pick out my own combinations and usually approves. Of course, color combinations and fit are the most important ... adding style for our Real Age dictates social friends in their fifties not the seventies though we can mingle with all age groups without being stereotypical.

CLOTHING – dress for effect

Guy Talk (Jerry)

My wardrobe has changed dramatically since we sold our businesses. I had worn a suit and tie since 1961 when I took a job with Arthur Andersen & Co. in Chicago. Being a public accountant then demanded conformity to a certain style ... business yes but more extreme. White laundered shirt, conservative colors for the tie, wingtip Florsheim shoes, a summer and fall and winter hat, clean shaven, with short cropped hair and no sports coats. They called us the Androids ... IBM had similar standards (rules).

This look lasted until I changed jobs then started my own CPA firm. But not much. As late as two years ago when we sold the nursing homes, I religiously wore a suit and tie (Jerry Garcia instead of Tommy Hilfiger) and continually had people compliment me on my professional look. And now I don't own a pair of wingtips.

Girl Talk (Shari)

Choose colors you've always felt good about. I never wear red because my skin has a yellow tone and it doesn't work. However, I can wear off shades of red and feel good in them. In your sixties, I don't recommend dressing like the teenagers. It's much better to be modern but more sophisticated and appropriate. I still wear jeans but never the ripped or ragged ones.

Now the fashion for jeans, slacks and evening wear is tapered skinny, modern flare and palazzo. Dress lengths go from four inches above the knee, an inch below the knee, seven to eight inches below the knee, or full length. That is why I say you can find pieces that work from your closet and add some new touches here and there.

Like Jerry, I always dressed my best at our nursing facilities. Our sweet patients would say "you always dress up and look so good, why?" I just told them "I do it for you because you're worth it." I always got an understanding smile which made my day.

COSMETIC SURGERY (face care)

Guy Talk (Jerry)

As for cosmetic surgery, I don't have a good reason to do it ... my neck needs some work but my exercise program seems to keep me muscular and without jowls. Like Shari, I haven't used any Botox or unnatural cures for wrinkles because I don't need them due to good cleansing habits but I do use her massager on my face to reduce the droopiness.

Girl Talk (Shari)

I'm for natural beauty techniques so I don't have nor plan to have Botox, implants, surgery for wrinkles or eye work. I shouldn't say never but for now Jerry says it's not needed and I leave it up to him not the mirror that says more than others. As someone in their seventies I have always taken the time and money to prevent rather than just maintain. I may think about injections to my face some time in the future as needed. It seems like a simple solution to erase a few wrinkles and years. However, Jerry and I still prefer natural remedies such as exercise and having fun.

HAIR CARE – different for the guy and the girl

Girl Talk (Shari)

To top it off think about your hair. Is it dull, does it make you feel good, do you get compliments on it? Many women look great with long hair that is worn up or pulled back. If you like short hair, there are many hair styles that are easy to care for. If your hair is in the middle of being long or short and you aren't happy with it I recommend going to a hair stylist with modern creative expressions.

As a cosmetologist, I can tell you it all starts with a great hair cut styled for you and your personal tastes. I've been going to the same stylist for twenty-five years. I consider it one of my best investment in being attractive. If you don't like your hair color, change it. I didn't like my color so have highlights done with it lighter around my face. If your hair is dark and/or you have it colored, I recommend some highlights to create a lively and healthy look. The best advice on "how often" do I need to spend money on my hair ... all I can say is "how often do you want your spouse to remark on how you look"?

Guy Talk (Jerry)

I've been graying gradually since an early age and only tried once to darken it ... leaving the product on too long and had purple hair until it grew out. As for Shari, she isn't even gray at the roots or temple to boot. Now, with her counsel, my skin and hair look the best ever ... gray and it is all there thanks to my mother, I guess. As for my haircuts Shari is my barber and has been since high school ... the advantage of marrying a hair dresser. She also has been the hair dresser for all of our immediate family over the years. She has always advised me that conditioning my hair after a shower and shampoo to make it look shiny and highlight my gray hair. Fortunately, my three daughters and son have great hair as do their children and grandchildren. That is where genetics is really paying off for our family.

SKIN CARE – the same for the guy and girl

Girl Talk (Shari)

I also use a face massager twice per week and facile exercises daily to stimulate and reduce wrinkling. Thus, I haven't had to have artificial lifts or Botox injections. This is not to say don't ask for assistance, but to advise that there are other alternatives to surgery or other forms of face lifting. It is amazing how great people look when they get face injections ... something I might consider in the future. I've even got Jerry using the wrinkle massager and he says it's working.

Guy Talk (Jerry)

Shari has got me more concerned and committed to better skin condition. After seeing my mother's skin in her eighties that looked great and with Shari pushing me, I now use the skin massager and conditioner for tightening the skin and working on the sagging neck muscles that age you if not tightened. Facially this takes years off your real age look. Sun screen is also a necessity since I've had some skin cancer problems from the early days of working outdoors. I always shower and shave in the morning unless I work out later (in the past I always worked out at the break of dawn, before work). The jury is out on which is the best time to get the best results ... my opinion is, just don't miss out on a work out. When I take a day off (usually Friday after a Thursday dance night out) I actually feel guilty... it's as if I miss out on maintaining my self-image or will back slide and quit.

NAIL CARE

Girl Talk (Shari)

I still have natural nails. Fortunately, they grow and I spend the time caring for them. Jerry says they look so good they could be fake ... but they never have been. My nail colors are selected for the occasion and what I'm wearing. For years, I had to keep my nails short so I could type, and then use my computer but now I can let them grow. I have always loved nail polish. Mom said she got me to take my naps by promising to polish my nails when I got up. I guess I've always liked painted nails.

Guy Talk (Jerry)

My hand nails are in great shape and grow like weeds so I have to cut them every week. On the other hand, my toenails are a mess from all the running I've done and the sports I played. They are candidates for surgery but I don't want to be laid for six months recovering, so I just ignore pain from the bunions and hammer toes. Certain foot products do relieve the pain if I use them. My grandchildren all look at my feet and quickly say they are ugly and they don't want my feet. When one of my granddaughters was six years old and spent the night, she came into our bedroom in the morning, saw my feet and gave me a hug, and said, "Grandpa, I love you no matter what your feet look like."

TEETH CARE – for a white and healthy smile the first impression

Guy Talk (Jerry)

Shari and I are fortunate to have utilized medical checkups and dental services for ourselves and our children, even when we felt we couldn't afford it. Our thinking was and is, a hospitalization or having dental surgery is way more expensive than the preventive measures we have practiced since childhood. The difference is ... my parents weren't as fortunate, due to growing up during the depression, they both had false teeth by the time they were forty years old. I used to never floss till Shari said are you going to be like your parents who didn't know about flossing. Those are fighting words so I began to floss twice a day and haven't had any significant dental problems since.

As for my teeth, I still have wisdom teeth, have one implant and haven't had any false teeth or bridges. I learned long ago from my dentist and Shari that flossing is next to sex for scoring high on the Real Age test ... also it is solving my self-consciousness about bad breath.

POSTURE AND GAIT – stand straight and walk great

Guy Talk (Jerry)

Shari and I both feel that you show your age if you slump your shoulders and shuffle your feet. She also doesn't like seeing me walk like Groucho Marx without a cigar. Obviously, as you age the strength and muscle tone changes if you don't work them. Since we walk at least 3 to 5 miles on our walk daysnwe are building endurance as well as strength and muscle tone. Since we have been doing Yoga my sciatic problems have been eradicated allowing me to walk and run more in line with my other goals.

Girl Talk (Shari)

For women, it's even more important to carry our upper body straight and hold in our stomachs. The best lesson I got from my mother was "you don't need a girdle if you strengthen your stomach muscles". For myself, being just over five feet tall I wear high heels most of the time so balance is a high priority and a good posture for walking will allow for those three inchers if necessary. One of the benefits of doing Yoga is it puts an emphasis on posture and a strong core. It's important to walk with a long stride, little short steps conjures up an old persons' gait. You only need to concentrate on lengthening your stride for a short time, and it becomes a natural habit.

MAKEUP FOR ALL OCCASIONS

Girl Talk (Shari)

As for makeup, I always moisturize morning and night. If you choose a foundation color that looks and makes you feel good, then you are off to a good start. I use eye color that's complimentary to my foundation and eyes. I have a light, soft gold color by my lashes then a light touch of brown or plum above the first color as shading to give depth. The last color is a light pink under my brow. Lightly swipe over your eyelid to blend and prevent lines in your makeup. I don't recommend using blue or green because it doesn't look natural. I always apply my eye shadow with a brush (a different brush for each color). I use eye liner in moderation and mascara always. Keep your eyebrows simple but neat and defined. Make a nice arch and if you use color or pencil swipe with a round brush to soften so they don't look drawn on. Being a blonde, this is more important than if you are a brunette. Brunettes can just keep a nice shape and don't need color.

Then the final phase is in a corresponding tone of blush on my cheeks. And most importantly I fan a swipe of high lighter over the top of my cheeks. This brightens you face and gives a healthy glow. You can get assistance from the makeup department in the makeup store if necessary … and it's free … so you will spend on their products.

Guy Talk (Jerry)

Even though I don't wear make-up I do follow Shari's coaching on using either a face cream or lotion on my face and neck. I always use after shave and cologne. She is also making sure that my eyebrows aren't curly and the hairs in my ears and nose are trimmed when she cuts my hair. Even shaving my back is required periodically before I go to the dermatologist.

JERRY MET SHARI (get what we got)

It is reported in Prevention Magazine the things that most impress a woman are: flowers, surprise kisses, a night out to eat and dance, watching chick movies, surprise small thoughtful gifts, and pick out your mate's sleep ware to their surprise then hold hands in bed until you go to sleep or till it feels good … we have because we are attracted to each-others looks and preferences.

JUST THE WAY WE ARE

Lover's cannot describe
Through any poet or scribe
Why they are more alive
With a positive will to contrive

All the contradictions
Heightens convictions
Revealing the way, we are
Together never too far

But when you stand back
Saying the scale isn't exact
Waiting for better habits to react
Healthy becoming a new fact

That's the way we were
Please come forward
Tell me in your word
About the way we are

The distance isn't far
From where we were
For I love the way you are
It didn't just occur

Though a distant reality
It's the way we are
Loaded to my capacity
With your tenacity it isn't far

So forget the way we were
If you want to be sure
That now will endure
For beyond age is obscure

As tomorrow is unsure
Not far from the way we were
Finding that we're never far
From our past habits that deter

But lovers can describe
Through any poet or scribe
What our epitaph will inscribe
After we have died
that
"We are what we think we are"

SELF-EVALUATION

After reading this chapter take the following Self=Health quiz … update your Real Age calculation, put a checkmark for your answers and come back later to rate yourself for complying with the actions recommended in this chapter:

	Birth Age	Real Age	YES	NO
Beginning Real Age score	_____	_____		
1. Are you looking old and need a Real Age makeover?			_____	_____
2. Do harmful appearance habits discourage and cause you to hide?			_____	_____
3. Do others comment pro or con on your clothes or appearance?			_____	_____
4. Are you motivated to try a different look and style?			_____	_____
5. Do you now use the real age calculator to measure results?			_____	_____
6. Later Rate your progress (1/worst, 10/best)			_____	_____

Your rating and answers are your confession booth for judging for yourself where you are with your commitment to change your behavior and lifestyle at this point of your journey.

DAILY AFFIRMATIONS

Never give up … never fear it … just do it

For better than worse

* * *

Action with faith will try again

Purpose and principles will ever win

* * *

We live, we give, we care

Left to our dreams we dare

* * *

Sunshine is made by a better mood

Casting out doubt and a negative attitude

* * *

Search your mind for answers sake

Believe in those who learn from a mistake

* * *

Create a good habit and you have something

Create a positive self-worth and have everything

* * *

Faith, hope and charity heals the mind

A healthy mind doesn't leave the body behind

Marriage vow/Lifestyle Habit Number Three
SEX, KIDS AND ROCK-N-ROLL

"Sex is less than love
And more than hate
As if you romance
Your soul mate"

Jerry Rhoads

SEX, KIDS AND ROCK-N-ROLL ... our mantra

To understand this Vow I call our healthy journey "Our Apple Tree".

There's Shari a Sanguine Apple: 5' ½ inch tall, 112 pounds, 79 years young, fit, happy, gregarious ... a Libra all the way. Real Age calculated at 55 biological years of age. One year biologically older than Jerry because of a pace-maker for a genetic arrythmia.

There's Jerry a Choleric apple: 5' 7" inches tall, 175 pounds, 80 years young, fit, happy, intense ... a Sagittarian all the way. Real Age calculated as 54 biological years of age.

Different in every way except, values, habits, goals, parenting skills, beliefs, lifestyle and aspirations. Dedicated to fixing the countries reactionary health care system that's broken and bankrupt. We must get aging Americans upstream from chronic bad habits causing chronic diseases ... such impotence, erectile dysfunction, abstinence, loss of self-worth and sextual desires due to loss of strength and energy. We call this chronic aging that can be prevented with all of the above. The CDC (Centers for Disease Control estimates chronic diseases and mental health conditions account for 86% of health care spending and 70% of premature deaths. If ordinary people would work at their lifestyle habits, get off their expanding butts, and processed carbohydrates, 40% of those premature deaths could be prevented and the other 60% experiencing chronic aging could be reversed.

Our formula for this Apple Tree is LOVE: Life of Values Evolving in our eternal body and soul. The formula of L+V=E is the story of Jerry met Shari. Evolving into a lifestyle that produces life sustaining habits for procreating offspring who are good healthy apples falling close to the Family Apple Tree. The Apple formulation has taken 62 years to cultivate 4 children, 12 grandchildren, 8 great grandchildren. All evolving into their own Apple Trees. Thus, was Adam and Eve evolving through the good and the bad apples under a God driven sun as life begun. Our formula for daily living is "Sex, Kids and Rock-n-Roll Equals Love" where Sex isn't a fantasy but a much-needed daily body function for all species to sustain love of life. Our Kids are the result of that loving relationship and as we are the parents of genetic apples from the family Apple Tree. Rock-n- Roll signifies our need for rhythm and lyrics in our life to reassert love for each other and find fun in dancing and prancing our desires together forever. According to studies, listening or dancing to music appears to be very effective in reducing agitation, behavioral symptoms and anxieties in children and adults suffering from OCD, dementia or Alzheimer's. In our health care businesses Music therapy was a program that we offered in our restorative programming for nursing patients for reducing or reversing such maladies. With this approach we were able to reduce the use of antipsychotics by a thirty percent.

The most interesting facet of using the love formula for finding and marrying your soul mate is the more different the ingredients the better the ever-ending Apple Pie. In the book "Personality Plus" it establishes our dominant personality type (Choleric, Sanguine, Melancholy and Phlegmatic) if matched with opposites can be a predictive aspect of a lasting "soul mate marriage". Obviously, this isn't a medical prescription for loving life and living happily ever after, that you can get from a pill or diet. Nor is it the luck of the draw or where you are born or to whom you owe your birth or who you choose for a mate. Its effort meeting the right opportunity that provides the luck every time. If Shari and Jerry are so different how can differences evolve into love of needing to be and wanting the same lifestyle? Like in sports or business the love formula of a life of values evolving into a happy, healthy lifestyle pursues positive not negative results. It boils down to our marriage vows converted to how to's into compatible habits. That's in essence, converting a chance at what Jerry and Shari Got into a lucky (lucky me lucky you lucky us) relationship that takes a life time to untangle. For to be married 60 years as we have ever-after takes a commitment that evolves into compatible habits and a lifelong lifestyle of give and take. Give of your positive self and take out the negatives before they become destructive habits. That's the eternal LOVE formula. Love is then the reason for staying married ever after with the Apple Tree analogy as your life long reward …. eating apple pie with your family.

CHILDREN – THAT WONDERFUL GIFT

We had our kids
Without a second thought
Made without lids
We hadn't sought

Thank God for the spiritual lift
When we learned about this wonderful gift
They were so innocent
Not a negative act without our consent

But when we said " don't and can't"
They started to say "won't and shan't"
Then for some God sent reason
We discovered something pleasing

They were so good
Till we told them they were bad
They were so happy
Till we got sad then mad

Why must we all
Climb till we fall
Why don't we see
That the new born souls are born free

Released they need direction
But their wills don't need dissection
They'll grasp for a loving hand
They'll ask for the interested command

So why don't we just say yes
To the traits God does bless
Love and attention
Without guilt and apprehension

When you as parents covet your children
Like this
How can any future sin
Witnessed be dismissed

And then maybe
We can show all parents
About the goodness of their baby
Before their patience relents

With our consents
Giving a spiritual lift
To those dear children
That wonderful gift

A sweet apple with a core
Wanting to be loved forever more

Sex and aging are great bedfellows between the sheets and pillows. Your body is your castle and battle to be sexual and wise ... win that duel with love as the fuel. For it is more pursuit than positions, more romance than passion, more need than want, more fun than done...sex, kids and rock-n-roll is the romantic outcome.

Sex is the most important private topic in public and in person. If we admit our misgivings and reasons for not wanting to discuss it we would have to answer some private questions:

How *Often should we have sex?... if you don't have the time or energy any more ... get fit and there is no limit to what you will want from your sexuality*

Where *should we have sex?... if you don't have the privacy for intimacy ... get a motel room*

What *is our preference for sex? ... if you don't have the desire or compatibility ... watch an x rated movie or meet at a motel*

Who *is my sex partner?... if it's not your spouse it's someone you love and have passion, romance and fantasies for ... go on a date and neck in the car*

When is it the best time?... if you aren't reserving a time or place ... find an exotic place and find time

Why because sex is #1 affection for relationships, longevity and a healthy lifestyle:

It's an expression of love ... a physical relationship is a love connection

It relieves stress and frustrations ... satisfaction is a stimulant

It slows the aging clock ... the more often the better

It prevents depression and sadness ... passion and romance are pain relievers

It builds a strength in the person and the relationship ... holding hands forever

It builds endurance and a feeling of security ... a positive codependency

It makes or breaks passion ... saving the marriage is a top priority

It's a happy ending to the morning, noon or night ... romancing the stone anytime

It's a family that' loves together stays together ... your children will know you know

Like the scene in "Harry Met Sally" Shari and I often have people come up to us and say, "I want what you got ... what's your secret ... you look way too young to have been married 60 years looking as good as you both do." Tongue in cheek I always answer it's "Sex, Kids and Rock-N-Roll." But in essence, we have defied the conventional aging wisdom ... which is to retire at 55, 60 or 65 and start the dying process. Instead, we have turned on our genetic tendencies to youthful but mature sex habits and turned off harmful hidden inhibitions. Then sex, romance, passion, affection and love are all rolled into daily happy bedfellows where more is a function of our love than self-gratification.

SEX is ROMANCE and PASSION

If sex doesn't bring us closer
It does define our distance from one another
And if we don't meet some ultimate passion
In the process we do at least
Crash head-on into ourselves

While times technology and terminology change
Human need remains the same

*If passion is back
It's because we want it to be
And because it never was away*

*Affection isn't love or romance
But it's the source of love
Passion isn't necessary to be romantic
But it is the fuel to necessity
As Infatuation is the boutique
Of passion and sexuality*

*It's the need to express passion
Rounding out the act of love
But sex isn't love for the abuser
If it's used to hurt not assert
Sincere feelings upon the accuser
Such is for passion alone*

*And age isn't a de-facto reason
For gaining or losing passion
It's the spice for the deeds
Continuing sexual needs*

*If sex doesn't bring us closer to discover
It does define our distance from one another
Whereas passion motivates the search
For an affectionate and longing lover*

*But no matter how you
Define it or do it
Love sex and romance
Without affection and passion
Is a fireplace without a fire
A mare without a sire
A man and a woman who retire*

From their desire

SEX HABITS ARE ALWAYS A PERSONAL AFFAIR

In this chapter, we explore the one interesting thing the researchers note in their analysis that there are "three dimensions of loving sexuality

— behavior, attraction and romance." Then how to avoid or reverse the unhealthy life style habits and behaviors that result in broken marriages and divorce. Shari and I believe our relationship and marriage longevity are a product of our sexual attraction to each other, our children as a result of that relationship and our love of music and dancing a reflection of that attraction.

In other words, people's sexual experiences don't always match up with who they are attracted to or how they identify with desire ... and those are the three distinct "dimensions of sexuality" to be considered as we age. So, do we have an attraction and passion for romance. Also, there are body changes (ED and menstrual changes), attitude and turn-ons that evolve, with the right time and surroundings that impact opportunities.

The Man is visual and the woman is not. The man is physical and the woman is not. The light is on the light is off. Since this chapter isn't a scientific study of sex, we dwell on how it's important in our overall relationship. That's nothing new, but how each of us handles it isn't necessarily a result of good habits or bad habits either. Because, outside influences impact or contribute as ED or the inability to find joy in the act of sex. But Shari and I have found that it's a healthy habit to "get it on with affection, passion and love." As for romance it's still exciting as our aging has increased the frequency and methods.

Early in our marriage Shari and I never went to bed mad at each other ... it worked most of the time. I'm more likely to apologize than Shari. She is prone to want to have her feelings tended to and that's what I've learned to do ... it's getting past hurt feelings using affection, before we can get it on. Over 60 years of marriage this has happened more times than I like to admit. But the one thing that was constant in our volatile marriage was our sexual relationship rooted in the love, physical attraction, affection and romance.

Like Romancing the Stone (Jerry's favorite movie made in 1984) "A romance writer sets off to Colombia to ransom her kidnapped sister, and soon finds herself in the middle of a dangerous adventure. She is a dowdy romantic- adventure writer hurled into a real-life adventure in the Colombian jungle in order to save her sister, who will be killed if a treasure map is not delivered to her captors. She is helped out by a brash mercenary, and together they search for the priceless gem located in the map." And find a treasure they weren't expecting ... romance. This relationship almost fits Shari and I to a "t" in our journey to a long and fruitful life that we plan to have forever.

More books are written on how to than why not. The Fifty Shades of Gray" just happens to be the man's wish and the woman's fantasy. And we humans are the only mammals (other than chimps) who have sex recreationally as well as for procreation. So, how do we as self-conscious human beings have fun, healthy sex without a book. In our opinion the answer to this is experimentation for an act of love not just self-gratification or satisfaction. It's more romance than a ritual or dance of the mating season.

Shari and I have dated since I was a Sophomore and she a Freshman in high school. It didn't last that long due to my immaturity and my love of sports more than girls. Of course, that changed and by my Senior year she was my steady girlfriend and best friend ... that has never changed. After 60 years married and 62 years together, we are still as much in love but even more sextual than when we were seventeen and sixteen.

Shari is sexy in a cute and curvy way. I noticed that 65 years ago when she was in seventh grade and I in eight when my heart skipped a beat each time I saw her. I still feel it every day when I see her. She is the most attractive girl, woman and lady I have ever seen or been with. She doesn't have to try to be sexy ... it's natural with her figure and personality. She says it's "only in your eyes as my beholder" and I say no, "I'm beholding to your sexy ways."

Even though I have the good fortune of a full head of hair and still muscular due to the workout routine our attraction is not just physical. It's Shari's smile when I kiss her. It's her selfless thinking with her heart of others first, including me. Therefore, we are still attracted to each other and sexually active due to our romantic relationship. She has inspired me to strive to be more like her approach to giving and serving our family. To me, that's sexy.

WHAT'S SEXY

What is sexy
Is it nudity or prudity
Is it fire or burning desire
Is it in the bedroom or in the car?

It's not what you are
But how you are
It's not where you are
But why you are

What you are
Sexy
Foxy
Lovely
Beautiful

How you are
Fun
Loving
Loyal
Romantic

Where you are
Between
Betwixt
Distant
Detained

Why you are
Romance
Marriage
Children
Family

We all are stuck
Between sex and love
Wondering if its real
Until it becomes what we feel

Not the looks
Not the sex
Not the infatuation
But that intangible that makes love

It's how you feel in your heart
That would break if you part
That's sex romance love and soul
Rolled into your sexy mate's role

With family as its goal

In the book "The Secret" Rhonda Byrne puts it best when she defines the "Law of Attraction." Ironically, without knowing it, since the book came out 40 years after I utilized it, I attracted my life long soul mate Sharon Kay White Rhoads and have been attracted to her ever since. From a simple kiss to a lifelong commitment practicing the Law that attracts us all to a soul mate.

- Your current state of affairs will impact your lifestyle no doubt and your interests and hobbies will enable you to change directions, for better results. You must rework your goals, as necessary.

- When I saw her standing there It was then that Law of Attraction (like portrayed in the book The Secret that states what you want is what you get if you don't give up or give into rejection) set in … it was four years later when I finally got her to date me. I was a senior and she was a Junior. We were married two years later and have just celebrated our 60th wedding anniversary. I credit our marital success to "sex, kids and rock-n-roll" and our unceasing quest for romance and love for each other. We inherently have or do something romantic daily … music, nature, poems, love making, visiting our maker, dance, yoga together, walking together, talking together, being together. (Our children make fun of us for needing to sit together at the table and always traveling together … never to part) That's romance, the only known "DNA Fountain of Youth".

- As soul mates, sex mates and fate mates we have conceived four grown children, twelve grandchildren and four great grandsons. We are going for the record for length of marriage of 93 years so we must stay healthy and happy or die trying!

- My advice is to appreciate what we have … sex, kids and roll-n-roll yes but also happy work life with an active participation in some group activities (church, boy/girl scouts, political campaigns, dance clubs, theater, etc.).

If you are emotionally old…the sun is setting on your future. No hope, lost and retired, no marriage, no relationships, no quality of life … If you are mentally old, the moon has eclipsed on your past, no dreams fulfilled, no love gained, no successful events, no joyful memories, no happy bed time stories, no value of life as you know it. This state-of-affairs must be reversed for you to age naturally, happy, healthy, and prosperous. Many will just accept unhappiness as circumstance that one must endure, while in waiting for happenstance to change. Guess what, it does not happen if your stance is on blaming others or just good ole circumstance.

The cure is, as always, in your head … you either think young or feel old … why not feel young and forget thinking old. As we age, we realize that infatuation as a teenager or young adult is not the same as being in love with this person for the rest of your life. And in many cases, it doesn't last through high school. I guess Shari and I had both infatuation and love at first sight then first kiss four years later. So, I'm not suggesting that every relationship will be that way and last forever. In some cases, that young infatuation brings you back together if the later relationships didn't meet the bonding that young love usually does.

Getting it on with a prior girl or boy friend may be the current normal with only 50% of the marriages not lasting. Our advice, you need to be both lovers and best friends. Who else will care for you in the later years when the kids have moved on and your health is declining? Of course, you can limit the latter by getting it on with your current mate. Shari and I believe you can only have one soul mate but we are happy we don't need another …. Ever. She's a one- man woman and I'm a one-woman man … we just lucked out and found this eternal romance with the first kiss, in high school. This discovery is, by far, the single most important habit to develop … put romance in every aspect of your life and life takes on excitement, fun and worthy of your mortal time together. As for immortality that will take care of itself if you believe in forever after.

RESEARCH AND STATISTICS:

For example, 81% of women report feelings of attraction "only to the opposite sex," suggesting that 19% experience some same-sex attraction; 17.4% of women have experienced same-sex contact. Yet only 6.8% of women identify as gay or bisexual. Due to unemployment 9.3%, that means a loss of self-worth and 16% due to underemployment 16%, that means a skill is more important than relationships

- Life expectancy impacts sexual mores
    - Females 80 too old to make love
    - Males 70 too old to have sex
- Retirement contributes to feeling unattractive
    - Females 62 no longer sexy
    - Males 65 no longer a hunk
- Divorce at an early age due to promiscuity
    - Sex becomes the trigger for remarriage rather than monogamy or affection
    - Sexual preferences are rooted in convenience rather than romance
- Divorce at a later age due to promiscuity
    - Loneliness makes it harder to find a sexual companion
    - Attraction makes it harder to find a lasting relationship

LOVE ISN'T PERFECT

I called out the number 10
And no one spoke back
I called out with the voice of a friend
And I was alone on the flattest track
I called out for you to come
And you did not speak

I don't feel love is dumb
As it may be weak
I called again and heard no word
I flew to where I'd been
And checked out each roosting bird

And no one had heard of my love
It seemed only I could discover
Whom I was thinking of
As the vision of my last lover
As snow had parted the air

And spring was blowing breezes through my wings
Not knowing that you weren't there
My chill was wasted on other things
I didn't find you
You weren't there like in the past

I began to think that we were through
And that time had taken its toll at last
But lo as I headed homeward
I heard you from up above
And without so much as a word
We reconvened our perfect love

Only to awake in the morn
And find you again gone
Like most dreams which are newly born
It's only a chapter closed by the dawn
Here's hoping I can get you back
Hold you truly in my vision
Though reality may be the lack
Of love it's no illusion

It's more than an act to a distance romance
Until you got back (from Dubuque)
From your sabbatical called circumstance
(when Shari got back the ring was my rebuke)
So, love isn't perfect nor just a fact

Until together forever after is its final act

THE DO'S:

Love making and sexual satisfaction for you and your partner isn't our purview but the impact on your overall health is certainly impacted by your personal habits and practices. So, Shari and I have found the following:

1. First and foremost sex is more mental than physical due to the importance of the love making factor.
2. But it is important for both the physical and mental needs of all human beings to be able to love their mate and their life soulfully (creatively).

SOUL MATE

What Is a Soul Mate?

From day one
Something you can't create
Something you can't fake
Something you can't break

It's someone going the same direction
Someone pursuing the same destination
Someone feeling the same attraction
Someone loving the same affection

It's separate but together
It's an everlasting tether
It's a bird with its feather
It's love forever

IT'S A CHECKMATE

3. Our advice is more sex with love is better than less (at any age) and is a high indicator of having a healthy and happy lifestyle.

4. When you feel good about your physic, your looks, your mindset, your future, you generally will feel good about your sex/love life. They all feed off the same equation ... self-worth equals self-image equals self-satisfaction ... an investment in the first 7 of our vows/habits give you the foundation for Habit #8 ... not necessarily in that order but in that magnitude.

5. The other important stigma to overcome is that sex is for younger mates and it falls off dramatically after the age of forty. Shari and I believe that is due to stinking thinking and poor health rather than age. Most healthy people are more active sexually than ever before ... though in their seventies, eighties or nineties they don't plan to stop anytime soon. It's truly a significant part of our physical and mental exercise program. We have found sextual love to be the best stress reliever.

6. Since this is a very private matter, we will leave it up to you and yours to judge the results of being sexual daily (visually attracted with some form of physical contact). Just remember a soul mate is the sex mate for a loving fate. In our experience, the healthier and happier you are physically and mentally dictates your resulting sex life habits.

THE DON'TS:

1. Eliminate or limit sexuality as you age ... it should get better because it's more intimate.

2. Let the past dictate how you participate with the opposite or same sex ... we are loving, needing humans needing affection and romance ... just give it and you will get it.

3. Find ways to avoid having a physical relationship due to health problems or inactivity ... make it happen even if it has to improve in its results.

4. Treat sex and its importance as a taboo or never discussed ... never done ... never is a long time.

5. Look for happiness and sexual satisfaction somewhere else when it's already in your bedroom waiting for you to decide to communicate not just fornicate.

Simply said improvement in Getting It On is all any of us can live or die for. There is no perfect love, relationship, circumstance, happenstance that can stir the pot. Humbly speaking, Shari and I give thanks every day for our life and our Rhoads lifestyle. Sure, we have worked hard like most everyone else and have had some luck (effort meeting opportunity) but it boils down to a give and take partnership. If you are struggling with that try the following three things:

1. Walk one to three times per week for one to three miles, holding hands (yes people will look at you as if your just one-night stand lovers) and just talking about anything and everything but disagreements. Shari has on occasion walked away from me until I stopped wailing on about some sports team or some meaningless family problem.
2. Make love at least three times per week. No further instruction needed.
3. Hug (and kiss if you can pull it off) your kids, dog and wife every day. Our kids do kiss their dogs but after kissing their kids. I would add Shari kisses the sons-in-laws and I kiss our daughter-in-law … on the cheek.

VARIOUS WAYS TO GET IT ON:

Give Time to Romancing the Stone (1984) *Where Michael Douglas and Kathleen Turner finally find a treasure they weren't expecting … romance.*

As people age it is conventional knowledge that the libido wanes. Studies show that most couples that have been married over 10 years get it on at most once to twice per week. Some relationships of convenience once a month and some divorcees not at all. Sure, it's more than how often. Quality over quantity is what we all strive for. The true fact that we have found is getting it on depends on how we treat each other in getting along. And the one thing that our strength was our sexual relationship rooted in romance.

ROMANCE YOUR STONE

My advice to body beaters
And wife cheaters
Needs are in between where
You'll find desires and flare

Not really knowing where to light
But having the urge to take full flight
And as it's seen and said a lustful heart
And love will soon part

Seeking a portal and a port
Of a consistent relationship
A better way to court
Not a roller coaster trip

So maybe we all do need romance
Maybe it's the steadiness of love's trance
And not an erotic up and down
Pleasures now a fool's gold crown

The solution is to settle one's feet upon the ground
Then maybe we'll take the time to look around
And find romance together not to abscond
For something lost then found as monogamy will abound

With someone else and adventure there
If there's no warmth of love to care
That takes a heart and flare
To be a pair

And this is of what I speak
Of getting it on not with tongue and cheek
Conquering life's fondest peek
With intimacy at its peak

By romancing the stone we seek

Go to bed early with a purpose

Guy Talk (Jerry)

When answering "what's your secret for being married 60 years, I always answer Sex, Kids and Rock-N-Roll." We have defied the conventional aging wisdom ... too tired to have sex at 55, 60 or 65 and start the dying process. We, on the other hand, are sexually active as we have always been. But now it's in the privacy of an empty nest giving us more time and more often.

Shari and I aren't sex experts nor are we neophytes but we are a happy and energetic couple not having to have others involved for us to have a great time ... I've got one desire and her name is Sharon Kay and it's been that way since I was seventeen and she sixteen ... 65 years with my pursuit and her willing reception of our love making. When going to bed we hold hands and kiss ... the rest is private. No sex toys or porn to get it on. Just each other in love.

Most of our friends, where we dance, comment on how we seem to be deeply in love and not needing anyone else to make us happy ... how true that is. I truly believe sex is number one, at our age, in keeping us healthy, happy and prosperous. Number two is our kids and theirs, a result of the first, and number three our dancing to rock-n-roll together since high school.

Girl Talk (Shari)

Actually, we had never heard that before, and it certainly surprised me that anyone would say it, or even notice. We were just having our usual great time and dancing to great music. We talk, and holding hands is just something we've always done. I love having that connection with Jerry, and if that is something you don't do anymore, you should try it I'm sure you probably used to do it when you first started dating your partner or spouse.

Does that mean bed is only for sleep as you get older? No, Jerry and I have always slept in the same queen-sized bed and had four healthy children doing so. I don't ever see that changing because of age. On the other-hand the oldest person on record is 122 and they still sleep and get it on if they're healthy. Fortunately, we are healthy.

Surprise she or he with flowers

Girl Talk (Shari)

I love flowers! Fortunately, Jerry is a very romantic person, and I can't imagine not having this kind of relationship. Of course, I knew he was a romantic, when we were dating in high school. He always bought me roses, loved to dance, and was such a gentleman with great manors. He still buys me flowers, has great manners and loves to dance. He gets a little annoyed if I start to open the door when we're out on a date. (He has given up on that when we go to see our family and grandchildren because I'm always in a hurry and rush to the house and open the door for the hugs and kisses). He used to laugh at me because he said, "You've got your hand on the car door as soon as we arrive in their town" and he was right...I just couldn't help myself.

Guy Talk (Jerry)

I know she loves flowers ... but so do I because they are beautiful ... like our relationship. However, I have learned that you can never buy too many flowers or give too many kisses. Romancing the stone is the most important function of the soul mate to keeping their soul mate connected to your heart.

Compliment she or he on their looks

Guy Talk (Jerry)

Shari looks great all the time and I tell her so … she sometimes argues the fact but I prevail. I never answer the question "do I look too dated in this" or "do you like me in this dress". Do a Bruno Mars and say "I love you just the way you are"…

> She's so beautiful and I tell her everyday
> Yeah, I know, I know when I compliment her, she won't believe me
> And it's so, it's so sad to think that she don't see what I see
> But every time she asks me "Do I look okay?"
> I say
>
> When I see your face
> There's not a thing that I would change 'cause you're amazing
> Just the way you are
> And when you smile
> The whole world stops and stares for a while
> 'Cause girl you're amazing
> Just the way you are

It's obviously a loaded question where a positive affirmation is the only way to her heart … let her decide what to wear and you'll keep the relationship positive. She knows the answer but just doesn't want you to confirm it

Girl Talk (Shari)

I just read what he said and he also looks great all the time and I tell him so … he never argues the fact because he knows how to put himself together and only needs me to confirm that his taste is right on.

Wear something sexy

Girl Talk (Shari)

I dress for him not in spite of him. The occasion dictates what I will pick … never intending to be sexy except for Jerry. I also don't want to embarrass my children or grandchildren or great grandchildren. Sexy to me is being your natural self ... you'll know when you feel it.

Guy Talk (Jerry)

I dress for the occasion since I don't have to impress a sexy woman ... since she's already mine. I'm told all the time how lucky I am to have her ... and I always agree. Sexy for Shari is always in good taste and sensitive to her real age. That being in her mid-fifties allows her to be more aggressive current fashions but not gauche.

Say something sexy or alluring about her or just hug her

Guy Talk (Jerry)

I treat Shari with respect and adore her personality. She appreciates me being thoughtful and a gentleman when it comes to opening doors, walking on the outside, helping her with her coat, helping her with the car door, complimenting her on her appearance and ageless beauty and figure. Like her mother, she is continually laughing and smiling. A trait I wish I could emulate but that's her personality coming through and I enjoy having her keep me loose. There's a theory that laughing is therapeutic and those that can laugh will live longer and stronger ... after witnessing this in Shari (79, her mother (93), her grandmother (87) and her Aunt Edith (109) I believe we live longer if we can laugh at ourselves. So goes the saying "look at the mother and grandmother to see what you will get as they age" ... mine was a vision of the future of fun and beauty.

AUNT EDITH

(I met Shari's Aunt Edith at the age of 101
She looked and acted 75
A miracle we thought done
But her legacy is still alive)

She sits there
Holding her head high
Above the mighty weight of years
That fly by
Steady for a hundred and one

Slow but sure
Beaming like the sun

With eyes so clear
Chuckling is her style
Youth in her being here
Humor in her smile

Yearly her contract with life
Renews Aunt Edith
So proud to be alive
So humble to be here in faith
With her busy hive

Generations of love
To keep her near
The surface of reality
Never naïve nor feeble fear
Just the strength of longevity

Her conquest of age is incredible
As she lived to 109 chuckling every decibel

(I met Aunt Edith's great niece at the age of 14
She looked and acted so alive
An attraction I thought serene
And her legacy is still mine at 75)

Genetics is the law of evolution
Because she looks 45
Chuckling at my solution
Marry a smile and a laugh
As your other half

Girl Talk (Shari)

To me being sexy is a vision not a saying. I will leave that up to Jerry. But it makes me feel good when he helps me pick out clothes and oohs and aaahs when I wear them. He has great taste and I sometimes can't make a decision so I let him choose.

Being playful can be very sexy

Girl Talk (Shari)

To me being sexy isn't a game ... however, love making can be playful. I don't like discussing something so personal but whatever we are doing has worked for almost sixty years and we are still doing it ... but more often. But I'm only playful and sexy around Jerry not friends, neighbors or business associates ... Jerry and I both have avoided any such confrontations or invitations and believe it only hurts the true relationship.

With social media and the exposes in sexual abuse and inappropriate behavior we all must live by a higher standard than power corrupts and allow it to lower our principles of monogamy, commitment and loyalty after marriage. This isn't idealistic or virginity, it is for happiness, good health and longevity.

Guy Talk (Jerry)

Shari and I have been lucky because we have common interests while being able to balance family, work and having a lasting romance due to uncommon reasons. It's those uncommon reasons that we are imparting in this book. The results of us actually being younger than our chronological age is somewhat a puzzle to us. The reason I have given often is sex, kids and rock-n-roll needs to be considered by everyone who desires to live an active long playful life, not withstanding acts of God.

Confess fantasies and dreams

Girl Talk (Shari)

The experts say women have the romantic fantasies. The men have their sports and boy toys. It spills over into movies, books, topics of conversation and pursuit of happiness. What Jerry and I have in common is what makes us different ... we only do what we both want to do not what other people want us to do. We don't take separate vacations, we don't travel alone anymore, we have to be flexible on what we watch and eat ... this keeps us from getting bored. Jerry says this has kept us looking and acting young because we like the way we were and are.

Guy Talk (Jerry)

Jerry said "Shari we are friends and lovers will you marry me". Then we had sex, Children, grandchildren, great grandchildren and sixty wedding anniversaries. Our fantasy then and now is how we perpetuate this and not get bored with each other; the answer is the relationship is like a fantasy since we are beating father time and the odds. So, living together forever is quite an endeavor. It will take more than a wedding ring but no more than our eternal love can bring.

Harry said "Sally we can't be friends and not be lovers" while he thought about sex. Because, he said "that man the predator is thinking about sex every ten seconds and the pursued is thinking every ten days". "While the female is thinking romance and the man is on the advance". "When the female is wanting a fantasy lover the male is falling for another". "Only humans and monkeys have recreational sex" and never confess their fantasies and dreams. Far be it for me to think that this will change all preexisting habits. However, it most certainly will have an impact on your longevity, number of offspring and wedding anniversaries, and most importantly your "real age" birthdays.

Suggest going on a date and then to a motel

Girl Talk (Shari)

Jerry and I have always found ways to be romantic. I can only remember one time when he took me on a date to a Greek restaurant to rekindle our fire and It worked. That was when we weren't communicating and before we started to take long walks together. After that we are regularly going out to walk or eat or to a movie or a play ... these certainly are dates that result in romance if you let them.

Guy Talk (Jerry)

It does work to do something exotic like a blind date and love making. Shari and I had our honey moon at a one-night stand motel in Des Moines and our marriage has lasted all these years because we were committed to having and keeping a family ... when we had an occasional spat, Shari said get out then I said I'm sorry I can't leave the kids. Eventually, we stopped having to say that because we made it point to avoid conflict because we loved being together.

Take each other to a sexy movie

Girl Talk (Shari)

A sexy movie is one that shows true emotions and happy endings … known as chick flicks. We both like nonviolent out of the box mysteries … we don't like fright. Porn turns me off … I get embarrassed with current movies because they seem to be without love and feelings just the physical part. So, Jerry knows when it is time to change channels or get a different movie on Netflix.

I used to be pretty prudish but the culture has changed so much that anything goes at the theaters (even stage plays show nudity) and in the bars. A sexy movie is one that shows true emotions and happy endings … known as chick flicks. We both like nonviolent out of the box thrillers … we don't like fright except in true stories particularly war movies.

Guy Talk (Jerry)

Shari said it for me. I do like war stories (not sexy), business success, sports heroes, true stories and most chick flicks. I don't usually break a tear but it happens when something changes my view on effort and determination.

Let love be the reason and satisfaction the result

Guy Talk (Jerry):

Being a Sagittarian, poet and renaissance man, my heart is on my cuff as is romance … I also have some mannerisms for etiquette and being a gentleman. Shari wonders where I get my sensitivity … must be from my father and mother in different ways. My father was a quiet man but very sentimental while my mother was sensitive to her wants but neither very loving towards each other or my sister and I.

Since Shari and I met for the first time in High School … she claims she picked me and I know that isn't true because I saw her in seventh grade, in Junior High. The significance of who eyed who first is lost in the next 60 years that we have been together. Yes, it's unique these days for baseball pitchers to win 20 games and marriages to last 50, 60, 70, 80 years…the world record seems to be 93 so we all have some ways to go but we have a great start. When and If you read this far and think we are self-indulgent please forgive us for dwelling on how we are doing it … we aren't that unique when it comes to wants and desires … we just have had this time to develop our negative into a positive story. My parents were married 50 years, and I never heard them say I love you and due to poor health, they expired in their early 80's in nursing homes that were despicable to say the least. So that has influenced me to want what Shari brought to the table … love, loyalty, friendship and amazing children, grandchildren and now great grandchildren … we just found out on Valentine's Day 2018 that Alec our oldest grandson and his wife Ashly are expecting, in September, their and our third great grandchild. Maybe by the time this book is published we will know if it is a girl or boy.

Girl Talk (Shari)

Intimacy is an important part of any relationship. It's a conformation of your relationship and love connection to each other. This has always been very important to us and I'm convinced it's a big contributor to staying young. Sexuality is a natural part of love making. However, without the romance, it tends to be just physical. Jerry and I create our romance before we make love so the end result is always better. Romance is a function of the bond we have in daily activities and have had in business and parenting.

Jerry and I have always been attracted to each other. Physically and sexually. Jerry with his visions and me with my affections. Romance comes before any other stance … religion, politics, opinions, differences. We manage to find time for each other every day since we have spent most of our time together in business and fitness and wellness for the last 25 years of our marriage.

All of these priorities come after our family but before seeking attention from others. I love to visit and laugh with my yah yah sisters and Jerry is into sports, politics, business with his yuck yuck brothers. Yes, we are so different in most categories but alike in our interest and passion for each other. Vacations and social functions always together never going apart.

Guy Talk (Jerry):

Love making and sexual satisfaction for you and your partner isn't our purview but the impact on your overall health is certainly impacted by your personal habits and practices. So, Shari and I have found the following:

FRIENDS AND LOVERS

Lovers can be best friends
Can best friends be lovers
I thought when I looked at you
You were my best girlfriend

The more I looked at you
The more courtship came through
Friends and lovers are they two
Or are they just someone to date
Or can they be the same

When I asked you for your hand
And you said yes
I'd be your lover I guess
But there was no guarantee
You would be my friend
Not till time could tell us
What we mean together until the end

We held each other close
We knew what need could mean
That we needed one another
To us there was no in between
And our infatuation grew stronger
As we stayed together longer and longer

We needed more than each other
For the warmth of our lifetime affair
Affection needed to be much more
Much more than just the sexual pair
We needed to be able to talk and be aware
To walk and be together and really care

And this I guess you'd call friendship
Wanting to be together
But not just for the embrace
That could come in any case
And you needed somebody to talk to
Someone who wasn't impatient
And forgot to caress you

You needed someone to lean on
Someone to confide in
And pick you up when you're down
This is the friendship
That had to be found
If I were to be your last
While time past so fast
Leaving only bits and pieces
Left behind as life ceases

Unless we're friends
As well as lovers
Giving support versus
Just pulling down the covers
Friends must become lovers
Yes we found we could be
Lovers and friends in matrimony

So after 60 years of wiping away
Our fears with our kids on their way
I believe being best friends
And lovers is the best to all ends

Happy anniversary Shari
From your friend and lover forever

JERRY MET SHARI (get what we got)

Get it on by the way you communicate. Say I love you every morning, noon and especially at night ... also when saying goodbye or hi ... we have and reply I love you too! THAT'S ROMANCE. Get it on by loving the way each other acts and looks (habits one and two). Experts on Alzheimer's have found that listening to music, playing music or singing slows down the decline in cognition. Shari and I have music in our bathroom in the mornings and during the day. Shari also bought an exercise device where we boogie with the music ... so we call it the "boogie board". Fifteen to twenty minutes in the morning works up a sweat before our showers (together).

HAVE ROMANCE

Dance old man dance
There's no age to romance
Life has given you your last chance
So dance ole man dance

Some mortals trot and some prance
Others shoot arrows and others throw a lance
But I'm telling you to advance
There's no age to romance

When romance has been unkind
It can seem like yesterday
That you seek and find
That you've not been loved today
Letting me see before I go blind
Age and love are aligned

So be sure you tell your lover
About those things that years won't uncover
When you discover there's no age
To be a lover

As I stood by the altar of Time's best friend
Romance and love as a timeless blend
And age said, "I do" to a heavy wind
Marking the progress towards the end
Of just being a friend
Allowing me to take my frustration down
And set up the abundance
That I had found

With romance
As the crown

Since I live and die in an ageless prance
Telling those who see me by chance
That I shall not age as I dance
To that mortal song called romance
It's the love of my life that will enhance

As age does advance
So have romance

SELF-EVALUATION

After reading this chapter take the following Self=Health quiz ... update your Real Age calculation, put a checkmark for your answers and come back later to rate yourself for complying with the actions recommended in this chapter:

	Birth Age	Real Age	YES	NO
Beginning Real Age score	_____	_____		
1. Are you getting it on with your significant other enough?			____	____
2. Do harmful habits still control your sex life?			____	____
3. Do you converse about your desires and technique?			____	____
4. Do harmful habit changes impact you gettting it on?			____	____
5. Do score your real age calculator to measure sexual resutls?			____	____
6. Later rate your progress ... 1 being low and 10 being the best			____	____

Your rating and answers are your confession booth for judging for yourself where you are with your commitment to change your unhealthy habits and lifestyle at this point of your journey.

AFFIRMATIONS:

Sex is what you want

But love is what you need

***

Loyalty is the music of lovers

Making the music under the covers

***

Love and Life has no end

For those who an eternal friend

***

Love others as you would

Who love themselves as they should

***

The start of better sex is in the heart

Not in a position or as a possession

***

Just find someone that you can trust

For their mind not their lust or bust

***

If sex is love … what are you? A lover or loser

The beloved, the former lover or sex abuser

I OPENED MY HEART TO YOU

You knocked upon my chest with your pretty eyes
You tapped me on the shoulder with your promises
You asked me to open my heart to you

So you could come right in
How could I possibly know
That you already knew when
I'd been in love with you
Long before then

Yes, it's for sure
I caught you glancing at me in the hall
And while I took my turn scrimmaging in basketball
You must have had me on your list
Not dismissed as a possibility

Just because no one else would look at me
Small and skinny not too cute
Ill-fitting clothes I had no suit
But I did wear those homemade shirts
And I guess that's what attracted your skirts

Shy and not the least bit savvy
I circled the square in my Dad's black and white Chevy
For it was that car that gave me the Elvis hair
To let you know that I really did know you were there
And boy was it easy to open my heart to you

Cause at sixteen everything was new
Amazingly the things important then
No longer seem more than a whim
Cute as you were with a curvy body
It was still a long-ways from getting naughty

But that didn't mean your appeal went unseen
Because all I could think of was what you seem
How this little cute blond
Must be my true love
Now and beyond

And amazingly over the years
Through many ups and downs
And smiles and tears
Not the way it sounds
I still feel that same old way

Here and now on our sixty-first Wedding Anniversary Day

MARRIAGE VOW/LIFESTYLE HABIT NUMBER FOUR
HAVE A PURPOSE AND DESTINATION

*"Life is about balance. The good and the bad.
The highs and the lows. The pina and the colada."*

— Ellen DeGeneres

HAVE A PURPOSE AND DESTINATION:

Living and loving your life with your wife are two sides of healthy, happy Aging. Your life and marriage now is a reflection of your life now not tomorrow or yesterday … choose the right path now to get and like your journey to living longer and stronger. Ironically, choosing a mate is the most important step to getting a life for the long run. And it isn't necessarily logical or predictable … but for sure opposites attract and likes distract getting a life. For Personality differences (read "Personality Plus" by Florence Littauer) and incompatibility justifying a change. It changed our life forever more. Our individual roles are driven by our personality and determination that results in longevity?

DAREDEVILS OF LIFE

This describes Shari and I
The daredevils in life
Mates for the bigger pie
Daredevils till we die
Together is the why

Daredevils of life
Daredevils of faith
Overcoming the fear of life
I took a wife

Her name is Sharon Kay
She took me afraid to say
No to the future cast
We stood before the past

Looking back at a simple dot
Traveling our path
To the gentle shrug, of "why not"
As the wind blew us fro and aft

It's only a short distance to understanding
We were so sure we knew the journey
Because it seemed time to leave the landing
Gentle nest of a simple beginning for three

With tears for fears in the eyes of our past
We set upon the sea of circumstance
Riding out the storms not to last
With our small craft named romance

Hanging on to each other to row
The Ark to Chicago
There were three four five and six
Jobs would come and jobs would fix

Rocky Rhoads that daredevil
And his mate of love avail
Together risk do dwell
In her loyal spell

For some feats caused thunder
In a cloud
Others stood under
Making the daredevils proud

To heal a blunder
Caused by the devils who dared
(Saying how can you get ahead by burying your head)

How *often do I check out my goals?... as often as you need reassurance*

Where *should I put my emphasis?... family first mate second and work last*

What *are the obstacles to my success? ... choose the path that most resist*

Who *is my best backer?... your mate, spouse, children and friends who believe in you*

When *am I the happiest with myself?... when I realize that life is meant to be good*

Why *is having a purpose important to a lasting marriage and happy lifestyle It's "Life is but a dream"... but having it as a purpose*

It reduces stress and frustrations ... satisfaction is a motivator

It slows the aging clock ... the right priorities create the biggest payoff

It absolves depression and sadness ... they are replaced by hope and success

It's the Law of Attraction at work ... for love, loyalty, faith are yours It's independence ... to live and age more slowly and surely

It's birthing the memories ... for later in pursuing your dreams

It's a sure way to be a good mate and parent ... replace can't with cans and almighty purpose

It's a family way to talk at meals... your children will understand you more then, than later

This Marriage Vow and Lifestyle Habit reveals important insights and ideas about how to find greater purpose and fulfillment in your life and marriage, no matter how young, or old, you think you are. It's also about how to avoid or reverse the unhealthy life style habits and behaviors that result in poor decisions regarding chronic aging.

Everyone, including Shari and I, goes through some type of nesting and de-nesting. For us, nesting was the process of converting marriage, as a two- person abode, to a family of multiple children that requires a nest, comparable to a mother robin in the spring that finds the perfect place for a nest to birth her children. At the right time, she nudges them out of the nest and teaches them to fly on their own. And eventually some type of retirement must replace work. But you still need some type of purpose, a reason to get up every day and some type of results to measure. hobbies, sports, charity work, helping your family out, etc.

Shari and I have created businesses up to and into our seventies to make life challenging without making it stressful. Now we're writing books and coaching others to be happy, healthy, and prosperous.

LIFESTYLE HABITS ARE THE PURSUIT OF HAPPINESS

What is valuable to you? Your answer to this question will have a great deal to do with determining your behavior and your destiny. Whereas attitudes of mind are important to the striving for goals and seeking of goals, attitudes are dependent upon the value structure of an individual. The proposition, "Which comes first, values or attitudes?" can be compared to the question, "What comes first, the brick or the mortar?" Obviously, we always need both to be able to build a strong, unyielding structure.

Therefore, both values and attitudes are needed to construct a character. The values are the bricks and the mortar are the attitudes. The word value is the base of the word "valuable". Values are also the base of a valuable character. To better understand this, I would like to discuss values. I should specify these are my values now; but it is my feeling to be able to grow as an individual, values need to grow and change.

The attitude to expand values is the stabilizer to the character we all are trying to build. My primary values are: self-acceptance through the establishment of worthwhile goals and striving to attain them; self-expression through the interaction with all kinds of people and the education of my family; self-respect through the appreciation of the accomplishments of others; self-confidence through satisfaction of worthwhile accomplishments; self-development through striving for new ideas and new ways of doing things.

(I think it is important to note in this summary there is no mention of money as a self-value. It becomes a result of applying values. It is the measuring stick of the progress being made in implementing values in everyday life.)

Values must be constructed by a set of attitudes in fitting together lifestyle. Values are important in work. Values are important in social life. Values are important in maintaining physical vitality. Values are important in constructing the spiritual side of your life. In the succeeding chapters, we will deal holistically with values as it relates to the 12 Rhoads vows/habits to prevent and reverse premature aging.

The values of work, social relationships, physical health and spiritual health are all connected to your habits and lifestyle. To change these building blocks into character, good health, happiness and prosperity takes a plan and a schedule for implementation. The rest of this book assists you in developing that plan (see Part three for those building blocks and measurements for reality taking and getting you in shape).

Work	Social
Body	Mind
Physical	Self
Psychic	Soul

Shari and I are opposites when it comes to personality. She is outgoing, giving, very personal, the life of the party and family events. It's her smile that lights up my life and the room so to speak. Like her Aunt Edith (lived to 109) and her mother Dorothea (lived to 93) she chuckles at most every chance. She is positive about most everything except business and she has left that up to her cynical, introverted husband. Having grown up in a negative environment as a child and teenager, I have had to work at being outgoing and positive. I like to believe I am now cured and have got it together. Our children lean more to Shari's personality and congeniality. They have inherited my work ethic and are great parents as well.

Shari and I found that allowing our children to pursue their dreams, not just a money paying job, encouraged them to pick a purpose and work towards it ... if that changes in the process it's okay ... sometimes having a failure and getting back up is the first step to accomplishing a dream job or career. We can proudly say, as Grandma White said, there are no black sheep in our family. Each has their distinct personalities that reflect their dreams and our values and priorities ... that start and end with family. That's our best reason for getting a life we can be proud of forever. It's preparation for aging as happily and healthy as possible as the children leave the nest.

NESTING AND EMPTYING THE NEST

Nesting is the process of converting marriage, as a two-person abode, to a family of multiple children that requires a nest. Comparable to a Mother Robin in the spring that finds the perfect place for a nest to birth her children. At the right time, she nudges them out of the nest and teaches them to fly on their own. Then the nest is left to de-nesting until the next birthing. Retirement must replace work and its discipline with a purpose so you have something to get up for every day and can measure the results. Hobbies, sports, charity work, helping your family out, etc. Shari and I have created businesses in our seventies to make life challenging without making it stressful. Now we are writing books and coaching others to be happy, healthy and prosperous. Shari and I, of course, have been through the nesting process successfully and then had to emotionally deal with the de-nesting of our grown adults one by one. Christie was our first to venture out of the nest at the age of 19 (she was the first on everything since she was the oldest), then Kimber age 24, then Kip 26 and finally Kelli Jo 29. Each sought their higher education, each in the area of their dreams. Christie, a merit court reporter, created her own court reporting business at the age of 28, Kimber, a commercial artist, created her own collectible line "Circle of Love", Kip a musician/computer genius, wrote and produced over 100 of his own songs and Kelli, a commercial artist and dancer, created her own jewelry line. They then created their own nests for their offspring and will be dealing with de-nesting as their children go off to college and/or careers. Now it's Alec, Chad, Leigh, Blake, Derek, Paris,

Nathan, Troy, Celena, Fallon, Nicholas and Tyler the grandchildren taught to fly and seek their fortunes; and now Carter, Jackson, Becket, Emmett the great grandsons and Mariah, Madison, Morgan the great granddaughters still in the nest awaiting their chance to sing and dance their dreams.

Successful nesting and de-nesting is what makes America great. Even with divorces occurring, the nesting is always the result of the marriage and de-nesting occurs whether the parents or the offspring are ready or not.

MY CHILDREN their NEST

My children are the chance
To prepare for the big dance
They represent a time to repent
For my youth misspent
Look upon my past
Good lord it's gone
Look upon today cast
Good lord it's just the dawn

Our children have been it seems
Passing us by in a flash
If you want to talk of schemes
Their life can be short story trash
But they've come upon us as a blessing
With hopes and fears that need addressing

All they really ask is a little of our time
Love and attention not a mime

And that's no crime
Just a little bit of love divine
And affection will go a long-long way
Such a very cheap price to pay

If you make this effort with your children
And give them what they need and when
The days of joy will be upon you
Given credit for what you do
For the likes of your children
Made without lies and sin

Are the likes and dislikes of you

If so their lives will also be true
They're the treasures in your quest
To acknowledge and hopefully savor
As you look upon your nest
With the pride you did your best
One moment at a time enchanted
Invested in their future
Never taking them for granted
The primary reason to nurture
Them ... on the other hand
You may have to understand
Any failure of the test

May be the way you've built their nest

RESEARCH AND STATISTICS

The American Psychological Association Help Center provided recent statistics that validate the importance of getting a life through mental fitness and mental health. The importance of the mind/body health are indicated in the following statistics from the APA Help Center in an article entitled Mind/Body Health: Did You Know?

Mind/Body Health

Psychological studies show that your mind and your body are strongly linked. As your mental health declines, your physical health can wear down, and if your physical health declines, it can make you feel mentally "down." A positive outlook can help keep you healthy.

Did you know: Behavior and Health

- 80 percent of Americans say that during the past few years they have become more aware of how their mental health and emotions can affect their physical health (APA 2005)
- Two-thirds of all office visits to family physicians are due to stress-related symptoms (American Academy of Family Physicians)
- 43 percent of all adults suffer adverse health effects from stress ("The Stress Solution: An Action Plan to Manage the Stress in Your Life", Lyle H. Miller, Ph.D., and Alma Dell Smith, Ph.D.)
- 58 percent of Americans believe that one can't have good physical health without good mental health (APA 2005)
- Men high in optimism were less than half as likely to develop heart disease than were the more pessimistic men (Veterans Administration Normative Aging Study)
- 64 percent of Americans said they are taking steps to reduce the level of stress in their lives (APA 2005)
- 86 percent of respondents to a 2005 APA survey on the mind/body connection said that a comprehensive physical exam should include some discussion of their emotional state and well-being.

With the impact of the aging process on cognition we are getting more and more blame on Alzheimer's than on brain health and its importance. Cognition is the first step to a healthy brain at any age. Simple brain exercises can improve later cognition and avoidance of brain related malfunction. The above statistics do start to deal with underlying causes that result in over laying solutions.

Such as:

1. Power of positive thinking ... millions of books have been sold on how to think positive and avoid negative results.
2. Self-destructive power of negative thinking ... millions of anti-depressants and opiates are sold to alleviate this subconscious trait. Also,

self-medicating these problems is resulting in overdosing and death due to stepping up into oxycodone, heroine, vicodin and fentanyl.

3. Use of games and hobbies to keep the brain and subconscious in a healthy mode.

4. Having love in your life to keep the brain positive unless it is broken off then a replacement is necessary for continued mental health without chemicals or other mind-altering drugs.

THE DO'S:

1. Your home is your castle, your restaurant, your entertainment center, your workout center, your resting place, your pride in ownership ... why not make it yourself=health and happiness center.

2. A place in the basement for some basic workout equipment as stated above.

3. A place in the kitchen for your restaurant serving the recipes for ingredients to health stated above.

4. A place for your entertainment center for relaxation and rest watching your best physical and mental health programs, such as Dr. Oz and Dr. Phil, to get a flavor of how well off you are now that you're becoming healthy and happy.

5. A place for your pride and making an impact on your Self=Health program is having your offspring, friends and neighbors remark how good you look and act. As a family, we have always taken the time to play games and have fun. We will help you form a 12-Step club in your home for others to attend and learn from using our LIFE STYLES Self-Health books and programs.

6. Practicing healthy habits is catching. Like smiling, listening, supporting a cause, giving to someone and voting your convictions.

7. Use a smile and praise as your response to confrontation or confirmation during family conflicts. Be the leader not the follower ... the head of the household must be bold in decisions and settling problems.

8. Be a follower as your children are becoming leaders ... coach them don't criticize their decisions.

THE DON'TS

1. Come off as arrogant or bullying.
2. Involve yourself in physical confrontations that are meaningless.
3. Get mad if you're wrong. Just admit and don't defend it.
4. Use vulgarity to sound tough or nonchalant.
5. Make war when peace is the required to make a point.
6. Say do, can and will if you're not planning on doing, finishing and accepting.
7. Make light of someone's opinion be it politics or religion or sports.
8. Be conciliatory and then renege on a promise.
9. Talk about the future without a plan or a goal … fate is playing life forward.
10. Let yourself be imprisoned by your own reactions and instincts called habits.

I'M A PRISONER

I'm a prisoner of my mind
I cannot escape myself
For the bonds don't unwind
Just for my mental self=health
Just like a prisoner in a cage
Held against his will
Angered by his rage

Swallowing the bitterest pill
Handcuffed to society
Yes, almost under lock and key
Thinking not in totality
But only concerned about me
Yes, a prisoner of one's own devices
One's own thought processes
One's own crisis

Serious not in jest
Imprisoned at the very best
Pushed here and there by the guards

Who block good ideas and zest
Forcing us to play their cards
For their pot of panaceas
And ironically to all the rest
If we can do what they see in us
We can strive to be the best

It's self that must be in good health
When the unbound mind is the wealth
Freeing you from the prison
Of doubting yourself

Shari and I are lucky because we have practiced a variety of lifestyle habits and career changes that influence our children, grandchildren and now great grandchildren. Following are suggestions to have your program ripple downward to your offspring as it needs to:

1. Enhance the experience with topics at the dinner table that implement positive life stories. All you need to do is tell oneabout yourself and it becomes one story after another. Of course, the great and grandchildren love to hear about their parents' escapades as kids.

2. How we should treat each other in a social setting and how to discuss politics and religion rather than push them off limits.

3. The content of our advice is positive. I seem to dwell on science, sports and/or politics and Shari on the art of acting right not being right. Since we aren't negative our coaching here is what works for our family and also works for other social settings.

4. We also have a few no no's ... no smoking, no drugs, no stimulants, no excessive use of pain killers, no excessive amounts of alcohol ... everything else common sense prevails. This is where you and your family's preferences will make or break your progress. The right habits at the right time are definitely stress breakers and friend makers.

5. Life style changes for the home environment play a role in how we and our offspring all feel. Cleanliness of the home, clothing and automobiles are positive acts that are being a role model for our Rhoads lifestyle teachings during our offspring's' upbringing. (Our only pet peeve is Shari and I always make our bed in the morning and our children do not consistently follow that habit ... but making the bed doesn't make a life so we turn our head on that ... as they turn their head on our and their children's minor disturbing habits).

6. This has resulted in our children wanting to bring friends to their home and then have the same environment for their children's' homes. This is taken for granted after a number of years of effort to be nice and productive human beings.

7. In other words, with coaching we leave the makeover of the family tree to each his own discretion but each should be aware that being nice affects everyone in your and their children's immediate families.

DIVORCING MYSELF

Books have been written
Enemies smitten
Over the topic of friends and lovers
Blooming flowers and bedroom covers

Do you live with someone?
Who doesn't talk to you and sulks
Even though he says you're the reason he balks

Do you sleep with someone?
Who doesn't kiss you except
When he decides he wants sex

Do you go to church with someone?
Who doesn't believe in God
Even though he professes religion with a nod

Do you go to PTA with someone?
Who doesn't participate never relaxes
Even though he gripes about taxes

Do you go to sports events with someone?
Who hasn't ever played the game
Even though he throws a fit when his son isn't to blame

Have you separated from someone?
Who always goes to bed mad at the world
Even though he says he's positive yet curled

Have you divorced someone?
Who you lived with for five years before marriage
Because of one or more of the above stages

*If not you are very wise
I confess to have had many of the traits stated above
Or I wouldn't have been able to recognize
The push and shove of lifestyle love
Thus being asked to let go
Of my ego and my head size*

*Fortunately I have a partner
Who wouldn't accept or put up with
What I would call a sniff and a sneer
Straightening me out with her gift
So I treated her as a peer*

*If I hadn't we would have been one of the fifty percent
Of the couples in the country being divorcees
Most are in blended families to have love's consent
Despite being asked to let go of past decrees*

*Yes I understand that every marriage isn't pure
The family unit bonding and being well adjusted adults
With our children feeling loved and secure
Come to the lucky man and woman who survive their faults*

*Commentary:
Okay we know as a country we have a problem
Would it be different if we just talked to our spouse
Kissed to make up
Make it a happy house
And Pray together
Participate in PTA
Play a sport together
Never go to bed without making up*

*Even then we may have reasons to break up
Family insecurity
Children's security
Finances
Job career and future Circumstances
Or mental and physical wellbeing
But you should be the last to cavort
After talking kissing playing conceding
And making up before we resort
To the divorce court*

Because this is what we vowed in our marriage
If you wonder why I think I'm qualified to write this advice
Because I had to learn to talk kiss pray without rage
And play with my wife and family so I 'm precise
60 years later married to that same someone
That held me accountable to the vows
And rewarded me with three daughters and a son

And the four stable grown adults
That allows
Twelve terrific grandchildren (three blended)
Eight (with one on the way) great grandchildren the results
Of having my best friend and lover that never ended

PS: by the way Ann Landers, if aware up there, agrees with me
Sorry If you think I'm judging thee ....
We all are what we decided to be
A defendant or a dependent happy family

VARIOUS WAYS TO ENHANCE YOUR LIFE

Here we are wanting to get under your skin and inside your mind about lifestyle habits that enable you to feel the difference in your days, nights and tomorrows. Make your Real Age the barometer of your genetic power.

Have a hobby (purpose)

Shari's hobbies *are sewing, reading, painting, scrapbooking, tennis, dancing, working out, gift giving, family dinners ...* **my purpose** *Is a happy and prosperous life with my husband and family. As we age and look at retiring life can become boring and meaningless unless we commit ourselves to the pursuit of our dreams regardless of age.*

Jerry's hobbies *are writing, photography, tennis, dancing, working out, family functions ...* **my purpose** *Is a happy and prosperous life with my wife and family. If I don't have a purpose my life would be over. Now that we are retired, I'm in denial and call it re-hirement because I've always had a job ... now my job is how to spend each day productively. Hobbies are then not pastimes they are purposeful work times.*

Have a meaningful, fulfilling relationship

Girl Talk (Shari)

It's most important that you remember what it was that attracted you to each other in the first place. I'm sure looks had something to do with it, and personality. You need to like yourself, feel good about yourself and it is amazing how easy it is to be liked and to like others. I see so many women that seem to have lost all confidence and pride in themselves, and it saddens me to think what they have lost. It would be so much fun to take them and restore their confidence and self-esteem. No matter your size or your age, with the right hair style, a little makeup and a current clothing style, all women can be beautiful.

Guy talk (Jerry)

I repeat what Shari has said … I see so many men that seem to have lost all confidence and pride in themselves, and it saddens me to think what they have lost. It would be so much fun to take them and restore their confidence and self-esteem. No matter their size or age, with the right hair style, a little cologne and a cool clothing style, in my opinion, all men can be attractive to their soul mate or in their search for that "one and only". I'm sure looks will have something to do with it, if not your personality will have to carry you.

Make more friends

Girl Talk (Shari)

We always had friends. Usually because of school activities or new comer parties or church events. Now that our children are gone the friends have changed. No longer are our neighbors younger with young children. But they are friendly and willing to help. We are now active in nights out to meet new friends that like to dance and stay active by sharing our healthy habits. Jerry says I must have my Yah Yah time or I get antsy for female contact. I do appreciate having someone to discuss something other than sports or politics. Even though I enjoy talking sports and politics because they're stimulating and provocative I enjoy talking to other mothers and grandmothers about family. Also, talking about fashion, movies and home décor is very important to me in choosing friends.

Guy Talk (Jerry)

Usually Shari and I have the same friends. In the past when we were in different circles the number and type of friend were different. Now we are together 24 hours per day so our friends are pretty much the same. But we want a social life other than our family outings. So, learn to dance if you don't know how and you will find new friends.

State your purpose for living and pursue it

Girl Talk (Shari)

When Jerry said I could be a consultant, I doubted because I'm human. But he was right and I became a health care consultant. Then when we purchased three nursing homes he said I could be the conditional administrator of our Washington facility. So, my initial purpose was that of a wife and mother ... when that role changed and the children were out of the nest I thank god that Jerry believed in me. But that is the way he is ... don't doubt just do it. I am now enjoying helping him write his books. Either as an editor or writing the girl talk in this book.

Guy Talk (Jerry)

My purpose early on was to support the family. Shari was a stay at home mom and did a great job as I was pursuing my CPA career. When the kids graduated and left home, she had already been working part time as the office manager in our CPA firm. Then when we sold the accounting firm and moved back to Chicago setting up the consulting practice, she became a consultant. When we purchased nursing homes, she and I became the owners, operators and administrators. Now that we have sold them, we are publishing books on health care management and writing self-health how-to books for newlyweds and aging Americans.

Walk the talk and think positively at the same time

Girl Talk (Shari)

Without a doubt, our future will relate to managing our own aging and living longer and stronger ... this is our specialty and passion. Somehow and someway we are benefiting from our past ways of thinking and doing the right thing. Along the way were missteps, detours and changes of pace. But our everyday living is for better health not just living a unhealthy life in assisted living or a nursing home. Of course, we are wanting to stay independent and avoid chronic illnesses by practicing what we teach and preach. That's the spice of life and our goal is to live forever here and hereafter.

Guy Talk (Jerry)

My parents were pretty much fatalists. What you have is all you'll get and learn to accept that. Having been in sports I learned to set goals and pursue my dreams. As result Shari and I were destined to move from small town Iowa to Chicago. My future was set in motion by my degree from Simpson College where my accounting professor Mr. Sorden helped me get a job with the largest accounting firm in the country at the time, Arthur Andersen & Co. This allowed Shari, Christie (one year old) and I to take the first step to jump start my career for the future then and now. Up until that occurrence I was looking at jobs I didn't want … so getting the job I wanted was truly a break. I also learned business from the accounting firms I was in that I needed to be my own boss and have formed four different businesses since then. Our latest is writing, promoting books and developing a lifestyle www. lifestylesforaging.com coaching business.

Meditate on your strengths Mediate your weaknesses

Girl Talk (Shari)

My meditation is before going to sleep at night in the form of prayers for those I love. I haven't been the advocate of technical aspect of mind control. I leave that up to Jerry but I do believe in the process and the results. Our life in the past, now and into the future depends on our beliefs and goals. When we purchased our first nursing home our prayers were also for many of our patients that were troubled or deathly sick … we were very much involved with their families as well and the funerals that were destined to happen. Had a lot of tears for they were like family.

Guy Talk (Jerry)

I became an advocate of positive goal setting using affirmations (one each day of the year) and meditation. My use of formal meditation is when I'm striving to overcome adversity or a financial challenge from our business. This occurred dramatically when we purchased three nursing homes in a period of two years. They were financially and operationally challenged. We had to borrow extensively to fix them up and improve the staff and food quality. I had managed facilities for clients in the past but never had all the responsibility for finances. So, I meditated on plans and relieving stress every day of the six and one-half years we owned them. It was very traumatic when we decided to sell them.

Tell your family often your pride in them and love for them

Girl Talk (Shari)

We are a lovey kissy family. We say I love you when we part, when we meet, when we telephone, when we text, when we email. Love is the glue and having a life for our family is the reason for living. We now have 12 grandchildren and 4 great grandsons to spoil, hug and kiss and love. They are our pride, joy and happiness.

Guy Talk (Jerry)

Shari is a gift giver. She openly praises our children and their offspring ... particularly on their birthdays ... we sing happy birthday and give them a gift each and every year. I used to write a poem for the occasion until there were too many to write. I now calculate their birth age in months, days, hours, minutes, seconds and heart beats with a short poem that goes on the back of their birthday cards. I call this their age-o-meter and now they expect it.

Every time we see our grandchildren and now our great grandsons Shari brings a toy or a gift of some game and we express our love to see them. They now expect it but still say thank you Nammy or Boo boo for the great grandsons. She would tell Alec (our first grandbaby) "Grandma loves you so much" and when he started to talk Grammy came our Nammy and at 30 years of age now he and all the other grandchildren know her as Nammy. She called Carter, our first great grandchild, "my little boo boo" and when he started talking he said one day "I want to go to Boo Boo's house". I catch the gift giving fever for birthdays and Christmas. Our children also have the same healthy habits.

Weigh your accomplishments

Girl Talk (Shari)

My greatest joy is our family and that we are still active when it comes to family gatherings. Our other successes are secondary but important. Jerry and I still wonder where we would have been if we hadn't stayed together during the hard times. We both can't believe our birth age since we don't think that way. We are very different from our parents at this age. I also think that because I still love Jerry, like I always have, with his strength and his tenderness, this makes us seem like we never change. People we haven't seen for five or more years tell us we always look the same. It must be our 12 habits that we practice that have contributed to this miracle. I also loved being involved with the nursing homes because it allowed us to help others with their problems.

Guy Talk (Jerry)

I heard you should be thankful for the things that haven't happened to you and for the things you don't need, to be happy. But at the same time be thankful for the future for the better. When I look at Shari, I can't believe we have been married 60 years and together for 62 years since she still looks 50 years young to me. We both agree our greatest accomplishment is our family that has reached 18 children, grandchildren and great grandchildren. After that, is the success we attained in our nursing homes despite the reluctance of the Government to acknowledge our quality of life principles and outcomes. In the three facilities using our 12 DNA Fountain of Youth habits for healthy living, we discharged over 400 people (40% of our admissions) back home. If you want more details on our experiences read "Restore Elderpride", "The Baby Bommers Are Coming", "Failing Government Taketh Away", "American in the Red Zone" and "The American Enterprise Manifesto."

Count your blessings

Guy Talk (Jerry)

Kelli, our youngest daughter, orchestrated an album for the members of the family to express their feelings about Shari and I, including how we feel about each other. She had each of us write a letter to the other, which neither of us saw until the book was complete and presented to us. Following are the love letters we each wrote to each other to celebrate our renewal of our wedding vows in Las Vegas at the Elvis Chapel on November 27, 2009.

To. Sharon White Rhoads

Love Letter

From Jerry to You

Dear Shari;

When I think of our love I first think of your loyalty. When I think of our life's journey I first think of your honesty. When I think of our children and grandchildren I first think about your strength and selfless commitment to them. That is why our fifty plus years together have been more than an adventure, more than a success, more than just infatuation, it is true love.

When I first saw you that day in 1952 in front of the Indianola Junior High School talking to Rosie and seeming too much for me to hope for…I set in my heart a place for you that could not be denied…even as I stole your picture out of Sam's billfold after our first face to face meeting on the square in 1953 I still could only dream of you ever being interested in my crew cut and horned rimmed glasses with a baseball mitt as my sole companion. In 1954, you then moved away and my heart went into standby. It hurt from what was missing…a chance to look at you from a distance.

When you returned to Indianola in 1955 I finally got a chance to ask you for a date…it was when you were a Sophomore and I a Junior but it still didn't seem even close to being permanent. I frankly did not feel worthy and you seemed distant…then that October evening in 1956 at the haunted house with Nancy as the connector you seemed to be attracted to me. Then it was our first real date at the Drive-In Movie in Des Moines that next week, when we kissed for the first time, I knew that it was "that immortal feeling called love". Love at first kiss.

When we connected, it was your beauty, your personality, your search for fun that inspired my obsessions…you were a majorette and I was an athlete dreaming of being a major-league baseball player. Both of which were fleeting but brought us together in our interests and passions for each other that have prevailed for fifty plus years and have never waned in the five decades that we have been together. Marriage was not imminent after we split in 1958 when you went to Beauty school and I to Simpson College… but as I counted the 180 days that we were apart and quieted my anxiety by buying an engagement ring, forgetting to kneel and giving it to you in the car, our November 27, 1959 marriage finally became real.

When our children came (Christie October 31, 1960, Kimber October 19, 1962, Kip July 19, 1965, Kelli November 28, 1970) and we were focused on them; even now we still clung to each other, for them and with them. That is the glue that made us more than human … It makes us an eternal family … it makes what we have today … healthy, happy, successful children that are passing that same morality and loyalty to their children (twelve beautiful and inspiring youngsters) looking for that same moment I had when you caught my eye) as our legacy. From Indianola where divorce and teen pregnancy were distained to our struggles to be *good parents without being obtrusive we have loved our life's work while working together to make our love for the elderly work.*

When we are moving on to the age of doubt and mystery Shari we will be there together forever ... because we have always been together from our birth to now we were destined to be one. I will love you forever and forever is our destiny.

Love forever, Your husband and partner, Jerry Lee Rhoads

Girl Talk (Shari)

To: Jerry Lee Rhoads

Love Letter

From Shari to You

I am so happy to have you. You are positive, determined, hardworking, devoted and the love of my life. I love that we can spend so much time together and not tire of each other. I miss you too much when I'm home alone. I think people grow apart when they don't spend much time together. I love being able to work beside you and share your passion and goals which have become my passion also. I love that we can share our down time because our interests are the same. I love that our beautiful family is the most important part of our lives and a constant topic of our conversation. I love exercising with you, watching sports, dancing and having a romantic dinner.

As I reflect on the fifty years we have been marrieds I've a kaleidoscope of cherished memories. We were so young, in love and sure it would last forever. Remember when Christie was born and we realized that we could actually love someone else as much as we loved each other and to add three wonderful children, making our family complete. When I got mad and told you "to get out", your response was "I'm not leaving the kids so you get out". My response was "I'm not leaving them either" and we stayed. We have always been able to get past our differences because of our love for each other and our children. Our love has expanded to our son-in-law's and daughter-in-law and our twelve grandchildren. Can life get any better? Well maybe ... such is our history.

I loved every minute of our trip to Las Vegas to celebrate our 50th wedding Anniversary! Renewing our wedding vows was beautiful and it felt even more perfect than our original wedding day, because I love your so much!

My Love forever, Shari

Also, the essence of Motherhood can't be understated. The creation of a family is the ultimate reflection of the spirit of love and endearment. It changed Jerry and I from a focus on the future to a commitment to the present. Over the years, we always put our children's wants and needs above ours. This is paying us dividends every day. Following is Jerry's view of the laurels of motherhood.

LAURELS OF MOTHERHOOD

Motherhood steps no meter
Nor can setback defeat her
She lives in the cribs of children
Yet turns away life's fear and sin

We catch her on the minds of many
Forgotten in the hearts of hardly any
She is illusive but there to clasp
If only the mind can grasp

The positive acts she gives as a wife
For problems are the scale of every life
And from the weight of the blues
As hope we lose from bad news

She makes her own potion
Bottled in her mind
And cached in emotion
Fettered with devotion

"We are what our parents
Never could be"
But "we will ever be
What they were to me"
"Better lives and habits are we"

For motherhood steps no meter
Nor can loss defeat or succumb her
She lives in the minds of sister and brother
A fostered home or a biological mother

With a reformed reliance
For a child of the ' hood

Pledging allegiance
To which she stood

The laurels of motherhood

JERRY MET SHARI (get what we got)

Walk and talk with your partner for 1 to 2- or 3 or more-miles holding hands and finally feeling attached ... Shari and I have since 1989 to get our life on track and keep it there! It saved our marriage and our lives for a longer and stronger future.

SELF EVALUATION

After reading this chapter take the following Self-Health quiz ... update your Real Age calculation, put a checkmark for your answers and come back later to rate yourself for complying with the actions recommended in this chapter:

	Birth Age	Real Age		
Beginning Real Age score	_____	_____	<u>YES</u>	<u>NO</u>
1. Are you avoiding habit changes because of your home life?			____	____
2. Do problems at home control our behavior and thinking?			____	____
3. Do you hear your kids say "get a life and leave me alone"?			____	____
4. Do you doubt you can change your life for the better?			____	____
5. Do you update the real age calculator to measure your results?			____	____
6. Do you now feel compelled to improve your life style?			____	____
7. Later rate your program ... 1 being low and 10 being the best			____	____

Your rating and answers are your confession booth for judging for yourself where you are with your commitment to change your harmful habits and lifestyle at this point of your journey.

DAILY AFFIRMATIONS

Habits are the reasons that don't lie
With us needing to know why
* * *

Critique yourself as the cause of deceit
Rescind your flaws from the jaws of defeat
* * *

To stop thinking is unthinkable
To think of not stopping makes us capable
* * *

Align yourself with those who can and do
Then do what you say you can't
* * *

Hello sweet reality, goodbye insecurity
 A change is overcoming the can't in me
* * *

Winning isn't everything But the will to win is
* * *

Life is an exciting journey for those who find their way
And get it back as pay

A LIFE LONG LOVE STORY

Romeo and Juliet in all their glory
Formed Shakespeare's life-long love story
It has lasted through the ages
It's still told on crisp poetic pages

It's the deepest love known to man or woman
Telling others how to understand
That romance and all its glory
Is a life-long love story

Holding hands under a tree
Or just looking at the sky with me
Wondering what will ultimately be
But enjoying this moment of being free

Free to fly just you and I
When time is just a passing thought
Passing as memories we sought
Finding that love cannot be bought

Life is so short it seems
Without romance and the help of dreams
Something simple is not exactly as it redeems
Like a shock from weather in New Orleans

It can go from good to bad
From happy to sad
Or loving to mad
Making up is so hard but glad

Then with a family to blend
With rock-n-roll and a boy friend
Challenging us to the very end
Until our grandchildren are to descend

With parents having the responsibility
To manage every possibility
We Grandparents can relax
While others must deal with the facts

Yes, life and all its glory
Exemplified in our life-long love story
From Junior High to Indianola High to Chicago Sky Way
Our love story is unparalleled till we die our way

Holding hands in bed and kissing lips
Aborted flights and meaningless trips
Until rainy days became blue
When Shakespeare's love came true

And I found out Juliet is really you
And Romeo is me too

Marriage Vow/Lifestyle Habit Number Five

MY BODY IS AGILE, MY MARRIAGE IS FRAGILE

"My jeans are the size of my altered genes"
"I'm forgetting why I can't remember"
"Sweat is just fat crying let me out"
"You don't get the butt you want by sitting on it"
"Fit is not a destination it is a way of life"

Posted on the wall at a gym

Get Moving Your BODY BY Not Sitting On Your Booty and Your Brain BY Not Sitting On Your Duty

We all exercise our right to live but do we exercise our privilege to live longer? You were born to be free of doubt, fear and compulsions that age you too fast. To control your health, happiness and prosperity you must slow down and replace your doubt, fear and compulsions causing stress with physical and mental exercises. Feel the accomplishment of having done something positive for your well-being and prevent a chronic illness or reverse those you have. That's the epigenetics of lifestyle.

This marriage vow and lifestyle habit is how to avoid divorce or reverse the unhealthy life style habits and behaviors that result from mental and physical inactivity. The realization for us who are aging too fast isn't new … A recent expansive study says not exercising is worse than smoking. Dr. Warl-Jabar co-author of the study called the results surprising. It's common knowledge that there are many benefits from being fit. But one large study found that skipping a workout is the worst thing you can do for our health. New findings published in JAMA detail how researchers at the Cleveland Clinic studied 122,001 patients from 1991 to 2014 putting them under treadmill testing and later recording mortality rates. Researchers found a clear connection between a longer healthier life and high levels of exercise.

The report calls Health Care Professionals to encourage patients to achieve and maintain a robust fitness routine. Another study revelation. While many of us are coping with a health problem, doesn't mean we have to continue to live unhealthy lives. In fact, the survey revealed that 67% of Americans believe it's possible to balance being healthy and dealing with chronic illness, some saying they have never felt stronger in their whole life. Other highlights of the Cleveland Clinic Survey: 80% of Americans surveyed are not eating sufficient servings of fruits and vegetables, 49% aren't getting a good night's sleep, 52% aren't drinking enough water per day and 49% aren't getting an annual physical or check-up.

More importantly 66% want help figuring out the best methods for improving their health ... and the Health Care Professionals aren't providing this advice. In reality from our experience of 60 years marriage the following are the risks and the rewards for staying married and healthy for they are interconnected with your lifestyle:

What are the Risks	**What is your Choice**	**What are the Rewards**
Loss of spouse	Replace	Security
Divorce	Stay Married	Security and happiness
Smoking	Quit Cold Turkey	Love longer, stronger, younger
Obesity	Replace food with love	Security, self-worth, self-image
Inactivity	Replace couch with exercise	Feel good, look good, be good
Loneliness	Get Married	Security, happiness, healthy ever after
Stress	Like or leave your Job	Future looks bright and secure
Drugs	Replace with exercise	Mind is in sync with the body

Loss of sleep	Meditate then sleep	Body is in sync with the spirit
Loss of Job	Jobs can be replaced in time	Finding a job you love is very healthy
Fear of aging	Read and reread this book	Thinking is the best path to the goal line
Chronic disease	Be Active, Positive and Happy	Disease avoids a healthy body and mind (prevention is the pill)

Shari and I love to walk, which we do in our neighborhood or on the beach or at the gym. We hold hands and walk for at least an hour. Usually two to three times per week during the summer and in the gym during the winter. We love this time together ... we're walking and talking. We have this time to visit and have many topics to discuss. From politics and our businesses to our children, grandchildren and now our great grandchildren. We reminisce about how we met, the fun we've had over the years and the vacations we took. It's great exercise for the body and the mind come rain or shine. We keep reminiscing on our childhood just to stay connected and thankful for where we have come from.

Originally our walking was to solve a lack of communication and feeling disconnected in our marriage. It has been the best solution to being on different planets and enabled us to agree we needed to purchase our own health care laboratory, nursing homes. In this chapter, we relate to what the experts on life styles and behavior have found; that the body's fitness is connected to that portion of the brain storing subconscious beliefs.

The body doesn't move until the mind tells it to. If the mind is fat so is the body and its future. If that is acceptable so be it ... but later there may be regret when life ends too early. It's hard but I look at being fit as a friend to my family, work and marriage. So, rather than threaten you into compliance I look to relevance as the motivator and elevator to your own health, wealth and longevity. Your real age is your mental conditioning not your physical conditioning. Think and grow fit then rich.

LIFESTYLE HABITS CAN BE A NEW TO DO LIST FOR FITNESS

As you read this book, you'll find that it's the number of steps you take not the inches of your waist line. It's the effort you exert not the pounds you lose. Luck is effort meeting opportunity. It's the feeling good you attain not what pounds you gain. It's the time you spend on your health not the money you misspend on self-gratification. It's replacing harmful physical and mental habits with healthy happy and prosperous life style decisions. The ripple effect is better personal relationships, enhanced career advancement, better marriages and family life and most importantly living longer and staying youthful, forever.

The fanatic in me says just do it … but each day I put it off until I feel guilty then I just have to do it. Shari on the other hand can take it or leave it. She does yoga with me, walks 5 miles and dances every Thursday night for four hours. My regimen is routines that vary each day with cycle training.

- Monday, ab work, push-ups, crunches, weights for arms or an aerobic of tread mill or elliptical or stationary bike.
- Tuesday, yoga with Shari ending with crunches and light weights,
- Wednesday, we walk at least four or five miles.
- Thursday, we dance four hours at the club.
- Friday, we usually take the day off after dancing.
- Saturday, I repeat the Monday workout and go dancing if there is a good band.
- Sunday, we usually walk or play tennis (in the season).

The irony is I have to work out daily to keep as trim as Shari who knows how to eat, sleep and work at her best pace … and she's aging slower than I am. We have our gym in the basement and walk in the neighborhood. We have been members in a number of tennis clubs that included a running track that we use for walking in the winter and my attempt at running once again. (I spent 20 years running everyday hoping that I would eventually enjoy it … it happened when I finally quit).

It is amazing that the well-developed value system and attitude of mind carries through to a concern for physical well-being. Most people healthy mentally, are generally healthy physically. The desire to maintain oneself mentally carries through to the body fitness. Physical well-being is a release of mental frustration. It allows the body to throw off tension and nervous anxiety. Physical fitness or mental fitness go hand in hand. To look at the embodiment of success is to dissect a healthy brain and body.

If a body isn't resilient, it is difficult to imagine it having the energy, the drive and determination it takes to have a healthy mind. Interestingly, I see a correlation between the person who likes to compete and stay physically healthy, and the person who likes to compete in life and stay mentally healthy. The person who avoids physical competition and challenge more than likely will avoid responsibility, authority, and the challenge of self-health practices.

In physical fitness, the concern should be more for the results you're trying to attain than the means you use. Many endeavors are status symbols which don't provide good physical fitness. You should choose the activity which will stimulate both the mind and body. There also must be enjoyment. Without the capability of attaining some feeling of release and achievement, it's hard to imagine the activity will be worthwhile. Look at children. It's just as important for them to be educated physically as it is to be educated mentally. Unfortunately, our society isn't giving as much priority to physical well-being as it should.

Our society does have a love affair with athletics, which is good. It trains the body as well as the mind. The physically fit person will also be able to function at a higher energy level and is likely to have a fuller sexual life. Sexuality has a great dependence on the body's physical wellbeing. The healthier the body, the healthier the sex experience. All, are ingredients to a full life. Wellbeing is what wellbeing does.

WELLBEING

What I'm seeing
Is a need for individual wellbeing
We're a nation of individuals
And the isolation swells and swells
Beyond the proportion of achieving

If you can't climb outside yourself
Take a step or two towards others
And I don't mean mothers and brothers
For a family counts to be sure
But they're not the real cure

To the unwell being syndrome
We must dedicate ourselves
To Self=Health and fitness
For as our family and friends
Are witness
Our good health wins out
Over fear sinful acts and doubt

For in the end it's our mortal spirit
That's overseeing our fear of it
And in death we partake in its wellbeing

For after death we mortals aren't seeing
The rewards that its freeing

As the lifestyle habits we're now receiving
By being Healthy, Happy and achieving

The experts on life styles and behavior ..have found that the body fitness is connected to that portion of the brain storing subconscious beliefs. Though there are physical maladies that effect these it is the unhealthy habits that create the problems. The body doesn't move until the mind tells it to. If the mind is fat so is the body and its future. If that is acceptable so be it … but later there may be regret when life ends to early. It's hard but I look at being fit as a friend to my family, work and marriage. So, rather than threaten you into compliance I look to reliance as the motivator and elevator to your own health, wealth and longevity. Your real age is your mental conditioning not your physical conditioning. Think and grow fit then rich.

FITNESS

Are you in shape
Do you pass the battle of the tape
Or are you always sick

Because exercise is what you skip
Are you a frequent flyer
With a spare tire and a stomach on fire

Are you a chronic complainer
And a manipulative grandstander
Or are you in sync

With a smile and a wink
Are you a lover or fighter
Laying low till you find a lighter

Feigning motivation and ambition
While the body does deteriorate
And the mind will need to hibernate

Or Are you getting smarter
And seizing time as a self-starter
For fitness isn't for a martyr

But if you wait
For enough time on the clock
And the will to take stock

Then Slowly but surely
Either late or early
Your always surly

When fitness becomes apathy
Taking happy away
Weigh in makes you PAY to play

Then you must
Not let the rust
Wipe away your gut and lust

In being fit bit healthy or bust

RESEARCH AND STATISTICS:

Do our muscles remember routines and does this memory last? "When you move, you activate sensors (called proprioceptors) in your muscles, tendons, and joints that constantly give feedback to your central nervous system about where your body is in space, so it knows what muscles to fire next," says Adam Knight, Ph.D., an assistant professor of biomechanics at Mississippi State University. It's a continuous feedback loop from your brain to your muscles and back. "Your brain creates pathways through your central nervous system, and movements become automatic," adds Wayne Westcott, Ph.D., fitness research director at Quincy College in Massachusetts. Those well-worn pathways essentially become your muscle memory.

It's a phenomenon aptly called muscle memory. Simply put, when you teach your body how to do something—ride a bike, surf, strike some yoga poses, run a few miles—it creates a physiological blueprint. So even if you take some time off, you'll get back to where you were faster than it took you to learn the exercise in the first place. "Muscle memory stems from your body's learning not just how to perform a task, but also how to break down muscle tissue and then repair and rebuild it," explains William Kraemer, Ph.D., a professor in the department of kinesiology at the University of Connecticut at Storrs. "That physiological knowledge lets you come back from injury, surgery, and even pregnancy faster, easier, and often better than before," he says.

Researchers at Salk Institute for biological studies are close to developing a drug that has the potential to reprogram genes and recalibrate muscles in a way that mimics exercise that may one day be instrumental in helping those with muscular diseases such as Parkinson's and Huntington's or those living with paralysis function at much higher levels. At Northwestern University scientists are using genetic profiling of joint tissue with rheumatoid arthritis patients to see which drugs will help improve the trial and error treatment approach which is the standard used on most chronic conditions. However, epigenetics is focusing on natural exercise remedies for reprogramming genetic based habits rather than using prescription drugs that have side-affects.

In the three nursing homes that we owned we were able to reduce the usage of prescription drugs by 60% and our patients immediately were more functional. In doing so we had to battle the physicians, patients and families due to the culture of drug usage for treating the prevalence of pain, depression, diabetes, heart conditions, strokes, cancers, obesity, etc. Many of our new admissions from hospitals required a thorough audit of the medications being prescribed by doctors who had never seen the patient. After they were admitted we had to fend off, using our Medical Director, inappropriate prescriptions that would exacerbate the chronic condition that we inherited. This is where we as owners and Administrators started to question all medication orders. We were backed up by studies showing that epigenetics were more effective in the treatment of chronic illnesses. Also, when the patient had a terminal disease diagnosis to justify the prescription order for hospice, it was challenged, the drug withdrawn and the patients would get better ... thereafter we made it a policy to do the same for all our admissions. Because the orders were usually for antipsychotics and opioids (including fentanyl patches) and the usual cocktail of blood pressure, blood thinners, cholesterol and insulin. Therefore, legalized drug addiction is rampant in nursing homes because of the chronic nature of the patients' problems that are left to archaic medical practices. We just bury the addicts as being too old to live a drug free life.

Our other discovery was the general use of special units to justify the drug use. The dementia and Alzheimer's units have been renamed Memory Care with medications as its base stabilizer and enabler. The only treatment for memory loss is not the latest pill but more activity, exercise, withdrawal of all medications, special diets, relationships, walking and talking with friends in the facility with an open environment and functions that draw them into using their hands and minds. Memory loss is not restored without this epigenetic approach ... the patient care plan must focus on moving the body and interacting with normal patients ... so the locked units keeping them away from normalcy makes the problems worse.

At our facilities we opened up the locked units and used natural remedies to restore the patients' functionality, not their memories. Memory is not a purview of environment but an inner view of the mind focusing on the past so the brain sees now better and adapts to the future without dwelling on " can't remember." The need for retention using past memories and current involvement in a quality of life with other aging human beings is not a unit it's a lifestyle. So, it boils down to getting the less functional involved with more functional experiences. Such as walking outdoors with groups. Locking them up in a closed environment has never worked but unlocking their memories with memorable events does work. Friendship is the main key for unlocking those new experiences.

In the book "Unbreakable Brain" by Will Mitchell, a microbiologist 25% of our body's metabolism is utilized for healthy brain function. Our metabolism is a function of our bodies ability to manage a complex of physical and chemical processes occurring within a living cell or organism that are necessary for the maintenance of life. In metabolism some substances are broken down to yield energy for vital processes while other substances, necessary for life, are synthesized.

If the body's not physically or chemically able to support our brain health, chronic disease is inevitable. The connection between physical fitness and brain fitness is necessary to avoid (prevent) or reverse dementia and Alzheimer's. Dr. Bredesen's book "The End of Alzheimer's" documents the reasons for combining physical fitness with brain fitness to accommodate the importance of sustaining optimal metabolism. His success has embraced the use of diet, supplements, reduction of stress, exercise of body and brain as natural remedies that can make or break your life whether you currently have what he calls the three stages of Alzheimer's or are genetically inclined to be at risk. All are treatable using his Re-code system. Following are more details on the interaction of genetics, habits, exercise and self-health remedies.

Per the President's Council on Fitness

Physical Activity

- Only one in three children are physically and sexually active every day.1
- Less than 5% of adults participate in 30 minutes of physical activity each day;2 only one in three adults receive the recommended amount of physical activity each week.3
- Only 35 – 44% of adults 75 years or older are physically active, and 28-34% of adults ages 65-74 are physically active.4

- More than 80% of adults do not meet the guidelines for both aerobic and muscle-strengthening activities, and more than 80% of adolescents do not do enough aerobic physical activity to meet the guidelines for youth.5

Why would life expectance take a down turn? Only one answer ... Chronic Aging and/or divorce!

1. Obesity ... average weight in nursing homes is 271 versus 150 20 years ago
2. Incurable cancers ... most cancers can be alleviated that usually cause other problems
3. Exacerbated diabetes ... type two diabetes is the biggest obstacle to better living
4. Respiratory failure ... apnea and shortness of breath are maladies of aging that generally are untreated
5. Untreatable infections ... nursing homes and hospital are breeders of infections
6. Strokes ... 45% of the baby boomers will suffer a stroke and/heart attack due to poor lifestyle habits
7. 3.2 million falls per year ... most are the elderly who eventually don't survive a fall
8. Complications of inactivity ... Baby Boomer Americans will have 4 to 5 chronic illness by the age of 85, most are in nursing home or assisted living
9. Chemical dependencies ... eight billion pills are pushed in nursing homes every year ... no more than legalized drug dealing by uninvolved physicians and families.
10. No preventive measures ... hospitals are paid for diagnosis not outcome, physicians are paid for encounters not cures, nursing homes are paid for maintenance not for discharge to home
11. No health preservation measures ... with aging Americans generally overweight and depressed the pharmaceutical advertising is on medication to alleviate not cure. Self-medication is prevalent with the elderly with alcohol or prescription drugs (patients hang on to drug use though it shows no improvement nor outcome)

12. USE IT OR LOSE IT

This adage is older than the TV remote, the driverless car, the escalator, automatic doors and windows in cars, power lawn mowers, snow and leaf blowers, personal robots, iPhone triggered security systems, auto parking, ... technology that does everything for us. As we no longer use it we will gain it and not lose it. Herman Ponteer, Ph.D. and anthropologist at Hunter College, one of the architects that established that calorie intake and output isn't the determinant of weight loss. The research showed that the bodyneeds calories to maintain body weight when it's not in motion. However, the data shows exercise is super important for health. The chronic health problems that people will have to deal with as they age (heart disease, diabetes, cancers, dementia) requires exercise as essential to use it so you don't lose it for preventing or reversing chronic aging. The magic pill, the DNA Fountain of Youth are all within our reach by using what we genetically inherit... an immune system that needs exercise and usage. Being active as we were in our childhood, early adulthood, will determine our future immunity to chronic aging. Use it don't lose it.

13. Prevent it don't abuse it.

According to Dr. Bredesen in his book "THE END OF ALZHEIMER'S" (Prevent and reverse Cognitive Decline), the solution is a very effective combination of DESS (diet, exercise, sleep and stress reduction) along with simple supplements. Have you heard sitting and texting are the new smoking habit? (Americans sit rather than move their bootie. Leading to a bigger and bigger bootie and a smaller cognitive memory). My words. Dr. Bredesen's 8 benefits of exercise:

1. Reduces insulin resistance
2. Increases Kerosis (liver function)
3. Increases size of hippocampus (memory)
4. Improves vascular function
5. Reduces stress
6. Improves sleep
7. Increases brain process neurogenesis
8. Improves mood

His optimal exercise: combine aerobic (jogging, walking, biking, dancing) with anaerobic weight training 4 to 5 times, 40 to 50 minutes per day. Workup slowly, stretch out and take care of your joints. The reduction in inflammation will improve joint function. Also use meditation for mental exercise. The benefits:

1. Lowers stress (stress kills the will and activates the last wills in testament)
2. Improves sleep (sleep apnea must be treated)
3. Trains brain for memory retention (games of chance and thinking)
4. Improves relationships (Fantasizing and love making is the best result possible)
5. Finds the inner spirit for relaxation (Dharma emerges from Karma from the inner you)

In Dr. Bredesen's book he proposes "targeting a symptom that appears after a disease has taken hold, as most conventional methods do, is very different from attacking the root cause of a disease at the cellular level. In other words, we want to get to the cause of decline, fixing any imbalances before it becomes irreversible. That's what we propose. We want to address as many of the 12 self-health habits as possible, not just one at a time, since each of the 12 affect the other 11. Our holistic approach of replacement of harmful habits with our self=health habits impacts the overall reversal of premature aging. We have seen in our lives that as we preserve your physical and mental health, we are preventing destructive illnesses that accelerate and exacerbate advanced aging.

INCHES

Progress is measured in inches
Plans are measured by progress
Profits are measured by dollars

Planning how to progress
Will unto thee profit

Clouds are measured by barometers
Temperature by thermometers
Speed by speedometers
Miles by odometers
RPM's by tachometers

Inches turn to kilometers
The physical can be measured
Dollars made can be treasured
And material belongings wagered
But life's dreams must be pleasured

They must be seen as real
They must be something you can feel
And pray about, as you kneel
For moments passed you cannot steal

The height of the man is measured by inches
And he is weighed by the pound
For results there are no cinches
Unless you bear your own ear to the ground

So listen to your spirit
Towards a future measured by happiness
At the height of never fearing it
And a past without duress

Above all ignore the mess
Count your miles traveled marking benches
And don't sweat the inches

We have chosen the Dr. Roizen's REAL AGE calculation as the analytical method (self-scientific based on current self-health habits) for measuring your personal habit immune system for preserving your health and preventing chronic illness. By taking one chapter at a time then recalculating your REAL AGE gives you the will power to continue with each succeeding chapter. Rereading chapters reinforces your establishing the routine and experiencing the rewards. Craving the success becomes the reason to continue the program.

As we do with the 12 Rhoads self-health habits, Dr. Breseden maps out the 12 root causes of cognitive decline into end stage Alzheimer's and solutions with his genetic ReCode system. They are as follows:

1) Diet, 2) nutrition, 3) regular exercise, 4) new sleep pattern 5) reduce stress through meditation, 6) brain training, 7) Resolve cellular inflammation, 8) healing the gut with biotics, 9) hormonal imbalance, 10) metal homeostasis using supplements, 11) detoxification, 12) avoid food allergies

His amazing success (700 to 800 cases of reversing Alzheimer's) has changed the conventional one pill approach for analyzing and treating other chronic diseases. We recommend you read his book in conjunction with ours if you are having symptoms of cognitive and physical decline. Dr. Bredesen's genetic ReCode system targets APOE4 (EPSILON 4) the most common genetic variable for predicting, treating, reversing and preventing Alzheimer's disease using diet, supplements, vitamins and exercise. What it does is reduce the inflammation of the circulatory system allowing the immune system to regulate the amount of APOE4 cholesterol and APO lipoprotein being produced to fight off fat metabolism.

THE DO'S:

1. If you have trended upward in weight and want to downsize our program of simple exercises using our downsizer spreadsheet will assist you in changing your weight gaining harmful habits.

2. If your goal is to add muscle in place of fat our daily exercise routines will establish better activity habits without having to go to the gym or suffer through the training. See Part three for suggested yoga, calisthenics, resistance training and aerobic training.

3. Body profiling using our Downsizer spreadsheet will focus on your current exercise habits and plan for a more focused approach to physical exercise.

4. See our website www.lifesytlesforaging.com

5. Only you can determine the before and after results. We will assist in the planning and tracking of results with the tools we provide in and on our web site.

6. Suggested programs: aerobic exercise using treadmill, elliptical, stationary bike, jump rope and walking indoors or outdoors. Resistance training using light dumb bells, bands, calisthenics, medicine ball, kettle ball, pull up bars, weight benches, etc. Palates, Yogi, Chi Ci, etc. (see the examples in the book)

7. You need to take a before and after picture periodically to show the transformation and your new look. This will confirm your belief that you can be whatever you want to be. Tell your spouse he/she looks great.

8. Put a reminder in your bathroom that my father's advice of "use your head change the oil in your car or pay the mechanic more" applies to our bodies and brains. If we do the right thing every day we have in affect used preventive maintenance on our most valuable assets ... our

body and mind. Like Daddy said: "you can buy a new car but you can't buy a new body or brain".

SUGGESTED WEEKLY TO DO LIST – BURN 600 EXTRA CALORIES PER WEEK

- Monday…walk as far as you can (in place or around the block)
- Tuesday…ride as far as you want (bike indoors or outdoors)
- Wednesday…lift as much as you can (pump something) … 5 to 10 pound hand weights
- Thursday … exert effort with resistance (sit-ups or crunches) … hook your toes under a couch or chair if needed
- Friday… push or pull with resistance (pull-or pushups) … can be done in the bathroom with the hands on the counter and the feet on the floor
- Saturday…run as far as you can (in place or around the block)
- Sunday… recite your best affirmative image then, meditate for the time it takes to go to sleep

These are options that are definitely stress relievers. By alternating routines either daily or weekly you will get better and more lasting results. You can pick two or three different routines that work for you.

THE DON'TS:

1. Don't weigh yourself every day and expect it to tell you what you want to see.
2. Don't set inflexible expectations that are not going to be started or accomplished.
3. Don't try to do it on your own. Until you have an unbreakable habit get a partner to keep you both committed.
4. Don't do exercises that aren't designed to get results … I read Men's Health, Prevention and any other information that I need to know what to do and how to do it.
5. Don't assume that others are going to see your results right away.

6. Don't fish for comments regarding your loss or changes in weight. You may not like the answers. Others who don't won't usually acknowledge those that do.

7. Don't set the goals to high or too quick ... consistency and persistence are the most important characteristics of a fit person. Then it's habit forming not habitual reforming.

Hopefully, by now, you are going to come up with your own set of exercises that are fitting your level of endurance and satisfaction. In time, you will find that you can increase the intensity and repetitions for faster results. Regardless make it a routine in the morning, noon or night. Go ahead with confidence that you are extending your age as well.

If you are exercising solo and don't have a partner to motivate you following are some ideas that don't require much time or physical endurance: deep breathing has been touted as a way to add oxygen to your blood stream and fight off inflammation, meditation or prayer has been credited as a way to fight off dementia, depression and negative feelings, isometrics that use your body weight and natural physical movements to tone muscles and strength, sexual stimulation relieves stress levels, attending a concert or play that relieves tension and negative feelings, any game of chance ... cards, video games, crossword puzzles stimulates brain activity, photography stimulates creativity, writing poetry or songs uses the mind for expression, or just working in a garden or mowing the lawn are forms of feeling a sense of accomplishment. All of these are a way to integrate exercise for the body and mind into the daily activities rather than having to decide to get up at 5am go to the gym. Then feel guilty all day and drink yourself to sleep that evening. That's habit forming at its worse ... compounding a simple decision into a lifestyle.

I just hope you have made the commitment to be healthy mentally as well as physically. What I've found is feeling better mentally having exerted myself physically attains my other goals ... acceptable weight, better attitude and gratitude for being healthy and living longer.

How fit is fit. Is it BMI, percent body fat, body weight per inch, bench press pounds lifted, miles run, steps walked, push-ups done, years lived, life expectancy, or your goals? You're the judge and the jury and the defendant. It's whatever you decide. But the Real Age calculator may change your priorities. It certainly confirmed Shari and I are doing something right.

Thus, this book on our lifestyle for Self=Health and living forever (a pseudonym for hereafter) will inspire some to a longer and stronger life. Those uninspired will be back for a cleansing after suffering one or more of the Chronic diseases and conditions—such as heart disease, stroke, cancer, type 2 diabetes, obesity, and arthritis—are among the most common, costly, and preventable of all health problems.

1. As of 2012, about half of all adults—117 million people—had one or more chronic health conditions. One of four adults had two or more chronic health conditions.

2. Seven of the top 10 causes of death in 2010 were chronic diseases. Two of these

3. Chronic diseases—heart disease and cancer—together accounted for nearly 48% of all deaths.

4. Obesity is a serious health concern. During 2009–2010, more than one-third of adults, or about 78 million people, were obese (defined as body mass index [BMI] ≥30 kg/m2). Nearly one of five youths aged 2–19 years was obese (BMI ≥95th percentile).

5. Arthritis is the most common cause of disability.4 Of the 53 million adults with a doctor diagnosis of arthritis, more than 22 million say they have trouble with their usual activities because of arthritis.

6. Diabetes is the leading cause of kidney failure, lower-limb amputations other than those caused by injury, and new cases of blindness among adults.

7. Smoking is the cause behind most of the above chronic aging events.

8. Divorce, separation and family dysfunction are the most prevalent costly and preventable cause of chronic aging.

TESTIMONIALS

Business & Industry Testimonials

We have presented seminars and workshops nationally to market Our health care consulting business from 1991 to 2009. The message was always the same restore and rehabilitate the elderly so they can return home under the scrutiny and care of their family. The seminars were for nursing home owners and administrators, using their management software, to make sure the Medicare and Medicaid programs paid for restoring as well rehabilitating their elderly patients. The workshops were presented to our own nursing home staff, patients, families and community caregivers on "Lifestyles for Aging" using the 12 vows/habits for living Younger-Stronger-Longer. We then linked this philosophy to our day to day operations that resulted in over 43,500 more of our 141 skilled nursing home consulting clients' patients and our own patients discharged back to the community. Now we plan to use "Lifestyles for Aging" as the 12 Habits for living Younger- Stronger-Longer as the learning guide to offer workshops to the general public (primarily for preventing chronic aging) with the theme STOP CHRONIC AGING NOW. The marketing platform for this will be senior centers, nursing home operators, AARP, Public Health Administrators, corporate HR directors and home-based caregivers.

"Jerry and Shari just presented their workshop 'The 12 Habits for Healthy Living' and had the audience calculating their biological age on their cell phones and answering a stress test to correlate real life to the "Real Biological Age". Then presented ways to replace their 12 key habits with the new ones."

Wendy Anastasia, HR for OneFP-USA

Patient Family Testimonials

"Jerry and Shari were the owners and operators of the nursing home in Muscatine Iowa for 6 1/2 years. My grandmother was in their facility for six of those years. She passed at the age of 99. They are the most caring and competent administrators of nursing homes in the State of Iowa. Our family cannot say enough about their facility."

Andrew Foster grandson of a former patient

Employee Testimonials

"Your nursing home is the best I worked in for thirty years. Your commitment to the patient's quality of life is extraordinary. No one is just left to a bed and a meal ... more and more are getting up and going home". Susie Davis, RN

"Jerry and Shari took over the failing nursing home in Washington Iowa. I became the Director of Nursing for Shari Rhoads who was the Administrator. I have been in the nursing home field for over thirty years and have never experienced what the Rhoadses brought to the challenges of nursing homes. Unlike the other organizations I have worked for they never said no to a need for delivering quality of life services. Their priorities were always for the patient, families and staff.

"They invested their time and money in turning around a failing business despite the attacks by regulators who didn't like their desire to fix the public disgrace known as nursing homes. They did it anyway until the regulators and politicians pushed them out ... the new owners then turned it back into a dirty, smelly hell hole that no one wants to visit."

Susie Davis, RN, former Director of Nursing of All-American Restorative Care of Washington.

"I am an LPN at one of the nursing homes Jerry and Shari owned and managed. When I read Jerry's first self=heath book it gave me hope that I could get back to my pre-pregnancy weight. He and Shari imparted to me the likely hood that having children and falling victim to conventional knowledge that I need to eat for two caused my continued weight gain. I took this literally since my pregnancy weight is where I now want to be. It wasn't as hard when Jerry got me to believe in myself again and stop stressing over my hectic stress filled lifestyle. By changing my eating, drinking and sleeping habits the pounds dropped off. Jerry told me I was a role model for his 12 habits for healthy aging plan ... so here I am enjoying life moving on to my goal of 160 pounds.

Ms. Martinez, LPN All-American Care Center

"Jerry's books have changed my attitude towards my current weight and dreams for the future." Sandy Volker, CNA.

Patient Testimonials

"I was admitted to the All-American Care skilled nursing facility in Muscatine Iowa after suffering a stroke. My wife of fifty-five years and 12 children were devastated. I had been active at this nursing home as a guest karaoke singer with a local entertainment group of seniors. When I was admitted, I thought I was being put in prison and wanted out. My children all thought I needed to stay. My physician ordered all these medications, without even seeing me, and as a result I couldn't even walk and was very angry and combative.

"After about a week of going downhill Mr. Rhoads the Administrator got involved, contacted the doctor and took away all medications and got me on a walker under strict supervision. In two weeks, I was independent and in six weeks from the date of admission I went home to my wife who was dying of cancer. My wife and children couldn't believe it."

Cecil Calvert

Shari and I call it better Life Styles for aging Americans. See our website www.lifestylesforaging.com. We use this book for educating our clients on the necessity and ways to stay younger than your chronological age. It has been established by Dr. Oz that approximately 75% of aging Americans are 10 to 20 years older biologically than they are chronologically. That's a big WOW for future health care costs in America ... this must change!

Finally, our society does not move the body or the brain enough ... Computers, autos, escalators, elevators, moving walkways, buses, trains, planes, all are making it too easy to DIE YOUNGER AND HARD TO LIVE LONGER. Using the exercises in and the Rhoads' downsizer algorithms for planning your course and plotting your success can change your life and health. See www.lifestylesforaging.com for downsizer.

THE BENEFITS OF SIMPLE MOVEMENTS, SUCH AS WALKING WITH YOUR SPOUSE OR SIGNIFICANT OTHER, CONTRIBUTE TO LIVING LONGER AND STRONGER CONVERTING TO A HEALTHY, HAPPY AND PROSPEROUS RHOADS LIFESTYLE.

PSYCHIC OR PHYSICAL

Tell me a tale or two
About what you believe and what you do
Are you more inclined
To view things from the front or the behind

Do you take more interest in a thing of beauty
Or do you get turned on by doing your duty
Or are you turned to a face that's kind
Or are you looking for a stimulation of the mind

Physical versus psychic
Skeptic versus optimistic
What really gets it on
The night-time or the dawn

Tell us pray tell us your story
Do you want moderation or glory
When you finally decide and commit to it
Try it for a while and see if you fit bit

Because if you don't and you start to hurt

Psychic will be a mind to avert self-destruction
Physical will be the body with no resurrection
Leaving results for your inspection

If you've picked the easier scene
Which only makes you mean
You may sacrifice your good wife
To be happy as a necessity of a crappy life

After all its your choice and gain
For which you've paid the pain

Just don't lose what you've had in full
Because dreaming is psychic
While doing is physical

To have it all " let go of not at all"

Your heart is the measuring stick for your longevity. Take care of it and your body can seek a better life style resulting in the accomplishment of living longer and stronger. One hundred and beyond is the mark of a life well lived if happy, healthy and prosperous. That's our plan ... what's yours? Jerry and Shari Rhoads.

100 years

1,200 months
5,400 weeks
37,800 days
907,200 hours
54,432,000 minutes
3,254,920,000 seconds
4,354,560,000 heartbeats

I calculate the real age (see the formula in the Appendix) of our children and grandchildren as they grow-up. Giving them the tool to track the result of their lifestyle and healthy habits. I also have what I call "The age-o-meter" to show the impact of time on their chronological age so they appreciate that using their time for practicing the twelve vows (habits) is to believe that their spirit lives forever and their physical body will be younger and last longer by being stronger.

What about you? Do you feel stronger every day? Do you have the energy you had in your teens? Does your weight bother you? Can you still compete in some sport? No confession needed. There is a reason that you're seeking a lifestyle change. Now with Shari and I doing Yoga together, walking together, dancing together, playing tennis together, vacationing together we are closer than ever.

VARIOUS WAYS TO MOVE OUR BODY:

Walking any distance regularly

Girl Talk (Shari)

We love to walk, which we do in our neighborhood or on the beach or at the gym. We hold hands and walk for at least an hour. Usually two to three times per week during the summer. We love this time together ... we're walking the talking and have many topics to discuss. From politics and our businesses to our children, grandchildren and now our great grandchildren. We reminisce about how we met, the fun we've had over the years and the vacations we took. It's great exercise for the body and the mind come rain or shine. Originally our walking was to solve a lack of communication and feeling disconnected in our marriage.

My main concerns had been raising our children and Jerry's was his work and with the last child out of the house, we realized we had pretty much lost our close relationship. In addition to our stimulating conversations and solving the world's problems, we also enjoy the scenery. It has been the best solution to being on different planets until we purchased our own nursing homes.

Guy Talk (Jerry):

If you are a couch potato, not an action hero and find it hard to get started. Try this ... my solution for dreading the workout focus on working it out with yourself and/or your mate if she or he will participate in having fun. Pick a workout for working out your differences. Shari and I were having our difference when I first started managing nursing homes. I brought the problems home with me and we were continually arguing about me not talking about us and my obsession with working out and sporting events.

The perfect solution was to walk together for our improved health, attitude, communication and friendship. Over the last twenty years we have walked the equivalent of 7,000 miles talking all the way to compatibility.

Jog then run a block, do more each day or week

Girl Talk (Shari)

I use to run with Christie, our oldest daughter. Then I had knee surgery on both knees for meniscus problems due to tennis and running So, Jerry and I have walked two to three times per week, holding hands no less, anywhere from 2 to 3 miles up to 9 when we were filling more time on the weekend. We would walk to a little restaurant, have breakfast then back home, totaling about 9 miles. We found that we were talking constantly about our mutual interests in the family and our businesses.

To us this time is used productively and look forward to good weather ... though we have walked in all kinds of cold weather but not rain. When we were doing all the traveling with our consulting business, we got up early and went out and walked every morning when we were out of town, so we had our routes in every town for our return visits. The most challenging route was in Salt Lake City... I called that hill a mountain, but the scenery was beautiful. During those out of town walks our conversations were mostly about our clients.

Guy Talk (Jerry):

I started running after five years of jumping rope. The next twenty years I ran everyday with time off for foot injuries. I stopped the everyday torture in 2001 and have ran intermittently since then. Since purchasing our nursing homes my running days are over. I believed the "Runner's World" magazine message that running was the best exercise for the body and mind ... however, after years of dreading the roadwork I found there were better ways to get rid of stress caused by our business. I thought that surely someday I would attain that runner's euphoria ... and I did ... when I quit.

My goal was to run the Chicago Marathon with my two daughters, Christie and Kimber but they told me later that they hated running and only did it to pacify my obsession with running longer and longer distances. We did run the Steamboat nine-mile race in Peoria a couple of times Kip our son is a tennis player and never got into running due to knee surgeries.

Don't Run a Marathon

Guy Talk (Jerry):

My favorite saying is "the day I experienced the "Runner's High" was the day I quit running every day." To me it was torcher to the body and a delusional satisfaction to the mind. Many a day that I ventured out into the early morning I wanted to skip it and didn't. After the run I felt that it was worth the satisfaction of accomplishment. Another story comes to mind about running a marathon. My daughters got into running and we did train for the Peoria Steamboat race … a nine-mile killer through the park consisting only of hills that we had to suffer through three laps before emerging downhill into the city. We did the race twice and each time I'm thinking the next race would be the Chicago Marathon that November. Until they told me they didn't enjoy running either. So, my marathon days were to run the last six miles of the Iowa marathon with my wife's brother- in-law, Rick Vandervelde, and watch him finish the Chicago race twice. But he and I ran a number of 9 to 10 milers until my only marathon came about in August, 1983 … when he and I, my two daughters, ran 9 miles on Friday night, he and I did a training run of 17 miles on Saturday in the heat and he, my daughters and I an 8-mile race called the "Ups and Downs" in Downs Illinois on Sunday. This total of 34 miles, over three days, is my claim to having run a special Rhoads marathon for the one and only marathon I was to ever run … after that tortuous weekend my running career was put on hold with a foot injury (planter faucitis) for one year, never to run the Chicago Marathon or any other until I stopped running in 2001. Over the 20-year running career I did a Forrest Gump distance of approximately 51,000 miles with the accomplishment of no other injuries except sore feet, while building a strong body and mind.

PAIN

Pain is in the person
Of each man and woman
Waiting to be undone
By being human

Pain is in every good
And stress must be
If you will and would
Live to be free

Pain is in the heart
For the sake of love
It's in every start
If you expect fit the glove

Pain is in the mind
That burns as we strive
Yet the ultimate we find
Is to be more alive

Pain is in the every life
Who cares enough to give
Creating rights from strife
And giving of self to live

Pain is in the effort
So we can feel good
And somehow resort
To doing what we should

Pain is in resistance
To being vain
Mindful that in each instance
We are to blame

For our pain
And will grow from it
Not in vain
But in spirit

Welcome pain don't fear it, invest it in gain

Girl Talk (Shari):

I hated running as a young girl due to a congenital heart condition that left me short of breath … but I do love tennis and have been able to play for years with Jerry. While he says he loved the running for what it gave him, I hated it for the strain it put on his body.

Swimming is one of the best for reducing body fat

Girl Talk (Shari):

I'm not an accomplished swimmer. I learned late and don't enjoy putting my head underwater. Our Villa in Cabo has a pool and I enjoy the water with the kids and grandchildren. Just swimming across the pool is great exercise.

Guy Talk (Jerry):

Swimming is not an exercise I have practiced since I graduated from college. I do swim in our villa pool intermittently when we go to Cabo. It's great exercise and I can see that it's better than running. But running is so easy to do anywhere and swimming takes an effort to find and get to the pool.

Resistance training of any sort will burn body fat

Girl Talk (Shari)

One thing I do every morning after my shower, hair and make-up is 40 push-ups at the vanity counter. (I never could do them on the floor). It gets my blood churning and gives me a feeling of accomplishment. It is also good for toning my arms and increasing my heart rate. I also have a "Fit Bit" that counts my steps clipped to my belt or in my pocket. It is fun to have and amazing to see how many steps I take in a day.

Once a week I lead Jerry and I in Yoga poses for one hour along with crunches, leg-ups and light weight training. It keeps him stretching and me straining. We now have added the "Simply Fit Board" to our program. I also use 4 lb. hand weights for toning, nothing heaver as I don't want to add bulk. We also do my leg exercises three times per week to strengthen the tendons around my knee … I had injections in both knees due to wear and tear on my cartilage and meniscus. It didn't cure it but did reduce the pain when we dance, walk or play tennis.

Guy Talk (Jerry):

A technique I use to get going with a dreaded workout is to say I'm just going to do a quick workout on the treadmill or elliptical … something easy and fulfilling … but I end up spending an hour lifting weights and doing ab work. Why does this work because I hate lifting and crunches but can look forward to cardio that's easy for me? As Jack Lalane who was well known as a body builder and lived to 96 said "I hate the thought of doing it but I love the results."

Yoga, plates, calisthenics, stationary bike, treadmill, rowing machine, elliptical … all contribute to weight loss, muscle toning and development and feeling worth-while" I've tried them all over the last forty years. It's my addiction … I have a problem taking time off even when I'm recovering from a cold.

Girl Talk (Shari):

Over the years I have taken Yoga, Platies, used the treadmill and tennis for my physical well-being. Jerry has been an inspiration to me as well as our children, with his encouragement to participate in organized sports and use different training techniques throughout our lives.

Guy Talk (Jerry):

Athletics and competitiveness drove me to an addiction to exercise. It isn't letting me go even at my age. It's an obsession with looking good, feeling good and being as good as I can be. That being said, I hate it and put if off till day's end sometimes. How can It be a good habit when I dread it and would love to avoid it? My sister and I have the same obsession and think it's looking for my parent's approval. To be honest I do appreciate the way I look after 40 years of it. Time well spent in my doctor's opinion. Even though he still is amazed that I don't need blood thinner, cholesterol medication and blood pressure pills. He even insisted that I get a second opinion at the age of 65 and I didn't go back to him for 12 years.

Finally, the internet has endless videos on how to put together a routine and I take "Men's Health" magazine and Shari "Prevention" magazine for inspiration on exercise, diet, supplements, love life, advice on clothing, Cologne and how to treat your mate. Also, the inspiration for this book came from what we were observing in our nursing homes that chronic aging in America is not a healthy exercise. It can be downright depressing and Shari and I believe that those last years should be the best years. For us the solution to slowing aging boils down, not to more discipline, but doing it together as part of love making so you can be happy now and forever after.

Dancing, skiing of any kind, play an hour of tennis, just move your body

Girl Talk (Shari)

Also, I consider our dancing one to two times per week, to be a part of our exercise program. We took lessons a few years back and have always been on the dance floor trying new steps that fit the music. Kip had a band since he was fourteen, that was in the entertainment business and we were always helping him set up and tear down his equipment for the shows; and he practiced in our basement for twenty years until he got his own home.

We've always attended our children and grandchildren's sporting events, dance recitals and beauty contests. Jerry was the family's photographer so we have thousands of pictures that chronical their growing up and having fun. With the advent of digital we can all share in the day to day special pictures and don't have to wait on them to be developed.

For years, I was a member at the tennis club and played competitively on a traveling team. Jerry and I also played doubles together and were a part of a drill session every Friday evening. Jerry's played at tennis clubs for years and has enjoyed teaching our children and grandchildren the basics while initially supplying them with tennis rackets.

Guy Talk (Jerry):

Every Thursday night from 7:00pm till 11:00 o'clock we go dancing at the Chicago Prime a restaurant and dance club. We also do the same on some Friday and Saturday nights. It's kind of a joke that we want to get in our 10,000 steps so we are on the dance floor most of the time, as we have since high school. Our friends that we have met there are amazed at our energy and dance skills regardless of our age. Quite encouraging when they remark how loving we are and don't seem to need other people to have a good time. We do dance to most all the slow songs to be in a loving mood. Our new friends there are always asking us our secret for longevity and our loving relationship. Our answer is dancing, kids, sex and roll-n-roll. Occasionally, someone suggests that we write a book on how we do it … that has resulted in this prescription for health, happiness and prosperity with a goal of living forever. Repeating Harry Jaffe in his book "The Secret to Immortality" states: move your body, laugh, and find love. All is free"

JERRY MET SHARI (get what we got)

We continue to play whiffle ball and volley ball with our children and grandchildren for the family championship … in our 70's Shari and I are still competitive. I have given all of the children, grandchildren tennis rackets and continue to play singles with them. Shari also loves tennis but is dealing with knee problems that are being treated with therapy. Our son Kip has had similar problems but still can beat me.

SELF-EVALUATION

After reading this chapter take the following Self=Health quiz ... update your Real Age calculation, put a checkmark for your answers and come back later to rate yourself for complying with the actions recommended in this chapter:

	Birth Age	Real Age	YES	NO
Beginning Real Age score	_____	_____		
1. Do you now have a workout area in your home?			___	___
2. Does better us of your time help get you to work out?			___	___
3. Do you see results from changing your exercise habits?			___	___
4. Do you plan ways to reduce colories intake using habits?			___	___
5. Do you revise the real age calculator to measure results?			___	___
6. Later rate your progress ... 1 being low and 10 being the best.			___	___
7. Later rate your program ... 1 being low and 10 being the best			___	___

FUTURE INHERITED

We inherit the wind
The world
The future dreams
We inherit the genes not our jeans

The personality traits
The facial characteristics
The voice texture
The goals and aspirations
Career selection to be sure

We inherit the family environment
The home structure
The locale and Life Style
We inherit the future or
Reject the wind

In our sails
At the home stead

Such as two brothers
One an alcoholic
The other a teetotaler
One unemployed
The other successful
Why didn't they inherit
The wind in their sails

That the storm assails

Aren't we either the victims
Or the beneficiary of the inheritance
Read this observance
It's the choice not the genes
That makes the difference

The good dad and mom
Make the right choices
Their offspring typically
The same rejoices
With the same voices
And sail through life

The bad dad and mom
Make the wrong choices
Their offspring typically follow
The same path
With the same wrath
And fail in a stormy craft

Then we have the bad dad and mom
Giving their offspring the choice
Do I inherit the future
Or do I try to change the past
Or do I choose another cast

The irony here is poetic
And ironic
We all can choose a path
Despite our past

Reject what we have learned
For what we have earned
To inherit the wind then yearned

Good or bad
Happy or sad
Future inherited
Though indebted

It's our life

AFFIRMATIONS

Move your body and feel the music

Work out the mind to mold the psychic

***

Live as if you'll die tomorrow

Love as if you'll live forever

***

Cradle to grave, most don't take a chance …

Exercise your mind and body so life can find romance

***

Challenge your mind and body for your own sake

Otherwise your destined for an early wake

***

Surely you can't expect miracles

When you are overlooking the obstacles

***

Natural highs are speed for freedom

Unnatural highs are speed for a demon

***

For those who believe in the will

Will find their way to fit the bill without the pill

***

Know thyself and seek fulfillment

Through activities that are energy well spent

YOU ARE WHAT YOU FEAR

You become what you've overcom
(so you are what you fear)

Replace a no way
With a some way

Replace a not now
With a somehow

Replace I don't know how
With effort so will can endow

Replace an unhappy face
With a smiling grace

Replace fear
With good cheer

Character comes from a choice
To be free of fear's hoist

As fear is a mind's doubt
For things that never come about

Unless you're a lazy lout

(85% of what you fear never happens
And the other 15% is only half as bad
As you fear ... why waste away fearing 7 ½ percent
Rather than endearing yourself to happiness)

Marriage Vow/Lifestyle Habit Number Six
CONSUMPTION IS FOR LIVING NOT DYING

*"One cannot think well, love well,
sleep well if one has not dined well"*

Brainy Quote

GET WELL BY EATING, SLEEPING AND BEING WELL

Healthy aging is in the acts of the doer who is replacing harmful habits with a healthy lifestyle. You're not what you eat, it's the time you waste eating and drinking and stressing about unhealthy habits due to the size of your meals and your waist line ... then doing nothing about it. That's the problem and the solution. What if my genetics predetermine my build, weight and mental state?

This marriage vow and lifestyle habit is how to avoid divorce or reverse the unhealthy life style habits and behaviors that result from overeating, poor sleeping and voiding all connected the thinking process in the brain not the stomach will power OR GENETICS.

Though there are physical and mental maladies that effect our lifestyle, it's the bad habits and failing marriages that create the problems. So, we impart simple solutions that we use in our own life, which can be employed as healthy changes in any lifestyle. We believe" it's not the genes you have but the jeans you wear."

Our goal in the nursing homes Shari, Kip and I managed and owned was to have the patients eat well, sleep well and void well ... then we could keep them recovering from illness, restoring their functioning and rehabilitating their physical wellbeing so they could return to their highest level of functioning outside of a nursing home. In other words, we wanted to return their independence and open up a room and bed to get another chronically ill person in, get them better and get them out. By doing this more would come.

Doing it this way we were able to discharge 50% of our admissions in better health than when they came to us. In this chapter and in our nursing homes the solution is the same ... better habits at a younger age and stay away from destructive chemicals and drugs; thereby avoiding the nursing home. On top of the effect of chronic illnesses, the unfit elderly person is likely to fall at least four times in their lifetime ... usually after the age of 60 ... most do not recover due to their underlying chronic diseases and lack of healthy habits. The research shows that bad habits are a subconscious brain function not a body function so the solution is in how you think, act and behave that affects your GENETICS, sleeping habits, toilet habits, weight now and forever after.

THE LIFESTYLE HABITS OF GENETICS

Yes, each birth is burdened with their genetics. We are all born to a predetermined set of genetics that have a memory cell as well. (Some researchers of what causes habits have proven that will power is a function of our muscles not just the mind). Therefore, we are setting out with no inclination to age faster, then, we fall victim to our environmental influences.

As we mature our physical genetics take shape and our personality genes are at work. Of course, the physical traits and our personality aren't easily subject to change but the interaction with our brain is, when it comes to thinking and doing. According, to the behavioral experts, "we are what we think we are". They also attribute habits to a result of our thinking good or bad. These habits are subject to change for better or worse by changing our thinking processes, routines and turning our positive genes on and the negative genes off. If the habits are dysfunctional and stressful then we will need to work on improvement, every day, by pursuing goals for a more effective and satisfying look in the mirror. Miracles are attainable from my own experience. Many of the patients in our nursing homes were restored to home or a retirement community using the techniques we present in our 12 DNA Fountain of Youth habits to longer living. It is similar to the

Alcoholics Anonymous (AA) 12-step program used in changing alcohol and drug addiction habits.

It is reported that an estimated 2.1 million people seek help from AA each year and as many as 10 million alcoholics may have achieved sobriety through group therapy. This has been astounding because it's founded on religious and spirituality behaviors with no scientific evidence of changing the brain. Researchers say that AA succeeds because program forces people to identify the cues and rewards that encourage their alcoholic habits and then helps them find new behaviors using the same cues (cravings) and get the same reward but shifts the routine.

Though our proof of success is primarily with ourselves and our patients, it is usually done by individuals not groups but the processes can be carried out with a spouse, a friend or a group of friends. My past home life environment wasn't positive nor focused on spiritual feelings of self-worth or the practice of self=health. I don't blame my parents because they too were a product of their culture and resulting family environment.

So, I have spent hundreds of hours working on my attitude and outlook. I have found in that approach to being happy and the health benefits as the outcome is worth the dedication and effort. The remaining information is predicated on my and Shari's real-life miracle journey to self=health. We all have values within the framework of attitudes, holding the pieces of life together. Hopefully yours are healthy. If not, try our prescription for happiness. It has taken most successful, fulfilled people years of unhappiness and trial and error to discover the worthwhile benefits of positive mental processes. Their philosophy is at the point where they train their mind to attain worthwhile goals, and in setting worthwhile goals, they're able to help and influence people. They will also leave the world a little better place. In our opinion this is true happiness. For the attainment of a positive mind is truly peace and security.

In the attached daily exercises, routines and affirmations (rewards), in the back of each chapter, we must reprogram the brain from a failure mode to a success mode. But first we need to understand that failure is a perception not a permanent location in the mind. To brain wash the negative and input the positive will take some time. For me it took a year of writing down positive thoughts. After the year became history my mind was set on achieving and believing not deceiving my self-worth. All this is a culture change not a cult brain change.

Try it… it works.

YOUR LIFESTYLE HABITS

Your values own your subconscious mind
Your subconscious mind owns your habits
Your habits own your behavior
Your behavior owns your life
So you own your lifestyle
On how you choose
Good lifestyle habits
Or
Bad die-style habits

This means that our weight, appearance, happiness, health, relationships, prosperity, faith, sex life, intelligence, behavior are all dictated by our DNA and genetic response to outside stimuli. That response can be positive or negative depending upon our subconscious mind and its habitual routines. This is where the mind needs to be turning on the right response rather than the wrong reaction to determine the results. In effect you control your own DNA Fountain of Youth. The faucet, so to speak, is turned on by your reward and off by your negative reaction which means you are in control of how you age and how long you live.

Most Americans use weight loss diet plans to look better, feel better but never are happy or better … which means you use any unnatural diet you will DIE- TOO soon and living to 100 isn't a healthy goal if you plan on being unhealthy. A bothersome statistic is the average weight of American Men is 196 pounds, according to a look up on Google. The aspired weight is 180 pounds. The average height of the American Man is 5' 6". Women are averaging 174 pounds for an average height of 5' 2" with an aspired weight of 160. This means the men and women's average BMI of 32 far exceeds the 27 recommended. Anything over 27 is considered to be obese. Personally, my BMI is 30 due to the weight training I do … muscle weighs more than fat and looks better. For example:

"Jerry's book Never Too Old to Live was my inspiration for getting healthy, fit and happy. I am an LPN at one of the nursing homes Jerry and Shari owned and managed. When I read Jerry's book it gave me hope that I could get back to my pre-pregnancy weight. As a result, I now weigh 160 pounds rather than 360 after having three children, when I got inspired. It wasn't as hard when Jerry got me to believe in myself again and stop stressing over my lifestyle. By changing my eating, drinking and sleeping habits the pounds dropped off. Jerry told me I was a role model for his 12 habits for healthy aging plan … so here I am"

Ms. Martinez, LPN All-American Care Center

Shari and I have a philosophy that pregnant women have been misled and have gained three times what they should during each pregnancy. Shari weighed about 105 pounds when she got pregnant. With each of the four successful pregnancies she gained 17 pounds each time. Her doctor would not allow her to gain excessive weight or accumulate fluids.

After each delivery, she lost the entire 17 pounds over the first month after having the babies. Each baby was healthy and weighed about the same. 7 pounds 4 ounces. Today she still has that postpartum figure. In researching what causes obesity, pregnancy and subsequent inactivity are the primary reasons for women. Since having babies 46 years ago she has never been over 120 pounds and is 112 to 116 now. Admittedly, she is a role model for any aspiring or current mother who wants to live longer and stronger at their best weight.

We aren't gynecologists but there is something wrong about gaining 60 pounds to feed a 7-pound fetus. After three to four children there is usually an accumulation of pounds that are never lost without extreme dieting. If you are a victim of this calamity our program can't prevent the occurrence but will focus on 12 healthy habits that reduce the pounds gained through physical exercise and the daily activities that you choose to use.

Our eating and drinking habits are also inherited from our past conditioning then passed on to our offspring. Healthy habits are not the typical pattern of growing up with parents who have harmful eating and drinking habits. So, we need to reprogram our own eating habits if we want to practice self=health.

I'm not one to preach but would like to teach you what I have learned about eating. If it is artificially tasty it is probably not good for you. For instance, fast foods, that take the brunt of the harmful habits we form, are flavored for instant gratification…not permanent health. Sodas are sugar with some fluid. Calories do dictate weight. Exercise does allow and stimulate a bigger appetite by burning at least the same calories that are consumed. If you are overweight you need to burn more than you take in … it is a daily challenge you must win to be happy, healthy and prosperous. Other options are liposuction, binging on diet pills, hunger strikes, fasting and sweat tents … all of which take off the pounds and turn back on the harmful habits.

Okay this is just common knowledge and sense…so how do I break these eating habits so I am aging slower and more rewardingly. The fact is I won't live forever, so why shouldn't I just enjoy it and move on. Try being the Biggest User of this book and not the Biggest Loser of this LIFE! 100 years is an admirable accomplishment worthy of your improving heath.

1. Eat slower and more often (3 meals are for past thinking)
2. Eat between the hours of 8:00 am and 8:00 pm
3. Eat healthy meals not snacks
4. Only eat what you enjoy but healthy
5. Lose inches not pounds
6. Count grams not calories
7. Measure waist not weight
8. Focus on health not weight
9. Look for protein energy foods not sugar (average waist circumference increased almost four times more in the daily diet-soda drinkers) (Carbs kill protein and you if moderation isn't the rule)

I'm not going to give you a recipe for what you should eat...you know it already...we all have it in front of us daily and we just ignore the facts. If you don't know or feel you can't afford to eat healthy then you're destined to be biologically older than your chronological age.

For us, it's much more fun being at a BMI that is considered healthy. Studies show that for men 25 to 40 forty percent have BMI's well over 30 (anything over 30 is considered obese or headed in that direction) and that increases with age. Most of it attributable to sugar intake (soda pop) or calorie (fast foods) excesses. According to Darish Mozaffarian, M.D., dean of the Friedman School of Nutrition Science and Policy at Tufts University "sugary drinks are linked to high death tolls worldwide". In 2015 he and other Tufts researchers calculated that 184,000 adult deaths per year worldwide were attributable to sugar sweetened beverages, due to diabetes and other obesity-related illnesses. Like most men from my generation I grew up drinking Coke or Pepsi.

Then it was fast foods at McDonalds and lack of exercise. It literally took me thirty - years of training to get back to a muscular 175. Now at 179 and 5'7" (I lost an inch in height) my BMI is a healthy 29. But the hours it took me to get back my fitness can be avoided by following moderation in consumption and maximizing your health-related activities and buy your wife flowers as the key to Self=Health habits.

Shari on the other hand was 5' 1" and 104 pounds when I met her, 104 pounds when we got married during my Junior year of college, 121 pounds when she delivered our first, second, third and fourth children, 112 to 115 pounds for the next forty years. Some say she is lucky and she will say she is careful with her lifestyle. For whatever reason, I'm happy she is my wife for life. She has fun at any weight since hers stays the same within 2 to 3 pounds. What we're up against is the changing nature of aging America. In the past, the average of a nursing home patient was 85, now it's 71 ... it used to be the average weight of a patient was 150 pounds now it is 257 pounds ... it used to be that 85% of the patients were females who had out lived their spouse by up to 20 years now the average of all patients is 51% female, 46% male. We had patients that weigh up to 650 pounds, had five chronic diseases and had little hope of getting better. The solution of course is better lifestyle habits at a younger age and stay away from destructive chemicals and drugs. On top of all this the elderly are likely to fall at least four times in their lifetime ... usually after the age of 60 ... most do not recover due to their underlying chronic diseases and lack of healthy habits.

The Baby Boomers are just now coming of the chronic illness, nursing home age ... not very healthy and wealthy enough to ride out the cost of health care on their own. Up to 70% will have chronic illnesses because of past lifestyle habits. In my book "The Boomers Are Coming", we established that there are physical maladies that create the problems. However the research shows that habits are a subconscious brain function not body function so the solution is in how you think, act and behave that affects your sleeping habits, your toilet habits, your weight now and forever. If possible, get up and recite the following poem and change your world.

GOOD MORNING WORLD

Good Morning world
That is an exercise of shaping up an attitude
Deciding that what you give to life
It will return in spades with gratitude

Hallelujah, it's morning unfurled
The alarm went off and as I uncurled
I didn't feel like facing the world
Then it occurred to me
That I was foot loose and fancy free
That it's purely up to me

To dictate and set my pace
So I put a smile on my face
Exercised and shaped up my inner space
Knelt down cleared my mind and said
A few words of grace

That really amounted
To what I'm getting around to saying to your face

Staying in bed depressed and uncurled
Will not lead to any opportunities to fuel
Waiting out there in the sunshine of the world
Particularly if you only see it as cruel
The fuel to go to the trough
Pursuing every angle
And execute effort to get aloft
Above the fray and tangle

With your hope and dreams unfurled
To make every effort you can
Yes say hello world
To put life at your own command
Now you know how to pursue destiny
That each morning is left entirely up to thee

And it's free

My wife's Aunt Edith was an example of laughter extending life's journey... she died at the age of 109 after being married 80 years to Uncle Ernie who was 101 when he moved on to the next continuum. Shari's mom Dorotha C. White was another of life's miracles...she was prematurely neglected and abuse in the nursing home system and expired at the age of 93 well on her way to 100 if circumstances hadn't intervened.

However, Shari's sister died of cancer at the age of 66... a victim, I believe of poor disease management by physician's that focused on pain not the problem ... her history of back problems. By the time, they had treated her for pain her cancer was at stage four and metastasized. The irony is her father also died of cancer and so had her grandfather. I have written five books on why the medical profession needs to practice deductive processes not inductive ruling our irrelevant factors (in other words by using trial and error testing the final diagnosis is wrong 45% of the time. It has been proven that you have a better chance of the right diagnosis by defining your health problems on Google). Physicians aren't required to have a detailed care plan, discharge plan, an aging (living) will, nor a detailed problem list with anticipated outcomes ... they don't need to because they're paid regardless of outcome ... in their mind with the elderly death is an inevitable outcome.

Shari and I are approaching eighty and convinced we can live to over 100. Our marriage spans 60 years, after meeting in junior high school sixty-six years ago, we married young and had four children by 30 years of age. We have had some minor health problems but are extremely active for our age. We're a believer in natural remedies and supplements. Otherwise we avoid pills as the solution for health problems.

Is this approach right for you? You need to answer that for your own self- satisfaction. We only know what works for us. But we do know that life is a gift that comes from the feeling of doing good, making a difference in others' lives virtually every way and every day…a life of feeling love for life itself. You are never too old to live this way.

In summary, this chapter is probably the most important and the least likely to be embraced without failing forward. For us change came in thirds after reading the Diamonds nutrition book "Fit for Life" … one meal at a time and sometimes it was just one meal a day and one night a week. Then we found we could do it two a day then three a day … but that is progress. The focus must be on priorities: reduce intake of soda, fried foods, fast foods, processed foods, excess alcohol consumption, say no to drugs and cigarettes. My coach in baseball said, "a perfect practice gets a perfect result". We are what we practice and that makes our new lifestyle habits. If you are observant and look around in the fast food restaurants and pizza houses and donut shops and around soda machines and smoking areas and doctor's offices and hospitals, in nursing homes and gyms you will see what I see … harmful habits abound more than good ones. Why not be the good example rather the bad sample of over eating, over drinking, over indulgence in anything, and give them this book to read.

RESEARCH AND STATISTICS:

Do our muscles remember routines and does this memory last? "When you move, you activate sensors (called proprioceptors) in your muscles, tendons, and joints that constantly give feedback to your central nervous system about where your body is in space, so it knows what muscles to fire next," says Adam Knight, Ph.D., an assistant professor of biomechanics at Mississippi State University. It's a continuous feedback loop from your brain to your muscles and back. "Your brain creates pathways through your central nervous system, and movements become automatic," adds Wayne Westcott, Ph.D., fitness research director at Quincy College in Massachusetts. Those well-worn pathways essentially become your muscle memory.

It's a phenomenon aptly called muscle memory. Simply put, when you teach your body how to do something—ride a bike, surf, strike some yoga poses, run a few miles—it creates a physiological blueprint. So even if you take some time off, you'll get back to where you were faster than it took you to learn the exercise in the first place. "Muscle memory stems from your body's learning not just how to perform a task, but also how to break down muscle tissue and then repair and rebuild it," explains William Kraemer, Ph.D., a professor in the department of kinesiology at the University of Connecticut at Storrs. "That physiological knowledge lets you come back from injury, surgery, and even pregnancy faster, easier, and often better than before," he says.

Per President's Council on Fitness, Sports & Nutrition

nutrition

- Typical American diets exceed the recommended intake levels or limits in four categories: calories from solid fats and added sugars; refined grains; sodium; and saturated fat.2
- Americans eat less than the recommended amounts of vegetables, fruits, whole-grains, dairy products, and oils. Soda is the mainstay for most Americans needing sugar and caffeine to function. Sugar contributes more to weight gain than any other harmful habit.
- About 90% of Americans eat more sodium than is recommended for a healthy diet.
- Reducing the sodium Americans eat by 1,200 mg per day on could save up to $20 billion a year in medical costs.
- Food available for consumption increased in all major food categories from 1970 to 2008. Average daily calories per person in the marketplace increased approximately 600 calories.
- Since the 1970s, the number of fast food restaurants has more than doubled.
- More than 23 million Americans, including 6.5 million children, live in food deserts – areas that are more than a mile away from a supermarket.
- In 2008, an estimated 49.1 million people, including 16.7 million children, experienced food insecurity (limited availability to safe and nutritionally adequate foods) multiple times throughout the year.

Cognition

According to Dr. Bredesen in his book THE END OF ALZHEIMER'S (Prevent and reverse Cognitive Decline), the solution is a very effective combination of DESS (diet, exercise, sleep and stress reduction) along with simple supplements

His recommended diet choices:

1. Reduce sugar intake (eliminate soda pop and any artificial sweeten drink)
2. Favor whole fruits
3. Avoid simple carbs, saturated fats, and lack of fiber (beer, alcohol, soda)
4. Avoid gluten and dairy products except eggs
5. Reduce toxins by eating fresh vegetables (the greener the better)
6. Include good fats, (olives, olive oil, coconut oil, nuts)
7. Avoid processed foods (cereals, meats, chips, crackers, etc.)
8. Choose fish (smash ... salmon, mackerel, anchovies, sardines)
9. Choose meat as a condiment (for 50 to 70 grams of protein for men and 40 to 60 for women)
10. Choose pre and Probiotics for digestive health (fermented foods such as sauerkraut, pickles, yogurt in moderation)
11. Include digestive enzymes (plant based for control of acids and inflammation)
12. Include supplements from A to K
13. Include specific herbs (based on needs)
14. Avoid damaging food when cooking (minimize loss of nutrients and production of glycation, high level of toxins

WHAT DO I HAVE TO LOSE?

I talked to myself
Yes 'hello' I said
What's this life I've led

Ups and down
Thorns and crown
Pushed my way to bad health
There's some good to talking to one's self

Thinking back on promises made
Eating crow and drinking lemonade
Cuz my mouth is full of 'use to be's'
Wishes and shallow pleas

Making time with only the tapping of my foot
Dangling participles and no square root
Just some dreams of the 5 & 10
Not knowing how to win

If to myself I could talk back
I'd agree health can't be curried in a snack
It's not as if candy pretzels or chips
Are the half-baked diet tips

It's not handy like girls with false lips
On everybody's minds but not on their hips
The words gentle words that I prayed in bed
Self " have you heard what I've said"

You should covet thyself
To make a better bed
So you would lose weight
Rather than your head
And your mate

Then miss your next birthday
DOA is a pitiful price to pay
An epitaph of excess and decay

THE DO'S (Ten Commandments to a Longer-Healthier Lifestyle):

Diet and nutrition designed for an enjoyable experience is a function of common-sense solutions. Harmful habits lead to bad results (over weight just being the most obvious) so we must convert those habits to better habits for most of the days to get the positive results of a prescribed controlled diet plan that doesn't punish you. Remembering that compliance once a day is better than noncompliance all day ... of course there needs to be progression to full adherence for best results. Basic Rhoads Vows for best results:

1. **Eat and drink what you enjoy but in moderation.** Moderation such an indefinable word. What it really means can I live without

it. If so, leave it alone and go on without adding to the problem. Remember that the content of fiber and fats are very important for processing your food into the colon-aryl track. Weight management starts and ends with that process. Study: drink up, but only one a day for a longer life ... according to an international study, adults should average only one alcohol drink per day or live a year or two less longer than teetotalers ... a sobering guideline versus the two-a-day touted by other researches. Of course, the key is moderation for other reasons as well ... sanity, reliability, happiness, dependability, successful, prosperous and a better person.

2. **Eat and drink as much as makes you feel fulfilled but in moderation.** I am obsessive for cleaning my plate since my mom never served enough. So, if I leave it I won't be full or fulfilled. Also, I am obsessive about physical exercise so I can eat as much as I want ... but am obsessive about not throwing anything away or having to eat it as leftovers. Shari is one that only eats what she likes until she is full and is not bothered about putting it through the garbage disposal ... saying "if I ate it, it would be gone anyway".

3. **Leave some food on the plate and wine in the bottle to attain moderation.** Make it a habit to leave something on the plate so the people in Syria can be fed. My parents, as depression era young adults, were conservative with helpings and I never left anything ... but with my kids it was people starving in China to get them to clean their plates and avoid the harmful habit of overeating. Thank God, like Shari and I, they aren't anorexic or obese.

4. **Leave the table when through but never stuffed and uncomfortable.** And strive to be moderate in desert and drinks. In Iowa, we always had a big breakfast of unhealthy foods. Dinner was always at noon consisting of fried and baked meat and potatoes. Supper was something left over from dinner or something from a box. Now that we aren't on a work schedule we typically will exercise before breakfast (at about noon) and have an early dinner about 5:30 and maybe a late desert (before 8:00pm). Since we are technically retired, we have either the conventional healthy Iowa breakfast of eggs, bacon and toast late in the morning or an early lunch of a salad or sandwiches of smoked turkey or chicken. This depends on our exercise program for the day, then an early dinner of a meat, salad, vegetables and no bread and usually a nonfattening dessert. The weekends are for exercising then having meals when we get hungry. We are neither vegans or vegetarians or overweight ... and have stayed at the same weight for the last 20 years. So, it must be working.

5. **Family functions can take on a new way of creating food selections** that enhance the experience with recipes that implement the betterment of the lesser of two evils, over eating and wrong ingredients.

6. **Menu planning based on choices that carry lower calories and less sugar** is the first important step to better results. 40% protein, 35% carbs, 10% fat, 15% fiber.

7. **The content of protein versus carbs is a science and Shari and I don't dwell on the science** but on the art of eating right. For me I have to have 40% protein 30% high energy carbs and 10% fats. Shari just the opposite. Since we aren't nutritionists our coaching here is just what works for our family. However, our children have become rather expert on nutrition as they have twelve children between them and have done a wonderful job of teaching them the basics of the good and harmful diets.

8. **Read labels and become familiar with the impact of proteins and carbs** ... sugar and fat ... chocolate and alcohol ... vitamins and supplements ... calories and body fat ... muscle and toning ... eggs and cheese ... bread and sweets ... processed foods and unsaturated fats ... salt and sea salt ... vegan and vegetarian ... south beach and your beach ... educate yourself on setting up your 12-habit plan and make practice your best habit.

9. **Understand the latest food allergies that include food and drinks we ingested** as youngsters ... peanut butter sandwiches, white flour, white rice, white bread, gluten free wheat, gluten free anything, saturated dairy products, soda, red meat, salt, sugar, fats, corn syrup, on and on and on? And the theories change as fast as they make them. My question is where were these allergies in the past ... peanut butter the staple for kids now a threat of dying not a treat for living. Glutens in everything and shell fish can kill you.

   It really comes back to common sense ... our bodies have natural regulators and indicators if we heed them ... bloating, gas, constipation, weight gain, weight loss, skin condition, allergies, chronic coughing, wheezing, insomnia, and finally our immune system. And pills won't cure these ... they will mask it for a while then comes the bad news ... you're having a stroke or heart attack or ulcer or cancer or worst yet you are getting old before your time. And there is only one destiny to that. The ride on Chronic Aging goes nowhere but to the graveyard too soon.

10. **Sleep at least seven to eight hours a day** ... however, this commitment is such a variable in the busy working for a living lifestyle. Ours has

changed considerably since going into Re-hirement. We now can stay up late and then get up when we are ready ... usually 7 to 8 hours later. We wish that we had done this earlier. If you have a history of waking up in the middle of the night have a sleep study done to see if you have apnea ... that can throw your whole system out of whack. ED, low oxygen content in your blood, respiratory deficiency, heart arrhythmia, stroke due to insufficiency of blood to the brain, numbness in the feet, discoloration in the feet, so on and so on.

I found out at the age of 77 that I have sleep apnea ... I was in denial with Shari and Kip telling me to get checked. I did and they were right I was having 30 events per hour when my breathing stopped and then started a couple of minutes later. I have had the dreaded face mask and machine for 2 years now and can't sleep without it ... now averaging 2.5 events per hour and feeling more rested and not getting up multiple times for a bathroom visit.

THE DON'TS (We aren't, in my opinion, what we eat. We are what we don't eat and don't do).

1. Let no time for sleep get in the way of your healthy habits. When we were employed by our own business, we usually slept six hours and got ready for the world at 6:00 am and retired at midnight. Not conducive for good physical or sexual health.

2. Forget the no no's ... no smoking, no soda, no stimulants other than coffee and wine, no excessive desserts, no excessive amounts of red meat, no second, thirds or fourths ... everything else goes. This is where your preferences will make or break your progress. These habits are stress makers.

3. Assume that this 12-step program will catch on with the family. As for lifestyles changes, for exercise and affirmations, we leave the family up to its own devices after considering the role model we have played in our marriage and Rhoads lifestyle teachings during our offspring's upbringing. In other words, with coaching we leave the makeover for the family tree to their discretion but with our coaching when asked.

4. Be unconscious of what you are eating ... try to comply to a healthy meal at least once a day, then two, then finally three.

5. Forget to look at the labels and plan a better approach to consumption ... your figure, big or small or just right is what and how much you consume.

6. Go to the grocery store when you're hungry ... eat a nutritional at least one meal per day, then two meals per day, then three ... a

progression is better than no improvement at all for your own mental and physical health.

7. Ignore the scale ... make it the reason for healthy eating at your age not your weight. So, count the days you have eaten healthy not the pounds ... they will take care of themselves.
8. Let divorce destroy your appetite for healthy consumption.

Do you know someone that says they eat and drink whatever they want and are still healthy, wealthy and wiser than you will ever be? In my sports background, this is either a liar, braggart or a natural. The guy that says he never practiced in his life, never lifted a weight and has 20/80 visions due to his good looks is probably not the natural. But there are those that are blessed with more of the five tools if they use them. If it checks out do what they do.

THE NATURAL

The natural leader persists
As one of man's most cherished myths
Why he not me

Perhaps because it's easier for us to believe
That someone is gifted
A fixed quantity

Man is either born or made with or without
Being faced with the impending
And unsettling doubt

Why he not me
It's as simple as can be
It's the task of improving
What he's proving

The natural in him not me
Can I get it or not
Get what he's got
Like some dogs have spots

Probably not
Natural is a product of nature
So you better make do with what you got
Be it a hitter or pitcher or fetcher

Or dance better then David Ross the Cubbies catcher
Making good to avoid that old age stretcher

VARIOUS WAYS TO BE HEALTHY:

Eat to love food but not for over dosing on food

Girl Talk (Shari)

I lived on a farm until I was twelve, …we had two huge gardens and our own cows, pigs, chickens and always had fresh caught fish and never bought potato chips and very little candy … and no soda pop. At the time I didn't realize that I was leading and living a pretty healthy lifestyle.

I've continued that lifestyle and believe in eating healthy because it makes me feel better. Lots of fruits, nuts, vegetables, chicken, fish and limited red meat. Also, dark chocolate and red wine. It seems dark is the latest recommendation of the experts. I love holiday food but refuse to eat so much that I'm stuffed and miserable. I will take some of everything but small portions and always save room for a little desert. Mom always warned us about starving children in China but dad always said "if you take it you eat it" so I learned at a young age to take only what I could eat and it has worked … no waste and no excess weight.

I like new recipes but look for the healthy ones. Our daughter Christie gives me many good and healthy ones since she is also into eating healthy and goes to the gym six days a week (gets that from her father). Jerry and I take vitamins and supplements … vitamin E, D, HG-3, CoQ-10 and fish oil and read health magazines to guide us on exercises, recipes and meal ideas.

Guy Talk (Jerry)

A good indicator of your results, like your Real Age number, will be your natural weight, your best energy level, your improved strength, your improved skin and muscle tone, your improved feeling of self-worth…is it worth it…try it. Feeding the body, the right nutrients, is the quickest route for our spirit to cleanse our soul as well as our pipes.

We always have and do talk with our kids at the meal table. It was the one time when we were all together in a positive environment. We talked mainly about them and their school, friends, boy or girl, problems, opinions, complaints and most importantly their dating plans. We started the Fit for

Life diet during the 70's and in the early 80's we were called the Brady Bunch because of the size of our family and the relationships we had.

Also, our children were fortunately very good students, had nice friends and had positive thoughts about their futures after high school. As I had always encouraged them to do they all pursued their dreams in higher education and have been a pride and joy to Shari and I. Christie was already a terrific typist, always had a job and was a dancer, Kimber was also a dancer and is a professional level artist, Kip was a musician and song writer and Kelli was also an artist and dancer.

Sleep more than six hours

Guy Talk (Jerry)

We sleep better now than ever. At least 7 sometimes 8 hours. But we do stay up late and get up around 8:00am. It used to be I would get up at 5:30 or 6:00am to exercise before being at work by 9:00. Having our own business allowed us flexibility … the only problem was for twenty of those years we were traveling to the nursing homes to do our consulting and installing software. So, no staying up late and getting up early if it reduces your energy and motivation.

Wake up rested and cut our night time snacks

Guy Talk (Jerry)

We not only sleep longer we sleep sounder and never have been into nighttime snacks. Our calorie intake has allowed us to never be overweight nor hungry all the time. This is a carryover from our Rhoads lifestyle at home … clean you plate because that is all we have. So, to this day I religiously clean my plate of only one helping. But I do eat fast to make sure it doesn't get away from me … my mother usually was washing the dishes as we were finishing that one helping. Shari is a slow eater and only eats what she wants and how much is when she is full.

Sleep apnea tests should be done and heeded at any age

Guy Talk (Jerry)

Shari has felt for years that I had sleep apnea … I stop breathing during a sound sleep. But I get up too often and don't feel rested when I get up in the morning. Sure, enough I am having a sleep study to treat this symptom. Shari's glad because it was keeping her awake waiting for me to breath. I was having some reflux from eating too late so this has been solved.

Eat by the clock: Avoid eating after 8:00pm and before 8:00am

Girl Talk (Shari)

When we read "Fit for Life" we got into the habit of eating before 8:00pm and after 8:00am until our travel schedule messed that up. Now we are happily back to that regimen.

Regularity at all costs … and get checked for colon cancer early on

Guy Talk (Jerry)

I purchased another book on better recipes and how to decipher the data on the labels. Since neither of us are gaining weight we sometimes get lax in everything but fat and salt. The "Fit for Life" by the Diamonds, nutritionists, diet is still the driving force behind our eating habits. I also get "Men's Health Magazine" that has the whole gamut of foods, exercise and advice on lifestyle. I'm not an expert on the diet part of our regimen but the results have been good … for example Shari and I both had high cholesterol (in the high 200's. Our doctor wanted us to take a statin but we chose a Co Q10 and apple seed vinegar … mine is now 190 and Shari's trending that way too. When Shari tried to use a statin, she ended up with hives and immediately stopped and became more cognizant of her food choices.

Stay off the scale but check body fat and think thin not fat

Girl Talk (Shari)

I weigh what I have always weighed before having children and after. I'm fortunate to have my mother's genes … she weighed under 100 and was 4' 8". I do weigh myself every day to make sure I'm not retaining fluids. This is because of my pacemaker (due to a congenital heart problem). Fortunately, I inherited my mother's body shape and my father's skin tone … Jerry's thankful for that. I take a baby aspirin, vitamin E, Fish oil, for stroke prevention, vitamin D for bone health and mediation for my pacemaker usage. I have a tendency towards dehydration and low blood pressure if I don't drink 5 to 6 glasses of water per day … so I carry a water bottle with me at all times.

Guy Talk (Jerry)

I hate the scale. My weight will vary 4 to 5 pounds in a day depending on the calorie and water intake. On average, I stay around 2,000 to 2,500 (usually two meals per day) and exercise everyday doing something physical. If I don't get enough protein in the morning, I will get the shakes by noon. I've been that way since I was a kid ... had to have a peanut butter sandwich when I got home from school or sports. I take supplements for strength (testosterone) and healthy immune system, and anti-oxidants for heart health, vitamin E, baby aspirin and fish oil for stroke prevention, CoQ10 for cholesterol balance, vitamin G and H-3 for cognitive retention and a balanced protein (40,%), fiber (15%) and carb (35%) and fat (10%) and (4 to 5 glasses of water during the day and one glass of red wine at night) fit for life diet.

Regular exercise promotes eating, sleeping, voiding well

Guy Talk (Jerry)

I have a goal to get down to 175 pounds and not lose muscle. Also, I was experiencing wheezing when I went to bed. Well I decided to stop eating after eight pm. I had heard that it causes reflux and the doctor said it might be that. After three days, the wheezing was gone and the last time I weighted myself I weighed 177.5. Before I was around 182 to 187. Shari and I usually only eat two meals a day. A late breakfast and an early dinner with a snack in the afternoon. Shari never really liked breakfast until we changed to this fit for life routine.

Fortunately, Shari and I only take supplements and the only medications Shari takes is for a congenital heart rhythm. We believe that many of the prescription drugs are at the root of many chronic conditions and addictions (opiates, statins, psychotropic drugs). They don't cure and have side-affects that threaten your longevity and mental alertness.

I quit seeing a physician at the age of 65 when he prescribed blood thinners, blood pressure medication and cholesterol drugs as being preventive whether I need them or not. I did return at the age of 76 to be able to meet Medicare's protocols. Shari on the other hand has seen the cardiologist regularly to have her ejection fraction and heart rhythm checked.

JERRY MET SHARI (get what we got)

Until the age of 65, we would Roller Blade at the park, all while holding hands because we wanted to stay in shape. Or we would practice tennis drills for an hour then play doubles for an hour up to the age of 70. Now we go dancing twice a week for three to four hours for cardio. Endurance is a natural byproduct of being fit by eating well, sleeping well and getting regular exercise. It also promotes strength when its needed.

SELF-EVALUATION

After reading this chapter take the following Self=Health quiz ... update your Real Age calculation, put a checkmark for your answers and come back later to rate yourself for complying with the actions recommended in this chapter:

	Birth Age	Real Age	YES	NO
Beginning Real Age score	_____	_____		
1. Do you get physical and mental checkup every 6 months?			____	____
2. Do eating habits still control your thinking when hungry?			____	____
3. Do you sleep and void better after improving habits?			____	____
4. Do you list priorities and goal for changing your daily activities?			____	____
5. Do you recalculate and use the real age calculator for results?			____	____
6. Later rate your progress ... 1 being low and 10 being the best.			____	____

Your rating and answers are your confession booth for judging for yourself where you are with your commitment to change your unhealthy habits and lifestyle at this point of your journey.

AFFIRMATIONS

at as if you'll die tomorrow

From a meal you beg or borrow

***

Not accepting what you are as others for what they are

Be they too heavy or a chin falling too far

***

Looking in the mirror can be daunting

If you are looking to be flaunting

***

Losing something for nothing is nonsense

Losing more pounds for a sixpence is common sense

***

Rationalization is an invention of human faults

To answer why not and explain defaults

***

Enthusiasm is the fire to inspire

Sustenance to our fitness desire

***

Utterances of habits come from within

Speak of them and reality will begin

***

We mortal humans learned to ride

Losing initiative for walking that died

***

The day in the life dedicated to a healthy body

Will be envied by everybody

Marriage Vow/Lifestyle Habit Number Seven

FUN IS A REMEDY FOR STRESS AND DISTRESSED MARRIAGES

*"When he worked, he really worked.
But when he played he really played for fun"*

Dr. Seuss

GET WITH IT AND HAVE FUN THEN SLEEP IT OFF

Making fun and having fun are like aging twins ... no one wins unless fun begins. Your family is the tree and you're the roots waiting for their wings to sing your song ... about the journey to healthy, happy and prosperous with fun being the result not the reason. Then like a hangover from other means of relaxation you need to sleep it off with eight hours of rest. Again, the experts are emphatic about stress and distress in marriages causing 40% of chronic aging. So, rest and relaxation following mental and physical acidities completes the genetic need to rest.

This chapter is about the other side of everything we do ... and how to have fun doing it. It's also about how to avoid or reverse the unhealthy life style habits and behaviors that cause stress because of poor decisions regarding loving, living and aging.

Shari and the family are obsessed with playing cards, board games, trivial pursuit, Pictionary and brain games. I have learned to participate and found that it's more fun than just playing a competitive sport against myself. We just purchased a chess board to learn why everyone is obsessed with that game and we get out the Scrabble game when we watch sports (Shari will put up with some of my Cubs, Bears, Bulls sporting events if we do something, she likes ... such as binging on Netflix's Heartland, her favorite. We also put together the Chicago Cub 1,000-piece World Series puzzle).

So, raising the family has been the most fun as we became grandparents with no responsibility to be perfect parents and are proud of how our children raise their children. Ironically, the weight loss ads these days usually start out with an overweight woman saying she decided to lose weight when she couldn't have fun with her kids and grandkids anymore. A very good reason for making a lifestyle change. Though the weight loss usually isn't permanent the desire and results are the same ... we all need to have fun to be in physical and in mental shape. In this chapter, we find that Stress is the antithesis to fun and experts say it's the act of letting things get to us that causes up to 40% of our aging too fast results.

On the other hand, de-Stressors are the act of avoiding or counteracting things that get to you. Like replacing unhealthy habits with our 12 more healthy ones. We have the reader take a stress test to determine how this is affecting their Real Age Score and use it to give them a not so subtle nudge to change their stressful lifestyle.

OUR HABITS SHOULD DISPLAY A POSITIVE LIFESTYLE

I used to catch myself cynically complaining about things that seems outside of my circle of influence (as demonstrated by my frustration with oppressive government voiced in my other books). I'm working on being more receptive to what appears to be dumb and is another view point that I don't agree with. Frankly, I've found that writing, particularly poetry, has relieved my feeling of not having my thoughts listened to,

My first published book was in 1981 when I was representing nursing homes in political hearings and presentations. I didn't formally publish another until 2009 when I was purchasing three nursing homes. Of course, the books were about how to operate a nursing home in a regulated environment. I wrote five more on self-health, three on socioeconomics, one novel about George Orwell's predictions and five poetry books about the "Wonders of the World".

These are listed in the back of the book. None have been as challenging as this one. Here Shari and I as a team are writing about us, yes, but more so about you the reader and hopefully the believer in how humans can do anything they put their minds to achieve. Earle Nightingale, the most famous self-help writer of all time, taught me that anything you conceive and believe you can achieve … and I add receive.

Shari and I are daredevils. We are impulsive. We are having fun being reckless but not jobless or moneyless. We have taken risks and fallen forward. We always light on our feet. Now that we are on the other side of our Social Security, we are still taking risks for fun and maintaining the good habit of doing it together.

IMPULSIVE

What's fun
What's happy
Just ask if you want to know
It's what you do where you go

Take off on a journey
To nowhere but an impulse
I have been impulsive
All my life

Meandering here and there
Don't have a care
Until I met and married my wife
And found her impulse
Was as big as mine

A puzzle being completed
Against the winds that blow
Just going without doubt
Finding out what we didn't know
By trying flying crying sighing
All the way
Until it's play

For life is just a game
With fear of the unknown to tame
By knowing

What's blowing
Wanting the same
As the moving tide

We're named fun and happy
Without pride
Having fun is a diversion from boredom
Making scorn and porn ho hum

It's life's bastille yet undone
Happy is fun not to miss
Mine was that first kiss
Knowing that impulse was this

Shari and Jerry's 60+ years of marital bliss

When I think of fun I think of memories: birthdays, holidays, vacations, weddings of our children, babies born to our family, a night out and the positive feelings they produce. These feelings seem to build the future as we go and become positive outcomes. I can't possibly know how all this works … the mind, the heart, the soul and the spirit somehow respond to my thinking. If you get a chance to see the movie "Sliding Doors" with Gwyneth Paltro … it shows how fate sometimes enters our future based on happenstance. But it has a happy ending due to Helen Quilly's timely decision to catch a subway train, that changes everything. It was the choice to dart through the sliding subway door that was her life changing and saving event. Some would call it pure luck and I call it effort meeting opportunity.

Shari is also the humble one and fun one. She will not admit that it's her talents that support Kip's music and our two daughters' artistic ability. While Christie inherited my business acumen. Christie has her own Court Reporter company. And has her merit designation and twenty years of upgrading her abilities and technology in a very competitive field. Kelli, at the age of eight, won an art contest winning a Daisy Duster bicycle and continues to paint children's rooms with cartoon characters. She also has her own jewelry line manufactured in China. Kimber has made a career out of her art work. She has several lines distributed by Enesco … the most famous being "Circle of Love" figurines that are in Hallmark Stores all over the world. Kip found early on that his talent was music. He bought his first electric guitar after selling our dog Roan's red setter puppies. From that point forward he was a musician and song writer for life. This talent had crossover to computers and prepared for a life time of technology and being an entertainer. We are extremely proud of their accomplishments … it's our roots and their wings that have been fun.

ROOTS AND WINGS

Children either walk or run away
From home and adventure
What sets the gait of
Their departure
Ask the puzzle maker

Who shall be the richest
Ask the banker
When will they arrive unto themselves
Asks the Quaker
Where shall they go and why
Ask the undertaker

Should their trip
Be to history with misery
If given to the no roots plight
Or given to the no wings flight

As children who shan't walk proudly
And must put ink in their pens to write
About wishful stability
With bad dreams of insecurity

Finding no peace in the past
Planting no value or graces
Into their fear yet cast
By flocking to shallow spaces

No thrill free or flowing
Feeling no excitement as a lover
Finding no tranquility in going
Into the tailspin of reality's hover

The moral of the roots and wings

Those given to roots
Hold to the good earth
By their love for family and tradition
And those given to wings girth
Hold to the good wind's ambition
By their roots, even as they leave the mother's breast

And make their own nest
So those cocks and hens
With nests of futility
Feigning the faith of has beens
Feeling no need for security

Give those chicks roots
Give those offspring wings and boots
So they can hold onto self-worth
And the good earth
Bent on survival and defend
Their mother and father's birth
On wings finding the good wind
And the roots for the struggle with no end

Roots and wings will give them the feather
Through sunny and stormy weather
Making their moral trip with stability
And their risky flight with security

Whether from the mother or the father
Or both together guiding them forever after

RESEARCH AND STATISTICS:

- The weight loss ads these days usually start out with an overweight woman saying she decided to lose weight when she couldn't have fun with her kids and grandkids anymore. A very good reason for making a lifestyle change. Though the weight loss usually isn't permanent the desire and results are the same ... we have to have fun to be in shape ... we aren't in shape to just have fun or we would never do it.

- The experts on life styles and behavior have found that your social and marital activities are all connected to the brain not the heart. Just ask someone how they are doing ... oh, I'm doing great ... you knowing they're probably not telling you the truth unless they are smiling when they say it. What's in your heart is the root of a happy marriage of fun and games.

- For men, the challenge is in extracurricular activities surrounded by over imbibing and eating. The typical former jock will come out of high school (as I did) at 142 pounds wringing wet. After joining a fraternity in College, I packed on 33 pounds my freshman year of beer and partying. My goal was always to weigh 175 because I was skinny with little muscle. The problem was that the extra weight wasn't muscle. It has taken twenty years of exercise to get back to a muscular 175.

- Stress experts say it's the act of letting things get to you. Experts estimate that stress causes a 40% acceleration of the aging process and marital problems. De-Stressors...the act of avoiding or counteracting things that get to you.

- Aches and pains ... exercise until you avoid them

- Worries and concerns ... counteract them with thoughts of joy, happiness and hope with your spouse

- Financial and economic threats ... think about solutions not the problems ... creative thinking is spurred by exercise more than any other act ... being overweight isn't an issue it's very real negative financial problem funded by doctor bills and low energy

- Personal tragedies and emotional depression ... get the mind and body working for a common cause either in exercise or in work related activities

- Getting old before your time ... if you have abused your mind and body for years a reversal will take some stress relievers every day ... better activities of daily living (diet, exercise, meditation and hopefulness) ... if you are not able to do this you have given into the inevitable health and chronic aging issues ... stop them now and forever be grateful that you did.

- Regretting your divorce and wanting the next marriage to be stress free

Yes, there is much to complain about ... negative influences occurrences can put you in a negative frame of mind if you let it ... I am stopping that as of now. And so can you ... think better, live longer, happier, healthier more prosperous lives by having fun doing it.

The value of keeping your promise to enjoy life can't be understated. There are books written on the perils of stress related unhappiness. In my opinion that unhappiness related to harmful habits is the major cause of s stressful marriage. To find out your stress level take the following stress test.

STRESS TEST

Following is a simple twelve question stress test. Stress has been tabbed as 60% caused by harmful habits preventing having fun from living. Researchers have found that 40% of chronic illness and chronic aging is caused by stress. These habits are aging the typical American faster than their chronology. For example, if you are 40 years old and your rating is 120% of your actual chronological age using a real age calculator your biological age is 48 or if your age is 50 your biological age would be 60 and so on. This may be the most important information you will receive if you want to live longer, healthier and happier.

	YES	NO
Number One Stress cause: not happy with personal appearance	___	___
Number Two Stress cause: not happy with attitude towards aging	___	___
Number Three Stress cause: not able to get it on with anyone	___	___
Number Four Stress cause: eating, smoking, drug or drinking habits	___	___
Number Five Stress cause: little if any physical fitness activity	___	___
Number Six Stress cause: financial crisis or loss of job	___	___

Number Seven Stress cause: unhappy family life
or divorce   _____ _____
Number Eight Stress cause: unhappy job or job change   _____ _____
Number Nine Stress cause: death in the family or no
close friends   _____ _____
Number Ten Stress cause: no outside hobbies or interests   _____ _____
Number Eleven Stress cause: chronic illnesses or obesity   _____ _____
Number Twelve Stress cause: not believing in a
higher power   _____ _____
Total Yeses   _____ _____

What's you score? Any three to four collectively, of the above, can cause chronic diseases, mental duress and divorce if not alleviated. It's interesting that these stress problems are the same as our 12 marriage vows and lifestyle habits are designed to improve your stress and happiness scores.

Then how can we always be Happy so stress is sedated?

HAPPINESS IS

Reaching the destination of a long trip
As your children are losing their grip
Happiness is an enthusiastic compliment
By someone you thought you should resent

Happiness is the embrace of a friend
With whom you would face the end
Happiness is the pride you take in a child
Converted to being calm from wild

Happiness is the softness of your homeward bed
And the dawning of a day you don't dread
Happiness is the smiling face of your love
When she finds out its her, you're thinking of

Happiness is plotting out your erstwhile course
And the feeling you've been touched by the force
Happiness is many years of effort
That to a success you can covert

Happiness is a thought of yesterday with a smile
And a look to tomorrow's effort as worthwhile

Happiness is not being unhappy with yourself
Being content to spend time invested in your health

Happiness is a trip with interesting parking places
And a mind that is filling those spaces with glad faces
Happiness is the smell of a new car or house
And the contentment expressed by your spouse

Happiness is the ability to say gee whiz
I gave to the cause because it's his
Happiness is eat drink and merriment
And feeling your purpose is well meant

Happiness is a good poem sung as a song
And the fulfillment of wanting to sing along
Happiness is perfecting your golf stroke
With the feeling you can go for broke

So shoot the moon be nice roll the dice
Knowing final bliss
Is in the hands of who you kiss
While the urge to sin

Is of mice and men

Is fun a trait or a necessity in relationships and effective living. The story about chimps, monkeys and gorillas is they have to have rough housing and fun to be content. The trainers in fact wrestle and clown around with them to develop a trusting and safe relationship. It was determined that the lady in Connecticut that was killed by her husband's (he was the trainer and had died in 2004) chimp in 2009 was wrestling with them.

Having grown up among people, Travis had been socialized to humans since birth. A neighbor said he used to play around with Travis and wrestle with him. He said the animal always knew when to stop and paid close attention to its owner. "He listened better than my nephews", the neighbor said, after Travis had mauled Nash. "I just don't know why he would do that." We are the closest living creatures to the chimp and I am convinced we need to wrestle with our kids, grandkids and our wives (affectionately) for our animal instincts to be fulfilled. I personally wrestled with our 4 children, 12 grandkids and will now our 8 great-grandkids as they were growing up and believe that improved my relationship because of the fun we had. If your kids are grown it's never too late to play games with them either on the kitchen table or out in the yard or the vacation home.

The results are guaranteed:
1. You will be happier
2. You will be healthier
3. You will feel younger-stronger
4. You will not age prematurely due to stress and/or Chronic Aging
5. You will live longer due to your lifestyle
6. You will be married happier and healthier

Sounds good but what can I do to get there? GET RID OF THE STRESS AND HAVE FUN USING THIS SELF=HEALTH BOOK! GET WHAT WE GOT.

LIFE IS GREAT

Life is great if you don't weaken
So don't wait if it's fun you're seekin'
Everything we say and do
Is a reflection of me and you

In the mirror or the shadow following
Becomes your legacy without pride
You're Swallowing
In the wake of each day's plight
Is your history book's delight

With worn pages depicting longevity
And torn pages thrown to your destiny
So, take the time to be happier and healthier
Keeping track to see if your self-worth is wealthier

If it's not then your life is left up to reckless fate
But you can change it's never too late
Then all will agree without hate
Your married life is great

DO'S

1. Take time off from routines that are boring and replace them with fun and games.
2. Listen to your family for ideas on what to do and see.
3. Use the weekends and vacations for games and trips. Just get away from the usual.
4. Spend as much time as possible outdoors … fresh air is inspiring. When was the last time you did a picnic with your wife and kids?
5. Hold hands with your spouse when you're walking. Others notice and will commit on how good that is. Others always remark that they would like to have what we have…and it comes naturally to us after making it a habit.
6. Smile, kiss and hug upon meeting and departing with a final I love you for the fun we have.
7. Talk to your spouse when eating out … even politics, religion and sports are open to discussion unless it turns to shouting then it's a don't.
8. Communication is as good as fornication and more spontaneous.

DON'TS

1. Miss an appointment with fun … make the commitment then keep it at all costs.
2. Frown when someone mentions playing a game.
3. Tease someone that is rejecting your advances.
4. Push someone away that is trying to make up with you.
5. Act mad about taking the time to enjoy something.
6. Have hurt feelings if the decision isn't yours to make.
7. Expect the attention from your children that they expect of you.
8. Don't ever text or use cell phone while eating out or driving … it will eventually kill conversation and probably you or cost you "a driving with intent to injure" felony ticket.

VARIOUS WAYS TO HAVE FUN:

Walk and talk together

Guy talk (Jerry)

Shari and I do hold hands while walking anywhere. Is that silly or are we too old to feel close ... of course not. But we don't care what others do or don't do. It's interesting how many people stop us and comment that we are doing something they should do.

Play yard and sports games or ride four wheelers with grand children and their parents

Guy talk (Jerry)

Each of our son-n-laws have their boy toys and manly incomes. They all are successful in their day jobs (each with skills developed after going through the rigors of higher education). Mike Stephens Christie's husband is an electrician with his own business, Michael Lawrence Kimber's husband is a CPA and CFO in hospital administration, Dan Ahern Kelli's husband is an MBA who is also a CFO in corporate America. Thankfully we are so proud of them for the way they have become wonderful husbands and fathers ... Mike has built from scratch, I call this his Master Piece, a summer home in Farmington, Illinois where we hold many of our weekends and holidays. Michael on the other hand purchased a homestead on Shannon Lake in central Illinois where we go to play water games and bags. Dan has multiple outdoor interests that he uses their RV for ... traveling to the other two sons in laws venues for fun and games. Especially the four-wheeler courses in Farmington and bags at Lawrence Lake, as I call it.

Girl talk (Shari)

Our family is close because we are always hugging and kissing and playing. Even the little guys and teenagers are loving. Too us this is affection given that confirms our love for them. It's fun to see them grow up with a loving attitude and self-confidence. We have a bag game, a croquet set, tennis rackets for the park, footballs, basketballs, softballs, baseballs, exercise room with weights and equipment, etc. Our sons-n-laws have the guy toys ... Mike has four wheelers and fishing boats at the lake house he built. Michael has a fishing and motor boat and jet skis on their lake front property. Dan has an RV, mountain bikes, trampoline and a zip line. Wow what fun.

Go to a drive-in movie or stage play

Guy talk (Jerry)

When I started my second job we went to a drive-inn movie ... that's 50 years ago and I still remember it. There was drive-in movie in Muscatine, Iowa when we lived there and didn't take the time to go there ... even now I regret not going. Seems like a once in a life time for your kids since there are so few anymore. Shari and I had our first kiss that has lasted 62 years, at the Drive-in in Des Moines, Iowa when we were 17 and 16 years old. We have been active members in a theater club. Since moving to Chicago in 1961 we have gone to plays. The first down town at the Civic Opera House where we saw 45th Street, a musical and later at Steppenwolf for the last twenty-five years (even when we moved to Muscatine, Iowa to operate our nursing homes). So, for at least four times per year we go to an avant-garde play. My sister is a playwright and we have gone to her plays.

Go dancing at your favorite club and dance as often as you can

Girl talk (Shari)

Our Dancing every week is the height of our activity next to family affairs. We have met so many people at the venue who all want to know our secret and for loving and living. They have been the main motivation for writing this book. It also produces almost 10,000 steps each on our fitness counter in an evening. We choose walking, tennis, yoga and dancing as our favorite exercise times together.

Take a long weekend retreat or driving until you stop adventure

Guy talk (Jerry)

We have taken a family vacation every year. The latest was a time share in Cabo, Mexico that was upgraded to a Villa where we could sleep up to 12 people. We mostly walked the beach, played tennis and used the fishing boats for fishing. We caught four 50-pound Durados (Mahi Mahi), a 100-pound sail fish and a 190-pound marlin. The mahi was the best eating. We still have the timeshare points to use anywhere in the world ... the problem of course is the maintenance fee and travel costs so we haven't used it for a couple of years. We have the timeshare points for 100 years that means our family can use it when we can't. Recently, we visited our daughter in Louisville, Ky stayed for a few days and continued on to Florida for five days. We also like to take a long weekend down town Chicago to relax, dance and eat out.

Have a date night every week (a break from boredom)

Girl talk (Shari)

Some couples we know have a girl's night out and a guy's out or maybe trips to Las Vegas with girlfriends and boyfriends. Jerry and I don't feel we have to do that to have fun. If it's your husband or partner, what is one of your favorite things that you both like to do? My husband and I love to dance. We are sure to do this every Thursday night and sometimes Friday or Saturday night also. Since we have a favorite place to go on Thursdays, we have gotten to know many terrific friends. It's not only fun but also great exercise. We've been told that we don't seem to have to have other people surrounding us to have fun … when it becomes a habit everything else seems to come easy. For example, holding hands and smiling at each other after dinner out is never boring anymore.

Another favorite is a couple great restaurants we like. We enjoy a glass of red wine with dinner and great conversation without cell phones texting each other. We never seem to run out of things to talk about. We talk about what cute things our children, grandchildren and great grandchildren say or do. I've recently opted into Face Book and Instagram where we receive and post dozens of photos and videos of our family having fun as well. We usually talk politics and our early years with friends between dances.

We watch sports, movies and have a big competition going on with Scrabble. We are also working on Chess since it requires much concentration and strategic thinking. (Great for the mind). We play scrabble and chess while watching sporting events and we have a Monopoly Game Table for longer time frames.

Guy talk (Jerry)

Our date night is typically dancing nights. We always are there on Thursdays and sometimes Friday or Saturday nights at our favorite restaurants that also have dancing. We do eat out quite often as we used to when we had intense work schedule. Now with our writing and publishing still in its formative stage we cannot afford that luxury the way we used to.

Go out to eat with friends, spouse and family

Guy talk (Jerry)

We are always invited to eat out with one of the four families and then stay over. It is a treat to have special events then dine out for graduations from grade school, high school, college and additional schooling. Shari and I love to sit at high tables in the bar for dining with friends and couples. Now that our budget is tightening we love to go out for au devours, wine and a shared dessert. This is usually a Friday or Saturday night out with dancing at another favorite restaurant that has a dance floor.

Go to a "chick flick" and be touched by feeling it

Guy talk (Jerry)

Our favorite movies are those from true stories of over-coming adversity, love connections and happy endings. We're both romanticists at heart. Favorite TV shows are "Dancing with the Stars", Fox News, CNN (only for nonpartisan programs), sporting events and Sunday political commentary. Kip bought us Roku so we could binge on certain Net Flick series. Shari likes Heartland and I like Breaking Bad and House of Cards.

Develop a family diary of memories (photo albums, gift giving)

Girl talk (Shari)

I love to paint in oils. I took lessons years ago and our home is adorned with my work from then and I plan to resurrect my easel and paint supplies … and I did recently when Paris my granddaughter requested a reproduction of a set of paintings, we have in our dining room. Jerry and I have such great memories. We got married when I was nineteen and she twenty. Our honeymoon was not in the Islands or Miami. We went to a motel in Des Moines for the night and returned to our first apartment the next day … after buying Louie Prima and Keely Smith's album. Two years later, when we moved to Chicago after Jerry's graduation from Simpson College with Christie in tow, our parents were saddened to see us go at such a young age.

Christie was this curly blond-haired beautiful baby and we were so young we didn't know fear of the unknown. Another memory that comes to mind is the time in Park Ridge, where we lived, when Christie, Kimber and I picked Jerry up at the train station all dressed up. When he saw us, he smiled and said who do I have to thank for this …. and I said our fifth wedding anniversary. He almost cried he was so embarrassed that he had forgotten that it was November 27, 1964.

Then Kip was born July 19, 1965 fulfilling Jerry's dream of a son. And Kelli, our last memorable surprise, in November 28, 1969 … now four children, twelve grandchildren, four great grandsons and we will have three great daughters when Nick gets married … all from 60 years of marriage … fun and" Memories are Made Of This".

Guy talk (Jerry)

When I look back over our sixty years of marriage there are hundreds of memorable times and places that have gone on in our life together. From this we find so many great and warm conversations to talk about and many of them to laugh about when we are all the family is together. There isn't anything more important to the grandchildren and now great grandchildren, than to remember special times at our house. The grandchildren call it Nammie and Grandpa's house, and now the great grandchildren call it BooBoo and GPP's house.

Our family is close because of these memories and the fact that even now we spend lots of time together. Even the little guys and teenagers are involved. Too us this is the attention given that confirms our love for them. It's fun to see them grow up with the same loving attitude and self-confidence. It's hard for Shari and I to understand and accept how some families split up and aren't having fun observing lifestyle habits passed on to their offspring.

I refer you again to the song "Memories are Made of This" sung by Dean Martin, written by Gus Kahn and Water Donaldson says it best in the third and fourth verse:

Memories are made of us (this)
"Then add the wedding bells, one house where lovers dwell
Four little kids for the flavor, stir carefully through the days
Memories are made of this"
These are the dreams you will savor
With His blessings from above
Serve it generously with love
One man, one wife, one love through life
Memories are made of this

Focused on the wedding bells and good times are the making of fond first memories "forever after" … as the saying goes so goes the marriage.

THE FIRST

The first step The first words
The first teeth
The first day of school

The first kiss
The first ring
The first wedding bells
The first anniversary is here

The first days of trials and tribulations
Were to hold those proud memories near
The first and foremost passing sensations
Is the passing of experiences to hold dear

Can a push then shove us into maturity
Made interesting indeed
In our life with another insecurity
Cultivating a flower from a seed

The days of first love real
The first nights of a honeymoon
The first home cooked meal
The first spat then a spoon

Such sowing leads to a fertile egg
And the day of offspring is here
A cute face arm and a leg
Filling grandmother's heart with a tear

Ah yes first … first is the best
First born is by far the initial surprise
Even though it's by request
Each first is the start of a new sunrise

Of the next best
Memory

JERRY MET SHARI (get what we got)

Kissed her or him in the elevator going up and down to the dentist while she giggles ... we have a time or two! I believe in the old chivalry ... be sure to let her go first through doorways, follow her to the table, walk on the street side, take her coat off for her, don't interrupt when she is speaking and practice etiquette at the dinner table. Never be too old to have fun .., and sex.

SELF-EVALUATION

After reading this chapter take the following Self=Health quiz ... update your Real Age calculation, put a checkmark for your answers and come back later to rate yourself for complying with the actions recommended in this chapter:

	Birth Age	Real Age	YES	NO
Beginning Real Age score	_____	_____		
1. Are you now thinking of fun to eliminate stress and its impact?			____	____
2. Does your stress and time constraint prevent chances for fun?			____	____
3. Do you let your family in on changing their harmful habits?			____	____
4. Do you have a plan for fun on vacation or trip every so often?			____	____
5. Do a real age calculator to current measure stress results?			____	____
6. Later rate your progress ... 1 being low and 10 being the best.			____	____

Your rating and answers are your confession booth for judging for yourself where you are with your commitment to change your harmful habits and lifestyle at this point of your journey.

DAILY AFFIRMATIONS

Fun in the sun or on the run

Neither is forever done

***

If my life were to end on today's date

I would play, play, play … so why wait

***

Foster principles in my softer mind

To gain the gift of leaving hard times behind

***

Throw off the mental chains maximize your potential gains

For self-health has its pains … no gains without change

***

What a man thinks he will become are

Thoughts of what he is… until he finds he isn't

***

Foolish is the man who fails to take measures

For habits in his wake wishing away his failures

***

Growing younger-stronger-longer is exciting

While just growing older is inciting … chronic habits and broken homes

Marriage Vow/Lifestyle Habit Number Eight

BE BETTER SOUL MATES

*"Even in social life, you will never make
a good impression on other people
until you stop thinking about
what sort of impression you're making"*

C. S. Lewis

GET SOCIAL BY BEING SOCIABLE

"Selfishness and loneliness are a sign of unhappy feelings only about oneself." Socializing with friends and family is living with no age in sight. You're not an island nor the sea ... you're a charade of what you want to be ... let others see that side of you and set your Real Age free. According to the bible we are to be a province of redemption and love for others. What better place to start than with your marriage? Then happiness is a preventive and genetic drug for our mind. Relieving us of stress and worry.

In this chapter it is more about how we use our time to be sociable with our friends, family and employees rather than having a social calendar. It's also about how to avoid or reverse the unhealthy life style habits and behaviors that result in poor decisions regarding marriage and chronic aging. We feel the more natural the setting the better for having fun as well as being sociable, nice and involved in other people's future not their personal or health problems. Unless they read our books of course.

As I said Shari is the outgoing and personable one. She brings it out in me. Hidden in my id and ego is the ability to communicate and listen if I concentrate on the other person. But I'm better than she in remembering names. I never used to be able to remember but a few first names then I had to run a nursing home with 196 patients, 175 workers and 190 some families. It took a while but repeating a person's name a few times when I saw them and using relative visions to retain them, I was able to at least remember first names. Nothing I did as Administrator impressed my peers more. Even the surveyors liked the personal nature of my management style.

Shari, on the other hand also managed our third nursing home and was able to manage with a smile, a laugh and a hug. After college, we have belonged to tennis clubs in every community we have been in ... some more than one. We also joined the country club in Iowa for the contacts since we didn't play golf ... we thought they would have a tennis program until we saw the poor conditions of the courts. Growing up in Iowa we both participated in school events, sports and social functions. When I took a job in Chicago, with an accounting firm, we also attended business related social affairs ... with some enjoyment but more stress than fun. Shari, Kip and I have owned a CPA firm, a nursing home accounting firm, a consulting business, a software development company, a nursing home management company and three nursing home businesses.

Altogether we've had over 500 employees that required social functions at the holidays, at the nursing home week functions, the other national recognition days, for the patients' birthdays and funerals. It's fulfilling and challenging at the same time because it required preparation, money and being sociable. Shari and Kip carry that ball better than I do.

LIFESTYLE HABITS CAN BE "THE NEW YOU" FOR RELATIONSHIPS

Our social life has narrowed somewhat after going into retirement but is expanding the more we make the effort to mingle with people of all ages. Our family is the first line of a social life getting together with someone every weekend. We also go to our son's music gigs and rub elbows with his friends. It seems that life goes to fast if you're not busy ... it is quite a contrast to being in business with a career or raising a family. We often look at each other and say, "I can't believe we will be eighty ". It doesn't seem possible based on our health, happy life and independence so far. Most of our friends are younger than we are ... probably by our preference to look young, act young and be younger than our chronological age.

Ironically, the values of your social life aren't much different than values of work. There is the desire to be accepted. You will note I said accepted, not necessarily liked. The social system is a means of balancing our values. Without this balance, we wouldn't have laws; we wouldn't have rationality in our lives. We would have nothing to govern nor establish guideposts for a way of life. Acceptance then is conformity to social law. Amazingly, the values of our social life are similar, to the values of work. To practice good work values will lead to worthy social values. For the worthy, tenor of work carries through a soothing tone for all of life.

But the practice is entirely different. It requires more than one person being involved to create a valuable experience. Yes, acceptance is primary but the other is feeling what the other person is feeling. It takes willingness and desire to be together in body and mind. It's best done doing something fun and exciting. Shari and I are very impulsive so on a whim we may go on a vacation to Cabo or take off and visit Kelli in Louisville, Christie in Morton, Kimber in Naperville, Kip in Oak Wood Hills.

While we are there we are playing games inside or out, riding in Michael's speed boat, fishing in Mike's lake, doing bags at Kip's and playing tennis at Kelli's. We are a tennis family due to my obsession with the game and having taught the whole family the basics. I purchased a racquet for each of them and gave them lessons and drills so they could play anytime with anybody and be competitive. Kip was number one on his high school team and Celena was on her high school team. Kelli is a late bloomer on a traveling tennis team ... making tennis a passion for her two sons as well. Dan, her husband is a very good player and has been my singles opponent for many years. For a number of years Shari and I had tennis instruction and drills every Friday night.

RESEARCH AND STATISTICS:

You can be rich in dollars and poor in health and relationships. Is this speculation or fact? Look at the implied statistics.

- Divorces over 50% of those who marry get divorced (most have lived together before tying the commitment knot more likely than not) ... second marriages are 70% likely to also.
- Drug use over 75% of those depressed actively use drugs, alcohol or substances to just deal with it or drop out.
- A high percentage of the offspring of broken families are troubled and some follow the same path.

1. Shari and I can't possibly know enough about divorce since we've never had one. We aren't wedding counselors ... not even for our

married children. But if you believe the data, divorces and separations are triggered by five main factors:

2. Personality differences (read Personality Plus by Florence Littauer) and incompatibility justifying a change.
3. Infidelity for any reason, none good.
4. Premature sex act causing pregnancy and an unexpected marriage.
5. Violence in the relationship isn't acceptable usually not resolvable.
6. Differences in social interests ... men and women are becoming more sports and Netflix movie bingers and not having a productive social life ... this difference in interest is the first step to a distance that usually isn't bridged.

(Shari and I have compromised ... we watch some sports, some Heart Land and a lot of Fox News and CNN. She loves the true romances and I the true success stories) but we watch them together.

National Domestic and Social Abuse Statistics

- 1 in 4 women and 1 in 7 men will experience severe physical violence by an intimate partner in their lifetime. (CDC, 2010).

- 1 in 10 women in the United States will be raped by an intimate partner in her lifetime. (CDC, 2010) Approximately 16.9% of women and 8.0% of men will experience sexual violence other than rape by an intimate partner at some point in their lifetime. (CDC, 2010). Data on sexual violence against men may be underreported.

- An estimated 10.7% of women and 2.1% of men have been stalked by an intimate partner during the.ir lifetime. (CDC, 2010).

- The recent high #metoo profile expose' on sexual confrontations and abuse have brought an ever-present social problem to light. It seems women dress and act sexual to find the right man, not to be manhandled by just any man. So, if the woman says no it's no ... if she says yes then you may have found the right mate or the wrong result.

As a society, we statistically appear to be violent towards our mate and have a failure to cohabitate (a derivative of the work habit) when assuming we must be happy all the time. In interviews with couples who have been married longer than 50 years the consensus is that love must be sustained by common interests and activities, plus a cohesive, sociable family. Amen to that!

In our 60 years of marriage we find that when stress and anger dictates, it destroys feelings that relate to self-fulfillment ... a need that is always there. The family partnership is a process of maturing needs, wants and feelings for the spouse or significant other. Co-dependence is not independence and that is what every relationship needs to be able to come together and feel free to express disagreement and conciliation. Over the years I have hurt Shari's feelings and have had to let go of my pride to decide is it worth it to be right ... or am I wrong by holding on to a losing hand. In other words, I would never let her walk out the door for another man. Because there will never be another woman like her ... not even close. Since I first saw her in Seventh Grade at Indianola Junior High, I never stop looking at her and wondering how lucky can I be.

And when I look at her again, all I see is her inner and outer beauty. Always smiling at me and saying I love you so much ... so what do I say " it's the luck of the Irish" and she says "you aren't even Irish" and I say "oh yes I am, I have you" (really I've been told by my relatives that that I am of Scotch-Irish decedents, but my uncle Forrest researched our linage and claims we descend from France with the surname Rode as our proof of roots ... so what, I may be French, Scotch and Irish since I have their luck. For now I' ll go with the luck of the Irish until I become unlucky.

Since this hand is dealt to me
The rest is up to me to do
When losing my life folds them
While winning is to hold them
I deal with the risk
and fate paid for what I never missed

THE DO'S:

1. Find joy in the simple things ... walking, taking, dancing, singing, playing in a sociable setting.

2. Seek out new ways to be social ... dinners out, movie going, sporting events, family outings, school outings, or just sitting on the patio with friends, neighbors and family, or alone with a glass of red wine watching the moon, stars and satellites passing us in the night.

3. Play board games, play games of chance, play outdoor sports, attend concerts, attend church events, participate in political groups or campaigns.

4. Play in public pray in private ... the spirit needs kindling ... the mind needs relief ... the heart needs love ... the soul needs a mate ... the spirit needs fun and games.

5. Be positive on the current events and politics that trend towards negative tabloids but containing a need for participation on all our parts.

6. Stand up for and vote for better government. We have to participate in some manner or we don't have the right to judge the results. If you're interested you can get my opinions on government and politics in my other books listed in my author's bio.

THE DONT'S:

1. Sit in front of TV computer and become a couch potato.

2. Support cynical antisocial programs and events popularized by the media.

3. Ignore the erosion that is happening in our values and lifestyles.

4. Blindly vote for social issues (problems) that don't propose solutions. And don't call a problem an issue unless you have a tissue to cry in your milk, while the perpetrator steals your milk.

5. Complain if you aren't a part of the solution.

6. Assume your family is listening to the news or reading the newspaper anymore. It bothers us that our children don't seem to listen to the news or read the newspaper. To them it is only bad news but we still encourage them to continue to learn about politics and foreign affairs through the media ... even though it tends to be negative, political and violent.in its content ... that's the world around us that needs their ears and voice. They say it's all the same, and they are correct. That's the world around us that needs to change for the better. Hopefully, as more of their generation come to the same conclusion, they as voters can make the changes in our leaders as well.

Our culture and society are becoming antisocial and too violent. Our social media started out being positive and has degenerated to an exploitation of aberrant behavior of a few and over-look the physical, psychological, spiritual and behavioral positive aspects of loving thyself and they neighbor. Face

Book, tweeter, Instagram, snap chat, email, Gmail, texting, sexting, Google, Windows, CNN, Fox News, on demand movies, realistic video games, etc. have taken over the mores of our society in such a way to eventually destroy being nice, loving, giving and positive about politics, religion, friendship, lasting marriages and strong family units.

But maybe not. What if we realize we all will live longer and stronger by being positive not negative? Our important relationship with intimate partners is where we start and have it change the media. Make it become our new normal, our new culture, our new belief, our new religion for a better world.

VARIOUS WAYS TO BE SOCIAL AND SOCIALBLE:

People that shop and sleep together stay married together. Intimate together partners can include:

- Current or former spouses
- Boyfriends or girlfriends
- Dating partners
- Sexual partners

Girl Talk (Shari):

Our typical week will include shopping together, writing together, going out for breakfast, lunch and dinner once a week together, buying groceries together, watching sports and Netflix together, going out to the movies together, dancing together and sleeping together. Not necessarily in that order. These enjoyable functions are social by making friends and enjoying the company of others together. We don't ever text one another if we are together. But we are always together so it is easy to communicate real time.

Speaking of friendships, Jerry and I spend every Thursday night with one of our dearest friends. We have been friends for 45 years, and have some wonderful memories, past, now and in the future. Dee Wallace is the reason we got involved in dancing every Thursday night at the Chicago Prime where she is a fixture. She is a beautiful person and is like a magnet for attracting friends because she is out-going and friendly. What I call a feel-good person because she makes others feel good.

Guy Talk (Jerry):

One of my favorite things to do together is to shop for Shari's clothes. I know what she likes but many times she doesn't pick what is best for her figure and her real age, not birth age. She looks 20 years younger than she is so she should dress that way. She allows me to help her in this respect. Her favorite shops are where we go and it goes without saying she looks good in almost everything she tries on. She selects the colors and styling but allows me to accentuate her assets.

Throw a neighborhood party or a family dinner

Girl Talk (Shari):

When we were younger and living in apartments, we would meet other couples and have impromptu parties. Many of those friendships lasted for 16 years even when we moved away. The couples would come to our home and we would enjoy and reenact those happy moments. But like every good thing it began to ravel with divorces and conflicts in scheduling until it didn't happen. Every time we moved to a new community we belonged to "New Comers" and made many new friends that way ... and this led to more fun and parties. Those included our children rather than getting a baby sitter and have the kids not have their friends there also.

Guy Talk (Jerry):

We moved from a town of 5,000 to a city of 5 million so, we had to adjust to the speed of the suburbs. This forced us to be outgoing where Shari excels .... As a result, our neighbors loved her and accepted me.

Attend church services and participate in the activities

Girl Talk (Shari):.

Each community we lived in meant a new church and new acquaintances. Jerry and I participated in social and organizational function and our children were exposed to those social events. I even was asked to paint a portrait of the savior approaching the Sea of Galilee that still hangs in the entry way of the Methodist Church. Years after we moved and returned the painting was still there.

Guy Talk (Jerry):

We were married in the Methodist Church in Indianola, Iowa in 1959. Our daughters were also married in the Methodist Church. We haven't been active in church functions of late due to moving. In the past, we were active in the church in Morton Illinois and benefited from the friends we made there. I was on the planning and finance committee. Always a great way to be a family by going to church and eating out afterwards.

Join a health club, tennis club or country club

Girl Talk (Shari):

One of my favorite athletic and exercise interests is tennis. I didn't learn to play until I was in my thirties but being the mother of a tennis family, it was inevitable that I learn how to compete. I got good enough to be on the traveling squad. I also participated in yoga and palates classes over the years. Neither Jerry nor I are golfers but did join a country club for tennis and social events.

Guy Talk (Jerry):

We have belonged to tennis clubs in every community we have been in ... some more than one. We also joined the country club in Iowa for the contacts since we didn't play golf ... we thought they would have a tennis program until we saw the poor conditions of the courts. On the other hand, the course was beautiful and so was the clubhouse and the food excellent. There was always a social event going on and we participated in the fund raisers.

In my early years in business I did play golf but not being very good discouraged me from making it my main athletic endeavor. Of course, tennis is my first love and running became my fitness obsession. And in reality, it also become my source of injuries and false positive exercise program.

Don't assume that Shari and I spend 100% of our time together ... maybe 90% but she and I like some time with friends and neighbors when the other isn't there. I refer to it as Shari's Yah Yah time and Jerry's Yuck Yuck time. When we moved to Iowa in 2012, after owning the nursing homes, our social life revolved around a limited number of friends so she craved time to be spent with her friends and visit about family and common interests. So, she joined a book club through Herm and Louanne's Wine Nutz Boutique, a wine and cheese club. We both met several friends there and enjoyed the time we spent there many a night after work.

Go dancing at your favorite night spot or restaurant that has music

Girl Talk (Shari):

Thursday nights are our favorite night out. Dancing at the Chicago Prime lets us make new friends and get great exercise. We both have step counters and usually hit 10,000 steps on dance night.

Guy Talk (Jerry):

You already know our feeling about dancing. The reason it's so social is the type of place we go to ... the clientele isn't too young and not too old so we fit even though we are twenty years older than most of them. We are benefiting from acting younger, looking younger, being romantic and enjoying each other. I'm even getting Shari to try some new dance moves.

Attend social functions for your children or grandchildren at school or college

Girl Talk (Shari):

We were very active in our children's education. I loved being a room mother and we attended all PTA meeting (I was President in Springfield), and attended athletic events and fund raisers. We have five grandchildren (Alec, Chad, Blake, Derik, Celena, Paris and Leigh are college grads) and three grandchildren (Fallon, Tyler and Nicholas high school grads). We have enjoyed going to most of their school programs and functions also. Nate and Troy are still in high school, but live in Louisville KY, so we don't get to go to their school functions, but thanks to the wonders of social media, we get to see videos of them with some of their tennis accomplishments, and trampoline tricks. We're lucky to be younger as grandparents so we can attend graduations at very level. It's our goal to be living and healthy enough to see our great grandchildren graduate from high school and college and start a family.

Guy Talk (Jerry):

Shari and I are adamant that our family be better informed on current events and socioeconomic affairs of the country. Our habits of the past, in viewing the news and current events, have changed dramatically with the social media and technology. Anymore it is all about the individuals not the world at large. Too much texting, sexting, tweeting, face time without seeing the big picture of our country in trouble and our future in doubt ... that politically needing all of us to be personally involved.

Also, with technology taking away any exertion of energy is self-defeating our purpose of living a healthy, active, productive life. Everything that used to take effort or some energy now is done for us ... (opening the garage door, raising and lowering car windows, collecting leaves in the fall, mowing the lawn, picking up groceries, driving and parking our cars, dialing the phone, drilling a hole, driving nails, riding everywhere, walking nowhere, having robots and drones) ... doing our work while we are watching others do it while we couch potato on it, looking, cooking, booking on a hand held, gaming, taming, framing on the cell phone, shooting selfies while leaving everyone more alone.

All very unhealthy habits that are going to break us before we break them. The positive answer of course is to change the routines not the messenger. It's still your lifestyle so use our 12 habits to a better utilize your life skills then factor in technology for enjoyment not ease of effort.

Run or walk in a race for charity

Guy Talk (Jerry):

When I ran the Bix, charity event in Davenport, I mingled with the other runners before and after the race ... most races have a social portion of the program. I have always dreamed of running the Chicago Marathon and would have if not for plantar fastidious and then giving up running for walking. I guess I guess I did effectively run a marathon over a three-day period in July of 1984 (nine miles on a Friday with my daughters, sixteen miles on Saturday with my brother-in-law and nine miles with them on Sunday). Or I could walk the 26.3 miles but probably Shari would not want to and my two oldest daughters confessed that they really didn't like running, so traditional marathons are out. However, Shari and I have collectively walked hundreds of miles over the last 20 some years and roller blades many more. Kelli, our youngest daughter, did run the Italian Marathon a few years back right after she sky dived with her husband without telling she was going to do it ... Kelli is the other daredevil of the family.

Girl Talk (Shari):

I definitely won't run a step unless I have to save a grandchild or chase a tennis ball. The next category would be a possibility if Jerry also goes. Over the years we have taken up roller blading while holding hands ... we have done distances of 12 to 20 miles without falling or stopping. Much better exercise than running (jogging) or bicycling.

Walk for cancer victims or breast cancer surveyors

Girl Talk (Shari):

Our daughter Kim walked the 32 miler and our son Kip 51 miles for charity causes. It might be feasible for us to do that in the Chicago Marathon someday. Kim says we should ... that is quite a challenge. You certainly meet a lot of good people and lose a few pounds.

Invite fellow employees to a patio party or holiday event

Guy Talk (Jerry):

Shari, Kip and I have owned a CPA firm, a nursing home accounting firm, a consulting business, a software development company, a nursing home management company and three nursing home businesses. Altogether we've had over 500 employees that required we conduct social functions.

For example: at the holidays, at the Nursing Home Week functions, for employee recognition days, for the patients' birthdays and funerals we sponsored parties and special events. It was fulfilling and challenging at the same time because it required preparation, money and being sociable. Shari and Kip are the socialites and get me to let my hair down and enjoy having fun.

Attend company parties, and class reunions

Girl Talk (Shari):

Jerry and I have so many things that we enjoy doing together and having a relationship with our employees, their families and friends. Also, and most important to us, it's a chance to hear different points of view and learn something new or just to visit and bond about ideas and opinions. My mom always said "you never get too old to learn something new. She was right. Whether it's a new receipt, a new restaurant, a different political view, or a conversation about sports or business, it stimulates your brain. That is why being sociable with friends and family is so very important to our well-being.

Guy Talk (Jerry):

Over the years we attended company functions for our employers then for our employees when we started the businesses. Social gatherings bond the team in a personal way. Most of our friends outside of work were our employees. For the last seven years we also met the families of our patients and they became our advocates for better care in nursing homes.

We also go to our class reunions … mine one year and Shari's the following year. This last two years were our 60th reunions … we've only missed one each when Shari had knee and gall bladder surgery. We love connecting with our classmates from the past grade school, Junior and high school days. Friendships play a big part in our social life and it doesn't take much effort but they're priceless.

Girl Talk and Guy Talk:

THE RHOADS FAMILY TREE

We planted the family tree early. We certainly didn't plan it that way. We had four kids by the time we were thirty and had grandkids in our forties and grandchildren in our sixties and great grandchildren in our seventies. So, unlike many families, our offspring will know their grandparents and be able to play and have fun with them. It is a joy beyond being older … matter of fact it keeps us young. At family events, we aren't shunned because we are too old. We are an active participant in the fun and games … even volley ball, solar ball and ping pong (now known as table tennis), bags, tennis, Cam jam, fishing, driving four wheelers, boating, whiffle ball, etc.

This picture was taken at Kip Rhoads and Karyn Oribello's wedding. Also, the Stephens family, Lawrence family and Ahern family are represented by the son-in-law's Michael, Mike, Danial and their children. Alec Stephens our grandson on the far right, second row is now married to Ashley and has three sons, not in the picture, Carter, Jackson Wyatt, Becket Stephens. Our other grands on Blake back row fifth from the right is now married to Danielle and have just had a baby boy, Emmett. Nick Scheibel, Kip's step son, fifth from the left back row just got engaged to Alyssa who has three daughters, twins Madison, Morgan and Mariah. Since they are Kip's granddaughters by marriage, they are also our great granddaughters. So, we now have 32 members in total and holding. In search of true fellowship is a goal of every family and attained by fewer each year that we have social media intruding into our privacy. I look at our results as streaming reality.

OUR KIDS' PICTURE SHOW

My goodness I'm proud of our kids
Yes, I'm really proud of them
Christie Kip Kelli and Kim
And though life's great

It's got its lids

But by golly it doesn't seem to have affected our kids

They've got their ups and their downs
They got to learn what's right and what's out of bounds
But for all intents and purposes
They've done great
They've learned to work and they've learned to wait

For the rewards that they have due
Accomplishments paralleled by few
Yes, I stand here proud of them
Thanks goes to Mom for
Christie Kelli Kip and Kim

She had the good sense of a marvelous mother
Holding their hand when they hurt
While I tamed their will to support each other
She protecting them at times behind her skirt
But making sure they were always learning and alert

Rocking them in that old rocking chair
Letting them know she was always there
And now it shows because they certainly are aware
That the family unit is more than individuals can bear

And as Shari's role nurtured them
To impart and make them upright
Christie Kip Kelli and Kim
Came in with my will to persist
And imparted sensitivity without spite

With this blend
We were then not hesitant to send
Them all kiting into the wind

Letting out the string just long and far enough
Letting them receive some scratches and bumps for
Getting tough

And though some of it was rough to get
We tempered it with our sincere family pleasures
Fitting them with this safety net
That protects them from undo mental pressures
But also opens their minds to life's treasures

This has been and it will always be
Pride as I see the jewels surface
Tough enough to win but with sincere humility
Showing we have accomplished our purpose

We'll always be able to feel proud
That our little birds had courage to know
How to fly through life's thunder cloud
And that's the way I see our kid's picture show

It's moving pictures we yet don't know

Guy Talk (Jerry):

Our family enables us to stay young by doing things and vacations with them. If anything holds a family together it is to enjoy free time together. I still like to go to sporting events with our son, son-in-laws and grandsons. I still play tennis with my 32-year-old grandson who has yet to beat me. He keeps saying this is the year. Shari and I have won some mixed doubles club events and my ranking in USTA is still 4.5. But the real joy is looking back and feeling good about the results.

I got my first Brownie camera when Christie was born in 1960 along with an 8-millimeter movie camera. My first passion was taking movies but found it too expensive to develop and used my little Brownie until we moved to Springfield, Illinois in 1969. Since then I have used photography as a hobby to memorialize our life using a variety of 35 millimeters with lenses of all brands to now, an Opus and a Cannon fully automatic digital. I'm not a professional with F-stop settings or light but the auto feature in today's cameras take care of that for me, but I do have an artist's eye for still life, candid's and sporting events of the grandchildren.

Over the years, I have taken about 10,000 pictures (now on my computer for reproduction) of family, holidays, birthdays, weddings, anniversaries and vacations. Thus, I became the photographer for the whole family and provided them albums at Christmas calendars to make the memories visible. We and they have hung some on the wall, sent copies to all the kids and I have used them for image illustrations in my books. I can honestly say that this is my major outlet to always have fun; since sports, my first passion, has subsided with age, photography is the perfect expressions of the eye, the heart and the satisfaction of creating something. However, the advent of the smart phone being a replacement for the bulky SLR has replaced me by anyone with a smart phone … my granddaughter in law (Alec's wife Ashely) has become the photographer extraordinaire along with everyone else on Snap Chat or Instagram.

Also, I use my photos as illustrations in my books and bonded with a few people who are reading my books … and have arrived at common ground on politics but not religion (that one is usually untouchable due to disagreement on how to live and how long we will live). In the last chapter, we deal with our views on How to Get Good with Your Maker.

Girl Talk (Shari):

Like Jerry, I also love to go to the high school class reunions. We have attended all of them except for two years when I had surgery. The next ones are September of 2022 and 2023 which is the 65th for the both of us. To put it in perspective, when my mom attended her 60th I remembered saying that it was unheard of and it will never happen to us … well never is now. As usual, when we attend, classmates remark how we haven't changed much at all. I agree we are still totally in love as we were back then.

Our solutions to being sociable is to not talk about politics or religion unless you are with people that share your views. Otherwise, the prospects of even being sociable is little if any. Being social and sociable are meant to be positive experiences. In the past, we joined the new-comer's clubs wherever we moved. This was a great way to meet people and make friends. Jerry joined Rotary wherever we moved and the Lion's Club once in Springfield.

In our early years, we socialized with friends in our neighborhoods because of our children and location. Previously, we lived on an acre and now a town-home and don't even know our neighbors, who are younger and have school age children. So, our social life is now with friends from the tennis club and two dance clubs we go to most every week.

Obviously, being social and sociable isn't the internet … texting, snap chatting, face book, tweeting and insta-gramming are all quite impersonal … not social as labeled. Personal is still eye to eye, face to face relationships. It's as simple as pursuing our do's and avoiding the don'ts.

JERRY MET SHARI (get what we got)

We have played a competitive sport with our children or son-in-law's and grandchildren … played tennis with our whole family in our 50's, 60's and 70's. We also spend all holidays together if possible. This last Christmas we had thirty-one guests including our immediate family, fiancées and future in laws. After Christmas we have to share our children and grandchildren and great grandchildren with the in-laws.

SELF-EVALUATION

After reading this chapter take the following Self=Health quiz … update your Real Age calculation, put a checkmark for your answers and come back later to rate yourself for complying with the actions recommended in this chapter:

	Birth Age	Real Age	YES	NO
Beginning Real Age score	_____	_____		
1. Do you smile more and look people in the eye?			____	____
2. Do habits now contribution to your being social and sociable?			____	____
3. Do you feel better being with friends, family and neighbors?			____	____
4. Do you plan to asking others to be friends and play mates?			____	____
5. Do you reuse the real age calculator to measure results?			____	____
6. Later rate your progress … 1 being low and 10 being the best.			____	____

Your rating and answers are your confession booth for judging for yourself where you are with your commitment to change your unhealthy habits and lifestyle at this point of your journey.

AFFIRMATIONS

Be social to the sociable

To do otherwise isn't negotiable

***

How smart can I be to ignore sobriety?

While wasting an opportunity given to me

***

I want to assume a firm tread on a path that love said

Would make a more acceptable bed

***

The feeling of love is not a dream

It's the very surge of friendly esteem

***

Give more of yourself and receive good health

For less material wealth and happiness is dealt

***

He who is sociable and likable … dilly dilly

He shall feast at life's happy, healthy table … dally dally

***

Give me the legs and shoulders of Atlas

So I can shrug off the burdens of friendly clashes

***

People bite off more than they can chew

Lord please fill my mouth until it comes true and rid my habits of these vagrants few

THE NEW YOU

Water over the dam
Spilt milk and mistakes can cram
A mind into jeopardy
Unless the past is reviewed posthumously

Is the past half full or half-empty
As the mind wishes it to be
It will be ultimately free
To view ecstatically

Because out of the past tenses
Love confidence faith and humility
Not to say the least sanity senses
The past is certainly the mark of me

But what if its ugly
What if it's not now the true me
What if it turned on me
And it saved the new me

I could have buried my past
Thinking it wouldn't last
Forming a new opinion of the Shadow I now cast
Does this change the past

No but it changes the present
Proving that the future
Is the new you
Awaiting the second feature

Is that a guarantee you've changed

No only if you are convinced
You're different
And you like the new you
Actually the old you never existed

After the new you persisted

Marriage Vow/Lifestyle Habit Number Nine
BE SATISFIED WITH YOUR LOVE LIFE

*"A little niceness goes a long way. Being nice
Doesn't necessarily mean you're weak.
You can be nice and strong at the same time.
That's a characteristic we need more of."*

Brainy Quote

MAKE BEING NICE AND SATISFIED A HABIT

Being Nice is the first step to being lovable and likeable to your life and wife. Your heart is the director and you're the moving picture while your mind controls the destination by being nice and the spice of life. Nice is a reaction to a moment and a response to another human being ... it should be sincere and instant if it is a positive habit ... if not you can't fake it and you own the results. And being accepted is the first step to being satisfied with relationships. Satisfaction is a process all based on a positive attitude, gratitude and being open to others.

This chapter about being nice, is more than developing a great smile. But that is a great way to start. It's also about how to avoid or reverse the unhealthy life style habits and behaviors that result in poor decisions regarding your love life and chronic aging.

The rule that applies to everyone is "smile first and often, listen to your companion or friend's problems and ask questions and wait for answers. I found out how to smile with conviction, listen attentively and my effectiveness exploded into more clients, less doubt, more hope and better outcomes and incomes.

IS BEING NICE A HABIT OR A TRAIT

Need I reiterate that Shari is much nicer than I am. Again, it's the personality thing. However, I don't like confrontation and am not a bully so I guess I'm too nice due to overcoming my shyness. In our businesses, we had to be diplomatic as well as sympathetic. Through 37 years owning our own business and having attended many educational sessions on attitude and its importance to problem solving, I feel somewhat qualified to express my experience in the books I author regarding health care services. Shari on the other hand has four perfect examples of the affect she has had on our children and grandchildren. They all are nice to be around and outgoing when it comes to communicating with others. We are indeed blessed.

Being contented and nice are results that guarantee:

- You will be happier and married longer
- You will live longer
- You feel younger and more virile
- You will not age as fast due to stress
- You will infect others with joy and fun

The beneficiaries will be

- Spouse
- Family
- Business associates
- Relatives and offspring
- Friends and neighbors
- Yourself and self-worth

Though all of this seems obvious we don't always live by the obvious.

Being nice is more than developing a great smile. But that is a great way to start. A study was done for physicians by AMA to determine who are the most effective doctors. The quality that was the most important was being nice and listening attentively to the patient's problems. Those that were the least effective were those who could diagnose their patients in 45 seconds to three minutes and give them a prescription for a medication or an order for a blood test then a hospitalization if they qualified for admission.

That same study found that physicians in general misdiagnose 45% of the time.

BUILD HOPE

Hope is built on trial and tribulation
Not just speculation
It takes faith to get it
The feelings want it and habits bet on it

For doubts wander
From thought to thought
While hope is built on work
Not wished or bought
Without effort we shirk…avert

One must exert time not fear it
Upon a persistent determined clock
While longings dispel the spirit
It takes time to unlock

History that is just one hope away
From senility
No… history says hope is built on trial
And error called reality

That criticism will always beguile
Human frailties to stop in terror
Relegating themselves to single file
Following the followers' error
Into the River Nile

Not to be baptized as hopeful scholars
But left behind to lotto's chance for dollars
This Hope is built on tribulation
Not just a trial's speculation

It takes faith to get it
Feelings to work for it and urges bet on it
Only a few healthy habits away
To be satisfied with each day

One good hope built our way

RESEARCH AND STATISTICS:

The psychological research finds that our current habits are influenced by outside environmental situations as well as our home life. Bullying and sexual abuse are a fact of life at schools, work, at the beach, in sports, etc. We all have been the brunt of it or observed it. Being nice and doing the right thing must be backed by the courage to confront and change it or just avoid it. Following are the impact of technologies that we and our children face … as this accelerates, they have a bearing on our current relationships and response to lifestyle changes.

National Statistics

1. Children that are Bullied also may have volatile behaviors: 28% of U.S. students in grades 6–12 experienced bullying 20% of U.S. students in grades 9–12 experienced bullying.

2. Parents have been Cyberbullied that also influence their behaviors: 6% of Face Book users experienced cyberbullying and/or hacking. 16% of twitter users were electronically bullied in the past year. 55.2% of LGBTQ users experienced cyber bullying.

Being a master of extraordinary habits (skills or abilities) takes, according to Malcolm Gladwell, a minimum of 10,000 hours (5 continuous years) of training and preparation … athletes, scientists, performers, politicians, attorneys, business entrepreneurs and physicians, if they are any good at all, must study and go into a timeless obsession to be the best at something and then they are what they are.

You're certainly not going to take five years to change your habits. However, what you expect to be and want to be is mastering your good habits, and not be a victim of harmful habits, by just doing them differently. That means beating the statistics by exercising your daily commitment to be nice to your children, their requests and your friends' needs. You won't even know when you have changed but your children and friends will.

THE DO'S:

1. Decide that you can overcome your harmful attitude and unhealthy habits ... write them down then confront and change them.

2. Set down actions for being nice that can be accomplished then savor more receptive listeners.

3. Find a place for your self-satisfaction by giving positive responses to your family members not the negative do this and do that.

4. Prepare a list each day a healthy agenda (age-nda means a health plan for the day including food, exercise, thoughts of love, acts of kindness).

5. Stick your neck out for causes you stand for then take action to help others find their agenda (age-nda).

Following are suggestions to have your program ripple downward to your offspring as it needs to:

1. Family functions can take on a new way of creating synergy that enhance the experience with topics at the dinner table that implement the betterment of the lesser of two evils, stress and wrong doing. Topics should include all age groups at the table so all can participate. We have some standard funnies about our children, that we all laugh about. We call them table talk stories. All you need to do is tell one about yourself or another family member, and it becomes one story after another. Of course, the grandchildren love to hear about their parents' escapades as kids.

2. Behavior has choices that carry lowering stress and promote friendships that reduce insecurity and confront bullying where it starts. How we and others treat each other in a social setting. As the saying goes "if you don't stand for something, you will fall for anything".

3. The content of our advice is positive. Shari and I don't dwell on the science but on the art of acting right. Since we aren't negative our coaching here is what works for our family also works in other social settings.

THE DONT'S:

We also have a few no no's ... no smoking, no drugs, no stimulants, no excessive use of pain killers, no excessive amounts of alcohol ... everything else common sense prevails. This is where you and your family's preferences will make or break your progress. The right habits at the right time are definitely stress breakers and friend makers.

Life styles changes for the home environment play a role in how we and our offspring all feel. Cleanliness of the home, clothing and automobiles are positive acts that are being a role model for our Rhoads lifestyle teachings during our offspring's' upbringing. This has resulted in our children wanting to bring friends to their home and then have the same environment for their children's' homes. This is taken for granted after a number of years of effort to be nice human beings.

In other words, with coaching we leave the makeover of the family tree to each his own discretion but each should be aware that being nice affects everyone in your and their children's immediate families.

IF IT WERE EASY

We take up arms to protect freedom
We put down weapons to protect peace
We put our arms around each other
So, love won't cease

Saying " if it were easy everyone would do it"
While the defeated cry out
Praying " if it weren't easy no one could do it"
And the risk takers and doers
Baying " if it were easy no one would do it"

Change is easy if you just do it
Habits can change if you just do it
My feeling is just get to it
Then try and try and try again

For life is more than hope with schemes
And loving the effort it redeems
It's the path it's the value of life
Being of Nice my Friend

Of Mice and Men

VARIOUS WAYS TO BE NICE:

Donate some time or money to a needy family or charity

Girl Talk (Shari)

Committing our time to running a nursing home wasn't in my future until Jerry took over a despicable facility and turned it around in 13 months. Then did it again. It then occurred to me that this is a mission that needs to be done. I loved being the Administrator of a 100-bed skilled nursing facility. We were able to take an ugly building with odors and inadequate lightening into a warm and inviting place for the patients to live. This represents the most satisfying and enduring gift I have made other than being a mother, grandmother and great grandmother. The families of the patients were the most gratifying aspect of being nice and getting their loved ones better and going home.

Guy talk (Jerry)

Shari and I set up a foundation in memory of her mother who died prematurely in a nasty nursing home. It was this event that convinced us to acquire a facility and prove that this shouldn't and doesn't have to be the result. Well, we ended up owning three hell holes and turning them into what we called The White House after Shari's mom's last name (Dorotha C. White).

The company was called All-American Care (AAC) to mean the best care available in America. This ended six years later due to the regulator's retaliation for our fighting for better support to the independent operators versus the mammoth corporate owners. My book "Failing Government Taketh Away" tells the story best. We are still committed to exposing this travesty.

Give out tickets to your kids for a sporting event

Girl Talk (Shari)

Jerry is an avid Chicago Cub, Bear and Bulls fan. We can't afford the exorbitant tickets anymore nor can the average fan. If you want to make a kid's day give them a ticket to the big game. That's really nice. As for the Bears, we optimistically sit at home and watch a team that needs a new owner, as did the Cubs, as do the Bulls.

Guy talk (Jerry)

Shari loves to gift everyone she meets. She doesn't need a reason but does it for everyone's birthday, weekend visit, Christmas, etc. I lovingly call her a gift- a-holic. It's an admirable habit. In reality, the recipient always smiles and says thanks … that's nice. I, on the other hand, need a reason but have improved being nice by being an author of this book. I'm amazed how good it feels.

As for a Cub ticket, it's ridiculous to spend $200 to go to a baseball game that I used to pay $2.50 for a double header seat in the bleachers. But that was when they lost 100 games per year and never got close to being the World Series champs … so now I'm saving up to take my great grandsons to the ball game.

Make holidays special for special people – a family that parties together loves together

Girl Talk (Shari)

Christmas is my favorite holiday. I love to shop for gifts and then watch everyone open what I chose for them. Our children, their children and grandchildren all will remember how we felt that special day. Even in the years when we felt we could not afford much we did it anyway … somehow, we paid for it and benefited from using those nasty credit cards.

Spending time with our immediate family of 32 is my all-time favorite fun time. That's why we have always had Christmas and most years Thanksgiving dinners. Of course, every so often we will have birthday dinners, usually at our kid's homes. Now we obviously have to share our family with the in laws so it takes advance planning and working out a schedule of shared time together so everyone is served.

Guy Talk (Jerry)

Christmas is a great time for my photography and picture albums as gifts. I also create a Christmas Care every year and a calendar for the next year for the families. I have this self-serving habit of not being able to wait to give a gift. Shari, for example, always knows what she is getting and has opened it before her birthday, Mother's Day and Christmas. She then has to wrap it and put it under the tree or at the party so no one knows she knows what she is getting. Every national holiday is a chance to get together for visiting and games for fun. At our age we still participate in those games, be it sports or board games and we're healthy enough to participate.

Help an elderly or disabled person in need

Girl Talk (Shari)

Our nursing home consulting and ownership made us proud to be able to restore people's health and dignity so they could return home. This was always Jerry's dream to improve their quality of life by making sure they got their Medicare benefits and the nursing home delivered quality services. Ironically, it took us owning them to be able to utilize the management systems that he and Kip, our son, invented for directing the care and making sure it was documented for payment.

I have chosen the Veterans as my favorite charity so that is where my donations go. There are three Vet charities that I donate to. It makes me feel good to be able to help these people that have done so much for me. I also donate to cancer research in memory of my sister and father who died of cancer. My older brother, who was 85 passed away in an Iowa group home. Over the years I donated clothing and money to their causes.

Guy talk (Jerry)

Shari, Kip and I installed our software in 141 skilled nursing facilities over the twenty years before we purchased our own. It was designed to map out the care needed based on the patient needs and problems, assign the work to the appropriate staff and document the delivery of the care in pursuit of positive outcomes. It is revolutionary since the government pays regardless of result using codes not accountability standards for patient centered care plans. Also, there is no requirement for the providers to prove their costs for each episode of care. The current Medicare and Medicaid programs pay for average to minimal care with no measurement of quality related to outcome. Insurance companies are also using the same antiquated methods of minimum standards of care for poor and wasteful results. It's still our goal as stated in my books that this problem has to be solved or the Baby Boomers will swamp the ability for anyone to afford even the most minimal care. As for draining the swamp this is by far the biggest and most expensive at $3 trillion dollars per year, with no plan for balancing the health care budget with the Baby Boomers coming onto Medicare program.

Be a good friend and Samaritan when needed

Girl Talk (Shari)

Having a good attitude about other people is so important. Everyone may not share my opinion or view but I respect their opinion as theirs. It doesn't matter, because our lives certainly wouldn't be where we are today if we all thought the same. I've been known to change my opinion at times because I've found that mine isn't always the best.

If you can be open minded, life is a lot less stressful. When I'm out and about, I think people are so interesting. In the first few minutes of observing them, I find something interesting about their appearance; and is there something warm, happy or sad about them. It gives me a nice warm feeling to be able to communicate with them. When I smile at them, I always get one back. It's better than getting lost in your own world and not being aware of your surroundings and others. Though I'm not good at remembering names using this approach is improving my retention there also.

Guy talk (Jerry)

Our goal is to solve the problems not debate the issues. Problems require solutions not debate. Our current health care program needs to be turned right side up by using good business practices not politicians and academics making the rules and deciding how or when to pay. This is killing the Great American enterprise … the VA for instance doesn't utilize nursing homes for rehabilitating our vets. There are 16,000 skilled facilities that have 3,000 vacant beds and rehab units that can best serve the vets and get them functioning and back into society. Just like the Postal Service, the VA hospitals and extended care facilities must be privatized to be cost effective, profitable and successful.

Smile and speak to people in your neighborhood

Girl Talk (Shari)

We don't seem to know our neighbors anymore. Other than a friendly wave and smile. The bigger the lawn the fewer the friends. Jerry gets to know the neighbors by being out and about doing our lawn and flower care. I used to have coffee with the neighboring mothers but as our children left home that passed. I now need to have lunch with the fewer friends more often to feel like I am a part of society. I miss being in the book club in Muscatine before we moved back to Chicago. Now I'm busy cowriting them rather than reading them for a book club.

Guy talk (Jerry)

Being nice comes more naturally to Shari. She is thinking of others always before thinking of herself. It has a wonderful effect on parenting, dealing with her and my parents before they passed on and our business associates. But she is not a trusting person she says. On the other hand, I am just the opposite I trust everyone until they prove us both wrong then I'm not nice. This trait has hurt me on occasions but saved me in other situations. As for our employees over the years I tended to trust in our ability to overcome obstacles in a nice sort of way. The saying "if it were easy everyone would do it" is so true. But if it weren't hard you wouldn't learn or earn anything much, would you?

The neighborhoods we have lived in are all different depending on the age of the neighbors. I usually say hello, smile and talk to the neighbors. Everyone is nice if I take the initiative ... if I don't, I might get a wave and a smile or we can talk to others as we walk our route around the neighborhood.

Being from a small town moving to Chicago was a big adjustment. Then moving downstate to Springfield was another challenge adjusting to a smaller environment, then to Morton then back to Chicago then to Muscatine Iowa, then back to Chicago always waving and smiling but hardly speaking unless spoken to. Shari and I both miss the small-town friendliness. But somewhat resent the fact that everyone knows your business and private life. With Facebook, Instagram and twitter it is worse than when we were growing up. On the other hand we have pictures of our grand and great grand children instantly and hear about their wins and losses as well.

So using the social media should have the same rules as face to face ... being nice really boils down to making it a priority and then a habit that leads to happiness for all.

JERRY MET SHARI (get what we got)

Drink a glass of wine over dinner discussing our plans. Or get dance lessons and go out more ... it's good exercise to dance and have fun. Weekly we burn about 300 calories each just dancing and having fun and our friends who see us want what we get from that activity.

SELF-EVALUATION

After reading this chapter take the following Self=Health quiz ... update your Real Age calculation, put a checkmark for your answers and come back later to rate yourself for complying with the actions recommended in this chapter:

	Birth Age	Real Age	YES	NO
Beginning Real Age score	_____	_____		
1. Are you told you're looking and acting old and grumpy?			_____	_____
2. Do habits control your thinking about how your treat others?			_____	_____
3. Do you feel like you need more friends, associates, controls?			_____	_____
4. Do you plan to commit to better social life habits changes?			_____	_____
5. Recalculate the real age as you change to measure results?			_____	_____
6. Later rate your progress ... 1 being low and 10 being the best.			_____	_____

Your rating and answers are your confession booth for judging for yourself where you are with your commitment to change your unhealthy habits and lifestyle at this point of your journey.

DAILY AFFIRMATIONS

I got a life when my wife got me

And she gave me the roots to a family tree

***

Take only what is needed

For morals and moderation must be heeded

***

Upbringing and character, what's it to ya

Everything, hallelujah

***

Seek not friend or foe

Instead look for reason to know … the difference

***

The bible draws good signs

Many hidden meanings between the hard times

***

Raise up your eyes to find

Your habits of today are covering your behind

***

Damn you; I cry, I am! Listen doubters; I sigh, I can! I will!

Look World; I did

***

Born to be healthy and free nothing better to be

Than a moving part of a happy family tree

See the My Real Age app, Tool #2, for modifying your kindness behavior for living longer and stronger.

DON'T BELITTLE DON'T BE LATE

To belittle
Is to be little
Too late

The difference between
The right word and the wrong word
Is the difference between
Lightning and a lightning bug
A curse and verse
A smug and a hug

Be nice compliment others
Negotiation is just that simple and
To some just that bitter
Former friends and lovers
May be littler than you
Due to the liter you made

Our personalities induce
Defenses over offenses
Though never establishing
Being too little too late

Our habits commit us to little
More than opinions and wants
Avoiding responsibility is too brittle
Despite the fights and taunts

Our future is based on habits
And our personality can be bitter
Not usually a variable if it fits
Changing little isn't any better

For belittling others
Is being too little to late
Belittling yourself smothers
What means little to fate

For the little never change
While the bully can't wait
To promote hate
A little too late

As being little is their fate

Marriage Vow/Lifestyle Habit Number Ten
GIVE OF YOURSELF FOR STAYING MARRIED

"No one has ever become poor by giving"

Anne Frank

FIND SOMEONE IN NEED TO HELP

When you help someone without thinking it's like eyes blinking … it comes natural at any age. Your rewards will be commensurate with your gifts … give of yourself for the ultimate self-health habit of receiving health, happiness and prosperity. This marriage vow and lifestyle habit is promoting the genetic secret that giving to get is a philosophy not lost on lack of funds, lack of interest, loss of health, loss of loved ones, loss of job or loss of hope. (In sickness and health until divorce do us part). It is about how to avoid or reverse the unhealthy life style habits and behaviors that result from being a me person than a we person. For example: we explore the value of our helping nursing home patients regain their vitality in their personal lives. The art of helping others is not easy to come by. It takes a certain amount of self-sacrifice. We all have given at one time or another the opportunity to help somebody … most times giving life to a child or a dream or an idea or a promise or stepping up when there's threat of harm.

The traits of my wife Shari (is for Sharing) are as the GOOD WILL GIVER … always with a helpful, positive attitude. She is by nature unselfish and a true gift-aholic. Every grandchild can attest to that. She helps us all to see the other person's wants and needs. She insists we call everyone in the family (32 plus fiancés) on their birthday and sing to them. It creates a very good environment for sacrificing self for others since I cannot sing a lick. As a result, she is ageless, she is beauty, she is the smile that lights up the room, she is the center of our family's root system and my risk seeking wings. God has blessed us with her, her mother and her mother's mother who were all givers.

I am still learning the act of giving ... not just advice as I am attempting to do in this book ... but being better at being a human being. I personally don't willingly give money I don't have but I do give of myself even though I know it may be wasted. The nursing home venture was a great example of "good deeds soon get punished" according to my attorney.

We sometimes call it courage but most times it's just plain caring enough to give. No thought of receiving or taking something away from the event. Quoting the bible is the best example of how giving is the result not the means to an end. "The act of giving can be as the door opens thus life overlooks the selfish reproach to any endeavor".

HOW CAN OUR LIFESTYLE HABITS AFFECT OUR VALUES?

Well, it's the subconscious attitude affecting our feelings for others in need. It's a conscious act or a reaction to feeling guilty. How can we develop the feeling of true giving without needing a reason why? And we can change our attitude immediately.

Shari being the most giving person I have known ... everyone around her respects her opinion and her actions because she is we centered not me centered. I need to work every day at being as good as she is ... her first thought is of the other person. My first thought tends to be about my wishes, dreams and goals. Together we have built a wonderful life of having it out every six months because I step out of the acceptable bounds of what is reasonable and likely to happen...the dreamer brought down to earth. She the GOOD WILL GIVER stating the obvious to consider best decisions for all involved not just my limited perception and far out vision.

My break through was self-help tapes by Earle Nightingale "Lead the Field" who stressed that if you could conceive it, believe it you could achieve it. I wore out those tapes and bought the book and wore it out. Then I started writing and reciting my poetry onto audio tapes myself. At the time,

I was starting my health care accounting, consulting and management firm. During that time, 1100 hours per year, on the road in my car with nothing to keep me going but my brain I began to speak poetry into the hand held tape recorder.

I would then have my secretary type them on her typewriter. It was before digital so the end product was a sheet of paper. After seven years and 700 thousand miles I had approximately 2,500 poems of every possible word I could think of along the way. Today, they make up my poetry series listed in the back of the book. Most, if not all of them, relate to the values and habits we are presenting now. Hopefully, you are employing some of them based on your own habits or what we are imparting in this book.

This has become our way of passing on to you a formula of giving and receiving due to you learning the Secret of praying it forward with better living habits of the brain, the heart, the soul, the mind and the spirit (see Chapter 12 for the spiritual Secret) as the 5 Wonders of the World that we all possess.

So, if giving to get is a philosophy lost on lack of funds, lack of interest loss of health loss of loved one's loss of job loss of hope it is surviving not giving. I personally don't willing give money I don't have but I do give of myself even though I know it is wasted. We all have given at one time or another ... most times giving life to a child or a dream or an idea or a promise or stepping up when in threat of harm.

We sometimes call it courage but most times it's just plain caring enough to give. No thought of receiving or taking something away from the event. Quoting the bible is the best example of how giving is the result not the means to an end. "The act of giving can be as the door opens thus life overlooks the selfish reproach to any endeavor".

To me, the value to achieve results through helping others is the fulcrum for giving values. The act of helping others is not easy to come by. It takes a certain amount of self-sacrifice. But in the process, it eliminates threat and builds rapport. The helpful attitude is a positive attitude. It is basically unselfish. It helps one to see the other person's point of view. It creates a very good environment for cooperation and communication.

How can anyone refuse help and how could anyone that is offering to help not gain the other person's attention. Another important value of giving then receiving is competence. To strive for knowledge, in your endeavors, must pay off. This desire can only result in better skills. Better skills better results. Competence can only come from a systematic and habitual study program.

Self-development is a continuing every day process. It's like good physical conditioning, it takes self-discipline. It takes tolerance to discomfort and pain, and it takes the desire to improve. For the successful person, it is a habit attained. For the struggling person, it's a passing thought, for a successful person it is a lifestyle habit.

Another value of giving is teaching others the competence you've attained. In teaching others, you learn more yourself. In teaching others, you develop a sense of teamwork and cooperation. Again, it establishes the lines of communication on an unthreatened basis. Teaching is satisfying. Teaching is as natural as learning. All the teacher needs to do is have the desire to pass on the knowledge to others.

How can we have learning without teaching? Teaching requires the ability to communicate the giving, verbally and in writing. It stimulates the mind to think in broader and deeper terms. It stimulates ideas because it requires the capability to attract the attention of the student, retain attention and evaluate the results of the efforts.

To be a good giver (teacher) you must exercise the will to be good not just an "emotion giver". The emotional giver gives for personal reasons such as a disaster needing contributions, a tip for a table, a shallow commitment for volunteerism, small gifts to the pan handler, etc.

The traits of my wife the GOOD WILL GIVER:

- Doesn't consider the amount as being a factor
- Responds to need not who is needy
- Follows through on volunteer work
- Doesn't say no to the kids, grandkids or in laws
- Brings a present whenever she feels like giving, which is on all occasions, including vacation shopping for trinkets
- Always says yes to requests for the check (budgets are for later)

As a result, she is ageless, she is beauty, she is the smile that lights up the room, she is the center of our family's root system and my risk seeking wings. God has blessed us with her, her mother and her mother's mother who were all givers. I am still learning the act of giving and being better at being a human being.

The movie "Paying it Forward" is one of our favorites. The plot of this young boy getting it restores our faith in our own responsibility. Giving is a reward for getting it then paying it forward with your own gifts. That is in service as well as monetary or material gifts. As I have confessed my motivation has changed by being married to a true giver of self, love and money ... Shari, who is called Nammy by her grandchildren and Boo Boo by her great grandchildren, gives everyone her attention, love and would her last dollar if necessary.

As a gift-a-holic in our nursing homes, she would hug everyone and give attention to their needs and wants for holidays. I, on the other hand, made sure I remembered their and our staff's names and made sure that our focus was on patient care outcomes. But both of us got into the nursing home business, and it is certainly a business, to serve our elders much better than they typically are. It boils down to money when service should be payed forward to get the money.

TO SERVE

To serve is to give
To give is to deserve the right
To get
To get is the fulfillment for the moment

No other law of nature is more profound
Not even thunder and lightning on the- ground
Can override the words of God
"Saying to serve is to deserve"
"Saying be aware thou shall share"

To serve is the willingness to take a risk
To invest your time and patience
And believe success does exist
So, pick your path to service

Put your time into that commitment
Give it your all for better or worse
Feeling the wisdom to wit it's sent
As a giving passenger with a purse

Serving the good ship Earth
Navigating the stormy seas
Of giving birth to the worth
That nature's riches frees

When all is said and done
You have served
And then you've won
The right to sit next to the throne
You alone

With your maker

Girl Talk (Shari)

Jerry has had compassion for the elderly and made it his mission to improve their lives as they age. His parents died in nursing homes as did my mother. Ironically, we ended our work career owning three skilled nursing facilities in Little Rock Arkansas, Muscatine Iowa and Washington Iowa. It was our plan to demonstrate our model for improving the care and outcomes in the very difficult environment of long-term care. You can review in section II what we learned and how we view picking a nursing home and how to be healthy and stay out of one. I got involved with nursing homes when Jerry started the accounting firm specializing in them. I was the office manager, partner and confidant over the last 25 years then I became a Provisional Licensed Nursing Home administrator. I had never run a business before but Jerry said I could and I did. It was one of the most challenging and fulfilling things I have ever done. Jerry's passion and philosophy rubbed off on me after he took over administration of Fox Valley Convalescent Center in Elgin, Illinois. It was an accounting client of ours and was in decertification. I couldn't go there due to the odor and depressing conditions of the patients and employees.

After about six months Jerry wanted to take our grandson Alec to see the patients at the facility. He said he had promised the patients he would bring his grandson for them to see. I told Christie, his mother, that we would have to go with them to make sure he wouldn't be frightened by the patients or the odor. Jerry said it had changed since I was last there. When we got there and entered the lobby Christie whispered Mom this is nice and doesn't smell and the residents look clean and happy. Well I was flabbergasted because it had indeed changed.

When we sold our nursing homes, we felt we had failed in the sense that the regulators forced us out due to our beliefs that the quality of life and our employees' future can't be directed by a failing government policy. The State surveyors retaliated against Jerry's views, expressed in his books, listed at the end of this book. His philosophy is we must restore the elderly and disabled to their highest level of functioning so they can go home. If they have to reside in an institutional environment it has to be home like but doesn't replace their family and home life. The current regulatory system only wants compliance with minimal care and don't reward the good facilities for quality of life excellence ... just dictatorial compliance. How can anything be positive with negative enforcement without incentives for quality?

Guy Talk (Jerry):

I always had a place in my heart for the elderly. After taking over Fox Valley I found that I had inherited a business where 175 patients didn't want to be there, 175 employees that didn't want to work there and 175 families that didn't go there. It was truly a challenge, none like I'd ever had to overcome. Each day I would go there and make a mark for getting through the day by changing one negative into a positive. I guess it worked because the staff stepped up.

Why? Well it was Wednesday December 16, 1987 and we got 16 inches of snow overnight. I got a call at home from the acting Director of Nursing who said only half the staff was getting there and she was wanting to know how to handle this. We decided to only deal with the priorities for the patients and leave everything else go. The Director of Nursing never did get there and when I, after digging my way out of the driveway, walked in there was something different going on ... it seemed quiet and the staff members were all in the patients' rooms getting them up, dressed and into the dining room. For 72 hours, we worked night and day, sleeping in shifts in the facility to make things better than they had been with all the staff there.

From that day on when the rest of the staff returned, we organized the work in teams as we had those 72 hours. For the next six months, we completely reorganized and sanitized the place to the point that when Shari and Christie walked in it was clean, no odor and the staff was so proud of showing off what they made happen. I left Fox Valley six months later as it was sold after we got it cleaned up and recertified.

What I learned from that experience is the 175 employees were wanting to improve the conditions but were not allowed to by previous administration. And it was an epiphany to me that one-half the staff could run the business better for 72 hours than 175 could do all day ... and from that day forward we worked in teams not as individuals. As result, before I left, we got the six stars given to the best facilities in the State and 175 families wanted to visit their loved ones to observe our restorative programs in action.

I'm telling you this story because I want you to know that anything is possible if you want it bad enough. We hear this from celebrities all the time but there are us ordinary people doing extraordinary things all the time. I know, if you're reading this book, you're looking for a change. I want you to realize that you can do anything we propose if you want it bad enough.

RESEARCH AND STATISTICS:

Giving by individuals makes up the vast majority of contributions received by nonprofit organizations. Giving USA 2015 estimates that individual giving amounted to $258.51 billion in 2014, an increase of 7.1 percent in current dollars from 2013. This accounts for 72 percent of all contributions received in 2014.

The National Center for Charitable Statistics (NCCS) annual report on Individual Charitable Giving by State shows that total reported charitable deductions amounted to $174.5 billion in 2011. This represents an increase of 2.8 percent from 2010's $169.8 billion (in inflation- adjusted dollars).

The average charitable deduction per return was $1,201 in 2011; state averages ranged from $2,516 in Utah to $620 in West Virginia. Following Utah, the other four states rounding out the top 5 average charitable contributions by return are, in descending order, the District of Columbia, Maryland, Wyoming, and New York. NCCS will publish a fuller version of the report in early 2014. With the current 2018 tax bill the removal of the tax deductions for charitable contributions will change dramatically in a negative way the giving habits of Americans. Like my book says "Failing Government Taketh Away" and gives very little back to the Baby Boomers in return.

Of the 77 million baby boomers three million aging Baby Boomers will need nursing home care each year, escalating to more than ten million in twenty years. This is the challenge we have as a country since we all have to contribute to paying for the past bad habits that are causing chronic illnesses. Here is where prevention and preserving our health has to be the number one priority.

THE DO'S:

1. Look past self for my worth by standing up for a good cause.
2. Take time to volunteer for a charity or your favorite cause.
3. Take time to get involved in Governing either locally, statewide or nationally.

4. Take time to make a difference in the life of aging America by adopting a nursing home patient. (Ask the Nursing Home Administrator for the names of patients that never have a visitor. Meet him or her and visit for 10 to 15 minutes. You will soon know if this is someone that would enjoy your return visits ... once a week or month).
5. Contribute time or resources to a local charity.
6. Help those in need of clothing and support food drives.

>**G**ifts
>
>**I**mprove
>
>**V**irtuall
>
>**E**verything

THE DON'TS:

1. Forget that what you give determines what you receive in proportion to your desire to help. Sacrifice is giving without feeling, sincere is giving with the joy of living.
2. Assume that giving at church or at work or at the stop light is enough to fulfill your commitment. It is the feeling of being a part of the greater good for the greater need.
3. Forget that what you do is what your children will probably do. Make giving of yourself the point.
4. Assume that giving is an intended habit ... rather it's a part of your subconscious need to help.

Sam Walton in his book "Made in America" stated that his only regret was not discovering the power of sharing his wealth with his employees (associates) earlier. America's wealthy give more away than they keep.

But don't forget that Bill Gates and Warren Buffet give for their own benefit while you can give for the neediest need's not financial or tax benefit. Shari gives for the feeling not for the doing. I'm still trying to get there.

Since giving is such a personal trait the statistics don't reflect non-monetary giving of one's time. My business motto is "Outcome is Income" when you're doing it for the right reason. Results for providing restorative services was our way of praying it forward.

PRAY IT FORWARD

My will be done
My acts be told
Thy flock shall abound
As a magnet to the fold

The law of the herd
This to be magnetized
This to be a shepherd
For the love of life revitalized

Please us now and pray it forward
Belief in mankind as a positive force
To perform our humble work toward
Sharing ourselves to the righteous course

The cause and effect of our accord
Is the cost of being brothers
For the good of praying it forward
Pass on the lifeline to others

And you shall have the good life
Though you must perish of flesh
Get behind me and pray
It forward to mesh

And project our own good
For the good of others
Pray it forward
to
The ultimate reward
or
Follow my prayer in accord
Or
Pray tell
Get the hell out of my way

VARIOUS WAYS TO HELP SOMEBODY

Volunteer for raising money for the homeless

Girl Talk (Shari)

I will drop some money in a homeless person's can, and hope they use it for food. By not living in the city we aren't confronted with this social problem. My feelings go out to anyone that is homeless but a small donation will not solve their problems. My giving is to charitable organizations that help them get off the streets.

Guy talk (Jerry)

We took my grandsons to a Chicago White Sox game and was confronted by a homeless man selling the "Street" publication. I paid him $5 for the paper and for his pleasure, I'm sure. Blake my grandson was surprised I would do such a thing when clearly the man was going to buy booze. I explained the gift was for me not him ... I benefited from the act not the reason. If my intent is good the subconscious creates a habit of giving for the right reasons. I usually don't make eye contact with a homeless person ... that's my harmful habit. The fact that I feel guilty for not giving is the reason I should give regardless of the feeling of disgust. I could be there someday if I make some really bad decisions. I'm going to give it a try and see if it can benefit both of us.

Give to meaningful charities (St. Jude is a good one)

Girl Talk (Shari)

My answer is the same as the last one. I donate a toy for the Toys for Tots charity. I also donate to food drives and coats for the poor. Many of these groups are run by former homeless or responders to the causes of being without a home. I respect their good intentions and ability to get the food or clothing to the needy. We received clothing and books for our patients in the nursing homes we owned ... most of which was not appropriate for the elderly.

Guy Talk (Jerry)

Shari is the most giving person I know ... we are called constantly by charities she has given money to without questioning the intent until I look up their results and it becomes evident that it is a scam. The best gift is to give of your time for a purpose of helping others in need ... such as our nursing home venture. The pride of ownership in a profitable business helping others is, in my opinion the best way to maximize your talents for the use of others to use. Nursing homes are usually not charities but are in need of visitors and participation in money raising events. There is where we have put our minds and money to make the lives in nursing homes better. Unfortunately, we succeeded in making their lives better but didn't make ours better. Thanks to an over reaching State of Iowa regulators.

Giving from the pocketbook is gratuity. Giving from the heart is charity.

CHARITY

Give more of yourself
Take less of others
What a simple law

He who practices this law
Then preaches the
Simplicity of charity

The understanding
And use of charity
Leads to untold fortune

He who is charitable
Has lasting wealth
Friends
Love
Peace
Memories
Prosperity

My confession is
I give because
I feel I should
A gratuity

My wife on
The other hand
Gives because
She cares

That's the difference
Between a donation
And a charity

Intention is the clarity
Giving of the heart is the parity

GIVERS ARE TAKERS TOO

Reaching out has two meanings
You are either giving or receiving
In life we do both but with greetings
To some it's receiving by deceiving
I like to think I give to receive

Without deception
But I wonder why I believe
When others take exception
Principles and ideals are fine
They make you feel good

But is it a better life divine
By lending when you think you should
I wonder if I could live that way
Pleasing just myself each day
For the sake of my pay
Taking without giving my selfishness away

No from the faces I see
Of those takers on the run
I feel good about being guilt free
I can smile when it's being done

As for those takers justifying their case
They pay the final price
With loneliness of face
And graves of ice

Who shall remember Hitler's demise
He took from mankind
While giving in his name to despise
Leaving shame and hate behind
Who shall not forget Jesus' to resist

As our savior he gave his life for mankind
Without asking them to desist
He let the takers ease their mind
How To Live Forever
What is better is the question
To receive for your gifts
Or just take the gifts for compensation

Ignoring what good it befits
You have a choice my friend
It's ultimately left up to you
But remember towards the end
Your heritage will be held true

As your offspring follow you
Emulate you
Defend you
Give to receive as you do
Remembering that givers
Are deserving takers too

Help the elderly deal with aging

Guy Talk (Jerry):

We helped various patients in skilled nursing facilities to get their rightful Medicare and Medicaid benefits. These allowed thousands of patients to go home and not be stuck in an assisted living or nursing home. How we did this is explained in my book "The Boomer's Are Coming".

Work for a fundraising function or solicitation

Guy Talk (Jerry)

For example: Jerry and I started a Foundation in honor of my mother Dorotha C. White who was abused and killed by a nursing home. She was headed to being a centenarian like her Aunt Edit when we had to place her in a nursing home due to our travel schedule. In eight months, she was put into an Alzheimer's unit, though she only suffered from dementia, had her mediations increased from eight per day to twenty and managed to miss her diabetic medication 118 times.

We found her in her wheelchair passed out at the nursing station and called an ambulance and she died four weeks later after being hospitalized with a heart attack due to dehydration. We sued the Lexington Skilled Nursing Center and vowed we could run better nursing homes, then the 300 we had been in during our consulting business.

When we set up the foundation for her mother's memory it was also for helping other nursing homes improve their rehab and restorative capabilities ... we gave them Bow flex machines for their therapy rooms ... most of them didn't get used properly because Medicare and Medicaid (Big Government insurance) doesn't pay specifically for physical conditioning to prevent falls and strokes.

Help someone get out of a predicament

Guy Talk (Jerry):

I used my snow blower to clean another person's driveway without being asked. He did the same for me when I got stuck in the snow. It seems we all have the inclination when asked but not gratuitously. We made a career out of helping the elderly get better care and have the opportunity to get back home after a debilitating illness ... this was the byproduct of changing the hopeless paradigm they ended up in.

Give some money to a legitimate purpose

Guy and Girl Talk (Jerry and Shari):

I usually only give money if a homeless person seems really hungry but I've never been in that predicament so I should change my attitude and make a better habit of practicing what I am preaching on "giving to get". We live in a world of widening values that are no longer focused on humanity but money ... this isn't the fault of our culture it's the fault of our values. Shari and I believe that can change with each of us reevaluating our values and lifestyle ... be subjective not objective ... be trusting not doubtful ... promote empathy not sympathy … reward good health with lower premiums for the healthy. Vice versa for the unhealthy. To make national health care work we all must consider good health to be a privilege not a right and internalize the benefits of paying for our own care. Currently, the health care providers are paid for income not outcome regardless of cost or accountable for quality.

Give to the person that is down and out, hope by helping them

Guy Talk (Jerry):

Giving without a reason is the only gift that makes a difference in people's lives. I've been lucky to avoid most of the obstacles that the needy have. The parable of "judge and you shall be judged" certainly is a motivation to be a giver not a taker.

HOPE

My definition of hope
Is a way of painting
A vision to cope

With life without a picture
Where there's hope
There's a will

Where there's a will
There's a way
Don't think me a dope

When I hug and kiss you
And call you hope
Because will's looking for security

To replace doubt
Which has inhibited me
And you're the best thing

I've seen to take it away
From what life can't bring
That's what I mean when I say

Don't turn your eyes or
Drop your arms before dawn
Cause it's by the will to
have you that

I've got the hope to go on
So don't think me a dope
When I hug and kiss you

And call you hope

For where there's hope today
There's a will at play
So, we will find a way

Tomorrow or the next day

We did help the elderly and disabled in our consulting clients and facilities we owned. It was very gratifying and lasting though we didn't accomplish our goal of having nursing homes owned locally by franchising the systems, property and equipment, then supporting the local owner in meeting quality standards. We still have the hope that someday this will be the quality of life standard.

Bail out a family member when in trouble

Guy and Girl Talk:

Always help your family if they are in need or a tragedy should occur, whether financially or physically, your generosity will be appreciated, and you will feel good for doing it. Our family has now reached 32 with the grandchildren approaching or being married and having our great grandchildren. Shari wants and does buy Christmas and birthday gifts for all just to say we care and are there for them. Then it works in reverse if we ever are in need. I have a confession to make about not helping someone in need ... our son and some friends from his band were partying in Wisconsin and had been drinking when pulled over by a policeman .... Our son was driving as the designated driver and was arrested for driving while under the influence ... he called us to bail hm out of jail and we told him to have the other two guys use their credit cards and do it ... our son said that they had left him and would we ... bail him out holding to our guns we said it was there responsibility to get him out. Later we found out that they had been left with the car with no keys and could not get to the jail to bail him out. For years I've regretted not hearing our son out and doing what I should have done regardless of the circumstances and helped him.

I've tried to make it up to him by always being there helping him in his love of music and computers. He has also been a valuable part of our businesses for 30 years and forgives me for that indiscretion.

Serve on a food line or volunteer at a missionary or shelter

Guy Talk (Jerry):

My only time on a food line was in Phoenix for a Catholic nursing home client. What I saw were not hungry people but street people needing a free meal … they seemed to be well fed but it did give me a view of the other side of our society and economy. This not only makes for an act of personal caring but brings reality of our country being a nation of the haves and the have nots. The fortunate and the unfortunate for whatever reason don't meet very often but when we do it demonstrates that we are all human with frailties and differences that cannot be fixed by politics or economics … our value system needs culture shock so we find joy in helping someone worse off than we.

Visit a nursing home patient that has no one

Girl Talk (Shari):

When we started a foundation for my mother and I set up visits for those in nursing homes that don't have visitors or family. When we purchased our own facilities we were committed to helping them have visitors. The Dorotha White Foundation was funded by the wrongful death settlement and to fund Jerry's books and our "Adopt Nursing Home Patients" program … so those who have no one looking out for them would have one of our volunteers visiting them on a regular basis.

We also gave nursing homes exercise equipment to strengthen the patients and give them something constructive to do. I made visits around the Chicago suburbs and got some high schools involved to meet their requirements that their students have so many social project hours. The visiting program would give them an outlet for getting their credits.

For example: I, as a volunteer, was assigned a female patient that wouldn't converse with her because she only spoke French. After finding out that it was the problem, I had her teaching me French words and they became fast friends. We did receive some national recognition for the program but the regulations tightened and the nursing homes wouldn't let us in due to fear of reprisal by the surveyors and because of the privacy rules.

Guy Talk (Jerry):

Shari became a volunteer visitor for those nursing home patients that didn't have a visitor. For a number of years she got high school social studies students interested in her campaign. The only problem was the nursing homes were skeptical and not allowed by the harsh regulations to allow her access to their patients. You had to go through a regimen of being a Ombudsman that becomes a spy for the State surveyors not positive influences for the patients' or families' protection. We still believe that the survey process is for political purposes not quality of life nor care. Unfortunately, we became a victim of this reality.

Contribute to food and clothing drives

Guy Talk (Jerry):

Shari always contributes to the food drives. We had them for the nursing homes but it was totally regulated so it was impossible to take anything but clothes. We also held garage sales and bazaars for selling what the patients made in our activity programs. We had them donate to our nursing homes but it was totally regulated so it wasn't possible to take anything but books and clothes that fit older and heavier patients.

Give books to nursing and assisted living facilities

Girl Talk (Shari):

When we left Muscatine, Iowa after selling the nursing home we contributed over 100 books that we had accumulated but didn't have a way to display them. Our Activity Director took them and shared them with the patients. Our local library is having a donated book sale to raise money and Jerry plans to give copies of his books for sale.

JERRY MET SHARI (get what we got)

Most people don't work together. Shari and I have been working together for 37 years in the business of helping aging Americans! We still plan to coach aging Americans on living longer, stronger and happier. Our mission is to change the culture in nursing homes from a money machine to a restorer of functionality and get them back home; in a home like environment. We found that working for this purpose together made our relationship stronger so we ourselves were aging together, happier and longer.

SELF-EVALUATION

After reading this chapter take the following Self=Health quiz ... update your Real Age calculation, put a checkmark for your answers and come back later to rate yourself for complying with the actions recommended in this chapter.

	Birth Age	Real Age	YES	NO
Beginning Real Age score	_____	_____		
1. Are you now inspired to give something to someone?			___	___
2. Do money concerns still control your thinking?			___	___
3. Do you feel like you need more friends, associates, controls?			___	___
4. Do you now consult your spouse on money decisions?			___	___
5. Do you still use the real age calculator to measure results?			___	___
6. Later rate your progress ... 1 being low and 10 being the best.			___	___

Your rating and answers are your confession booth for judging for yourself where you are with your commitment to change your unhealthy habits and lifestyle at this point of your journey.

AFFIRMATIONS

***

The full heart holds out a hand

Be it needed by his fellowman

***

He is charitable that lifts

To choke off Poverty with his gifts

***

As in service you achieve

And in giving you shall receive

***

You can't give what you haven't got

Nor can charity be bought

***

Plato said of the price of charity

Even dogs will demand equality

***

When a grateful heart opens a mind

Fruitful acts aren't far behind

***

Goodness isn't in the reason why ….

Just as sight isn't only in an eye

Marriage Vow/Lifestyle Habit Number Eleven

BE SMART WITH YOUR MONEY AND HONEY

*"Too many people spend money they earned
To buy things they don't want
To impress people that they don't like"*

Will Rogers

GET AND KEEP YOUR HONEY

Gambling better habits for a chance at happiness relieves the pain of Chronic Aging. Your bank account isn't a reflection of your net worth its only one side of you ... the other side is your choices making yourself worthy of happiness, prosperity and longevity. Then money and your honey can have a happy marriage as they are emphatically connected.

This chapter is our story about how we handled the most complex activity in a complex and unbending economy as health care somehow chose Shari and I to solve the resistance to stop chronic aging in nursing homes. It's also about how to avoid or reverse the unhealthy life style habits and behaviors that result in chronic aging that results in institutional confinement.

People remark "how in the world can you work together" and our response is that it is an extension of our marriage partnership. It was this relationship that enabled us to enjoy travel and Shari to have her own career, after raising the family. Though we had our moments of disagreement like any good partnership we worked it out. Our advice "you are what you're willing to lose" comes from starting our own businesses four different times before we purchased the nursing homes.

Shari and I are impulsive which can be a two-edged sword. Our only regret is we didn't save more and take fewer risks but that just isn't us. It's the entrepreneurial spirt in the both of us. However, our daughters married men who are savers and more conservative, to balance our daughters, who are more like us. So, the husbands are the breadwinners and the wives are the artists and entrepreneurs, and risk takers making their own money. A very good blend and has made for great security in an insecure world.

Our son on the other hand was in our business and has learned a skill that enables him to be more conservative than we were in our business. Neither way is wrong or more right so long as we all finish strong. During the years of owning our CPA firm and a consulting and software business, Shari and I traveled to 141 skilled nursing facilities in 22 different states with our software and consulting service. Once we installed the software and setup the cost management system, we made quarterly visits (over the years 1,400 on site revisits) to audit the system. It also allowed our son Kip to exercise his expertise in computer hardware and software.

You don't have to be a CPA to start a business. But taking the risk requires certain skills. My start was graduating from high school in a small town and then getting a degree from a Simpson a small local liberal arts college. As a senior one of my last interviews was with Arthur Andersen & Co. the largest public accounting firm from Chicago. Unbeknown to me this would be the break of a life time.

LIFESTYLE AND BORROWED MONEY GO TOGETHER

LIKE BIRDS WITHOUT FEATHERS

Being scrupulous and being smart aren't necessarily the same. I can remember my father saying he bought a car instead of Winnebago stock that cost him a fortune. My father was very conservative and didn't like risk due to his being brought up in the great depression years. But he taught me how to use debt, take risks and work to better myself. He knew why, but couldn't practice, that being cautious is one thing and being risk averse is another. He was a man of quiet but effective wisdom. He taught me how to finance what I wanted then pay for it with a job earning the monthly payments. My first purchase was a Bulova watch that I couldn't have without using other peoples' money (in this case it was the owner of the jewelry store who gave me the time payment plan with a nominal interest charge). In the next 60 years we have utilized this concept to purchase and manage our personal and business expenses and investments.

And since Shari and I have learned being smart with money is such a personal trait initially based on personality then training then on circumstance and finally on necessity. I'm a CPA and business owner so my training is to deal with money for my clients which is very different than how I deal with Shari and our money. Being an entrepreneur developing startup businesses requires a more liberal approach to risk. Risk being the likelihood for failure as a percentage to the likelihood of success. If the risk is high and the reward low the percentage is going to be upwards to 100%. But if the likelihood for success is high and the reward is low the percentage will be down around 25%. The best place to be is likelihood for success is high and the reward is high the percentage will be 50/50 and a good investment.

You don't have to be a CPA to start a business. But taking the risk requires certain skills. The more knowledge about the business you are starting or working towards is essential. There are many courses independent of getting a college degree that await the ambitious person regardless of age. My start was graduating from high school in a small town with a liberal arts college. After four years at Simpson College and improving my GPA to a 3.5 out of a 4.0 I still didn't know where my career would be. I had a business degree and the liberal arts courses in sociology, psychology, history and English. Business math, taxation, business law and economics were for my future in my own business. My accounting professor Myron Soriden was influential in me being awarded the Wall Street Journal "best business graduate" distinction and he backed me for the best job offered to my graduating class. Arthur Andersen & Co., the largest public accounting firm, offered me a consulting position in their home Office in Chicago, This resulted in a lucrative Public Accounting position and a CPA certificate that formed my future into a lifelong career, not just a job.

I was at Arthur Andersen for eighth years then moved on to become a partner in two other regional CPA firms before starting my own firm in 1977. From that point on my entrepreneurial skills began to kick in. Raising money to fiancé my firm's growth was the most challenging task and rewarding for a successful business.

My specialty that developed at Arthur Andersen was health care and it created many opportunities for future growth. During the next twenty-five years, my wife and son both got involved in the business. We utilized the software that we developed to implement a revenue cycle system in over 141 nursing homes in twenty-two states giving us the where withal to raise enough to purchase three nursing homes. People remark "how in the world can you work together" and our response is that it is an extension of our marriage partnership. It was this relationship that enabled me to enjoy travel and Shari to have her own career, after raising the family. It also allowed our son Kip to develop his expertise in computer hardware and software. Though we had our moments of disagreements, like any good family owned partnership, we worked it out.

Now with retirement imminent we have time to invest in a new business, writing self=health books, Shari and I are wanting a work schedule that will result in helping others to attain what we have … good health, happiness and prosperity. Spend more time with the family and not worry about money or how to pay for retirement. But I'm also not promising Camelot to our readers or ourselves:

SPEAKING OF CAMELOT

Deck the halls with boughs of holly
Fa La La La La La La
Speak the vows of folly
Fa La La La La La La

We often speak of Camelot
In voices of grandeur
But more often than not
Our pursuit is unsure

We often speak of Shangri La
With words of love
Until the ice begins to thaw
Like righteous words from above

But too often we speak of fear
In voices trembling weak
Not so are we insincere
As much as not meaning what we speak

My dreams are mine to think
Kept in perspective light
And at no time can I sink
If my hope is bright

We often speak of Camelot
Then forget that actions are facts
And more often than not
Dreams are dust in our tracks

So sing on Jester of life
A breadwinner naught
For folly is a begetters wife
And shallow words are fraught

With thought and prayers of Camelot
Be it a President who has taught
Us that it is likely or not
That happiness can be bought

Or a forgiving God
Taking away our able thought
Making reality seem like a fraud
For accepting Camelot

Deck the halls with boughs of folly
Fa La La La La La La
Speak the vows of Pollyanna
Fa La La La La La La

When all we wanted is what we sought
A family a job a home to be bought
Not a dream of whether we like it or not
For someone else's Camelot

We have learned in the 60 years of marriage and 65 years working at jobs that the future holds what we're thinking about and planning for today … it's a plan to be altered due to circumstance and/or happenstance but not for the lack of romance. Being a dreamer, schemer and redeemer enables us to take life's risks and come out smelling like a rose … that's our family's prescription for happiness … hopefully it will work for your future.

Another lesson I learned was not every good idea will make money, fame or fortune. Having been in a family that was dependent upon my dad's factory job at Firestone in Des Moines, Iowa austerity was the way of life. Though we were not as poor as the nonworkers or the lazy element in Indianola, Iowa we didn't have any money to spare for even a night out at a restaurant. In my senior year, my dad was on strike and couldn't give me $2.50 for athletic insurance. So, I couldn't go out for a game I loved. I became the sideline supply manager. I was able to participate in basketball and baseball because they were noncontact sports. After high school, I wanted to go to college and Simpson was the choice because it was in my home town and relatively cheap if I lived at home and got a loan for the tuition and books.

The best decision I ever made was to get a college education. Then pass the CPA exam the first time after being out of college for eight years … and I had to take courses at De Paul University after graduation from Simpson to qualify for the accounting portion of the exam.

Over the years, Shari and I have not really lived by a budget or even thought of being poor. It has been our approach to make it happen and if it doesn't try harder until it does. Our children are somewhat more conservative in that they want to be more secure than we were. Even though we have sold our three nursing homes we are still not financially fixed and don't plan on retiring in the general way.

We are using our funds to finance a writing career that has been developing since I wrote my first poem in junior high school. I come from a family of writers … my mother was a poet, my sister a playwright, our son a song writer, our daughters are artists and entrepreneurs. Fortunately, they married well and have a financially secure life and future. Their children likewise by getting their education and having the right attitude and healthy lifestyle habits also are writers and artists seeking pursuing their dreams.

Shari and I have only invested in our own small businesses. No speculation in the stock market, no real estate ventures (except our nursing home acquisitions), no gambling at the casinos, no speculation in futures or selling short or long. This is high risk and high reward if successful. My accounting firm and consulting business allowed us to purchase three nursing homes. It was highly leveraged and short on working capital. Over six and one-half years we struggled to stabilize the troubled businesses.

Fortunately, I had a great bank relationship that helped to survive and sell them for enough to pay the bank and other creditors. We purchased them in our early seventies and had plans of creating a franchising solution for nursing home ownership. Also, our son Kip, who was a partner in the business, and I invented a software system of cost accounting for setting prices and competing in a very competitive business. I am still trying to sell the software to a larger developer. Have you ever wondered what it would be like to not have to worry about finances, bills and money? Our society's obsession with money over quality of life. For example: personal investing with your nest egg is a matter of relativity and your aversion to risk. If the investment is relatively low to your total nest egg the risk is also low.

However, if the investment is a threat to your nest egg obviously, the risk is high and the return must be high. Mutual funds are inherently low risk and low return. IPO's and startups are high risk and usually high return. Initial stocks offerings (Google, Facebook, high tech) on the major exchanges are also relatively high risk high reward.

Our next business is this book and the potential consulting that can come from it. Money is a conduit to opportunity and we have capitalized on the freedom to take risk in America and if you fail the bankruptcy laws are designed to help get a business back on its feet after a failure. Also, there are reorganization rules (Chapter 11) to allow the business to renegotiate its debt, spread out its obligations and go forward with a plan to increase business and reduce costs.

What does the human being really need for a fulfilling life? Rank these top twelve pieces of gold for your use in attaining a fulfilling life:

1. Money
2. Success in work
3. Notoriety
4. Celebrity
5. Role model
6. Legend
7. Family
8. Love
9. Happiness
10. Healthy
11. Wealthy
12. Independence

A recent study showed that you can invert the above list and have what most people really want. So, work ranks eleventh in our true wants even though we think it is the way to accumulate money, which creates happiness. However, that study also showed that as we age the real wants, we choose are in reverse. Then money is back on top and work moves up to second. Why would this be? Because the resources are being depleted and we feel that our health, happiness and independence are beyond our control.

What if you are never too old to work and independence isn't last and happiness isn't ninth? Isn't that a function of healthy living and wellness? Put yourself first. Be healthy, happy and prosperous first and the other wants will come naturally all based on your current lifestyle vows/habits.

SURE ... IT'S NOT THE MONEY

I heard this celeb on TV
Say "Believe me"
He said "Now that I've got it
I can forget it"
"It's not the money"

Isn't it funny
Me sitting here
Crying in my beer
About money

It's sure easy for him to say
He's got steady pay
Nothing but fun paying his bills
But what about us folk from the hills

We got nothing to look forward to
Except being broke and blue
What about you
You got troubles too

I just don't appreciate the guy telling me
"It ain't the money"
When he's got it made
While I'm shaving with a worn-out blade

Maybe that's the way it's gotta be
But please don't insult me
By saying " it's not the money" you earn
Sure, it is even when you have it to burn

It's called the greed gland
And now you make such a quip
To us paupers such a command
Will sink our ship

Because we don't get
That guy offering a split
With us folks from the hills
That can't ever pay our bills

That's the way it goes
Playing lotto and going to the casinos
Which of course " it ain't about the money"
Funny it's always about the money honey

Following the Golden Rule ... those with the gold rule

Sure, it's the pursuit of the gold driving our economy. Our country is founded on enterprise. The plantation, the gas station, the Dairy Queen, the farm, the country doctor, the local pharmacy, the retail stores around the square, local hospital and nursing home ... all now owned by out of town conglomerates. It is called a Monopsony ... the opposite of a Monopoly. It's where the government and big business collaborate to control the economy, the jobs, the wealth, the future. Monopolies are for control of the flow of products and services; a Monopsony is to control the people.

In my book "The American Enterprise Manifesto" I make the case for downsizing government at every level and upsizing enterprise for the sake of paying down the horrendous national debt by allowing 200 million enterprising Americans to be more involved in the legal infrastructure, governance and politics from the grass roots. The bottom line: "is America too big to fail"? In my opinion only if the individual Americans fail to act and take responsibility for their own welfare and wellbeing. In my book "The Monopsony Game {Failing Government Taketh Away)" I explore the perils of government becoming the purchaser of last resort (where government jobs are better than private enterprise jobs) for controlling unnaturally, the supply and demand for serving our consumer-based economy. This completely moves us away from capitalism and the pursuit of profits to measure success or failure of our collective efforts. The next step is socialism where government control of all facets of livelihood at the determent of our freedoms.

YOUR LIFE IS TOO BIG TO FAIL

American values are changing ...
Bigger is better
Live for today
And ignore tomorrow
Pay to play

Business is business
Divorce rate up
Satisfaction down

No savings or security
Obesity will abound

America is frail and will fail
In small towns thought better still
What happened to happy for the many
Working forever for the same money

Saying:
Be a patriot
Love thy neighbor
Pledge allegiance to the flag
Pray to God
Save 10%
Give 10%

Praying:
Believe the media
Life was too small to fail
The difference is due to
Money is God
Without faith we plod
Our jobs are boring
"My pay is abhorring"

Playing:
It's who you know
Not what you know or grow
College is too expensive
Debt is extensive
My vote doesn't count
Influence is clout

Decaying:
Our kids are distant
Their fun came and went
I don't know my neighbors
Texting sexting kills his and hers
Casting us all to join the flight
That life was what it was ... just right

Delaying:
Discovery stifles recovery

How do we get it back when we lack
Bringing talk at the dinner table back
Or focus on family so it will weather
Since offspring are birds of a feather
Playing together is staying together

Relaying:
Simple solutions through evolution
All should stop looking for a better spouse
Pride in our work each day never to cease
Bring faith in the President back into our house
Support our political leaders and police
When all lives matter
Then the criminals scatter

Replaying our values:

> *Less is more*
> *Simple sells*
> *Diversity is strength*
> *Equality is earned*
> *Faith is big*
> *Right size is small*
> *Freedom is not for sale*

Then life is too big to fail

Bottom line: Shari and I have been in business together for 37 years. My son Kip was also in the businesses that we started. Family business is a two-edge sword … the relationship between partners is very different from employee and employer. Most disagreements are handled as personal in a partnership and as non-personal in a regular business. However, they're truly the same when it comes to a fair resolution of problems … communications in a respectful manner is required in both instances. Because money isn't the reason it is the result. Just as good health is the reason and happiness with prosperity is the result.

RESEARCH STATISTICS:

Retirement and Finances

The retirement expectations are widely varied among Baby Boomers. Though attempts to save have been made, not many have saved the recommended amount. As of 2014 and according to the Insured Retirement Institute:

- Thirty percent of Americans don't have any retirement savings.
- Thirty-five percent felt comfortable with their efforts to save for retirement.
- Thirty-three percent believed they would have enough money to live comfortably.
- Sixty-five percent were satisfied with the way their finances were going.
- Twenty-one percent stopped contributing to their retirement accounts (10 percent even pulled money out) because of trouble paying rent.
- Forty-six percent were concerned with leaving an inheritance behind for loved ones.
- Fifty percent of first marriages end in divorce and 75 to 80% of second marriages call it quits … when that happens the female is left with learning how to pay the bills, invest any excess funds and put away for retirement … fifty-six present have left that responsibility to their male counterpart.
- Eighty-six percent of married Baby Boomers had retirement savings, while 70 percent of singles did.
- One hundred present of Americans lost equity in their homes and 401k accounts in 2005 – 2007 when the Federal Reserve raised the discount rates 500% to their member banks and saved the large banks and investment houses with government bailouts.

The Business Insider in their "Your Money web site" has estimated the following: an estimated 60-year lifetime cost of 13 specific harmful habits:

1. Paying for health care costs … $14,662 for doctors, drugs, hospitals and $78,000 per year for private nursing home care.
2. Playing lotto … $11,600 for a dollar bet
3. Paying credit card debt late … $18,000 in added interest
4. Using ATM's for cash … $19,000 being charged to withdraw your own money
5. Drinking soda … $21,000 plus the health care costs for obesity
6. Online Porn … $22,000 plus the cost of divorce when caught
7. Morning trip to Starbucks … $88,000 for a Latte

8. Not packing lunch and using fast foods ... $94,000 plus the health care costs for chronic weight gain
9. Smoking ... $116,000 plus the costs of a new lung
10. Wasting food ... $125,000 while people are starving in Africa
11. Drinking bottled water ... $131,000 when its free from your own well
12. Smoking or using weed ... $219,000 plus other drugs abused
13. Drinking too much booze ... $263,000 plus the cost of divorce and legal costs
14. Total lifetime costs of these 12 habits $1,127,600 if all 12 are an individual's lifetime habits

Just imagine if 1,000 of the 313 million Americans had all 12 bad habits the cost is over $1 billion dollars opportunity cost savings for changing their habits, plus all the complications that these have on our lifestyles and culture. If its 100,000 then the cost is $100 billion dollars over a 60 years' lifetime. Just as a U.S. Senator from Pekin said "A billion dollars here and a billion dollars there certainly adds up to a lot of money" that all Americans won't be able to cover.

The Business Insider also lists the 12 opportunity cost savings of being cheap (pay me now or pay me more later) (penny wise pound foolish):

1. Vending machines ... fast foods that kill you faster
2. Divorce ... legal costs eat up earnings, nest egg and destroy your quality of life
3. Insurance deductibles ... misleading as a savings if you cannot pay them
4. Opting for layaway ... incentive to buy more when you can't afford it
5. Variable rate mortgage ... misleading with a volatile interest rate the Fed can impose
6. Extended warranties ... usually never needed but cost you when they don't occur
7. Bulk purchases of food ... encourages waste unless you have kids at home
8. Skipping dentist ... classic pay as you go or pay me more later
9. Splurging on coupons ... encourages purchasing what you don't need
10. Shirking a pet's health ... pay now or get another pet later

11. Getting a prenup ... encourages divorce as a positive financial alternative

12. Leasing a car or not keeping up maintenance on a car ... pay now or pay the pauper later

National statistics are trending downward for small businesses ... more are going out of business than getting into business. In America, 60,000 new small businesses are started monthly and about 600,000 go out of business each year. Except in the health and fitness business. However, unhealthy aging is creating an opportunity for consulting and action planning for improving lifestyles for better heath, happiness and prosperity.

College graduates are becoming entrepreneur's due to technology and they're not being able to get jobs in their chosen fields. Anyone can write an app, setup a website, create an idea for expanding the digital applications to self-driven vehicles to national security to protect us from hacking, to home security systems, to robots, drones and advanced weaponry. Many companies are recruiting noncollege graduates for more scientific and trade applications based on IQ and acumen rather than waste four-years on a bachelor degree they can't use.

The internet has turned passed business practices into massive relics and making social media the driving force for recruiting, marketing, communication, surveillance, tweeting views, blogging for aspiring writers, photography for the iPhone, and video for anyone on earth to be a spy. We certainly live in a culture of great opportunity if we continue to evolve as healthy, caring human beings. Rather than suffer our later years in confinement or unmanageable retirement in a nursing home.

THE DO'S:

1. Both the husband and wife (or significant other) must have their own money and account for it. For obvious reasons, there needs to be a Marital bill of rights practiced not just preached.

2. Both parties need to consult with the other in making larger expenditures that affect each other.

3. Job opportunities are available to both in our nuclear society. Both need to take the step if it doesn't terminate the relationship.

4. Involve the whole family in money decisions so everyone learns how to manage their money.

5. Saving is as important as our other lifestyle habits. Commitment comes from withholding the money in a separate account each paycheck … just like withholding income taxes.

6. Risks with money will be available to all. The value of the return should be commensurate with the risk taken. This is the hardest part of managing personal finances and will take counsel at some point. Investments in a 401.k plan at work lowers the risk and puts funds out of reach if deducted from your paycheck. The fund managers are using the leverage of their investors to take moderate risk and maximize the long-term return … usually also coupled with a retirement pension plan that pays out upon retirement. Usually tax free.

7. Remember the basics: home, food, autos, insurance, medical expense, clothing, entertainment, etc. all are daily expenditures and your income is periodic … this requires some form of a budget that matches the resources with the likely expenditures leaving some for the future needs.

THE DON'TS:

1. Assume that someone else will bail you out if you make the wrong decision. It usually won't happen.

2. Plan on more money to cover future needs unless there is a fixed amount of income. Or you are able to borrow within your means to pay it back.

3. Make money more important than relationships. You "can't buy love" is a classic failure of the heart.

4. Let fear dictate your earning and use of money. Life is a risk so is living on the edge. But there is always a way to bail the boat … it may hurt but it will teach you a lesson that you need to know.

5. Make commitments to others for helping them through self-imposed money problems … they have to learn and earn the same lessons you've learned.

6. Forget that impulsive thinking habits dictate most money decisions so having a good set of financial goals will set in motion having better money results.

Various Ways to Better Manage Your Money:

Lose the Belly Save The Money Keep Your Honey

Body weight, belly fat, total girth and net worth are connected. Research shows that the more pounds people carry the less money they tend to have and usually their marriage has lost its passion and romance to weight gain. According to a 2017 study from Johns Hopkins University, your estimated lifetime savings in health care and productivity would be $28,020. For a 50-year-old it would be $36,278. Jay Zagorsky, Ph.D., an economist and researcher at Ohio State University, has been examining the weight-wealth connection for more than a decade. His 2015 study revealed several prices tags: for every pound of weight gained, $226 of wealth is lost, for every point of body mass index gained $1,900 of wealth is lost. So, if you're 50 pounds overweight you're cheating yourself out of more than $11,000 of net worth. If you need motivation tie your weight to a money goal for losing pounds and inches and keep track of the savings or spend it on a much-needed fun vacation … such as a tennis camp or hiking expedition. Probably avoid a cruise because of the temptations of the daily eat-a-thon and midnight snacks but praise your spouse for being fit and a great cook for staying healthy. It's not the money honey it's the healthy and longer sex life we have.

Prevent scams on the elderly and aging Baby Boomers

The most obvious way to prevent erosion of your earning and spending habits as you age are health care costs. Now and as you age into a nursing home. As stated before, the savings for staying fit are on average $14,662 per person in America. Some as high as millions and some as low as zero purely attributable to fitness. But the highest cost of all is fulltime nursing home care of $78,000 per year. Thus, the biggest financial motivator for staying fit should be the avoidance of a long-term stay in a nursing home. If that happens you will spend down all of your savings, assets, future income to a $2,000 burial fee then apply for the last resort for funding, Medicaid until you expire. Per the NHE fact sheet issued by the Federal Government the annual cost of Medicaid funding for the disabled and elderly in 2016 is $565.5 billion. Medicare alone is $672.1 billion per year.

The savings to the country for fitness far outweighs any other proposed reduction in the so-called entitlement programs … NHE reports the annual cost of the care of the unhealthy Americans is $4.2 trillion dollars annually.

Guy Talk (Jerry):

According to AARP, Americans over 50 are the prime targets of crooks who want to steal what they've accumulated over their lifetime. Number one rip off is the reverse mortgage. Why would you borrow more money against your retirement home that will trigger foreclosure with any economic down turn? The TV ads fail to inform you of this risk.

Number two is your Medicare coverage for expensive hospitalizations or nursing home stays. Your coverage rights will be made by a reviewer that is neither a physician or a nurse. Insurance companies administer the Medicare claims for the Federal Government and are given the authority to approve or disprove a Medicare claim. Over the last twenty-five years Shari and I, as consultants, have appealed hundreds of claims that were rejected for two reasons … claim is not medically necessary and the claim doesn't improve that patient's condition. Both of these reasons are illegal according to two court cases.

Fox v Bowen a decision by the Federal District Court in 1986 found the denial of claims for arbitrary and capricious interpretations such as "not medically necessary" and not "improving the patient's condition were depriving the Medicare beneficiaries of their rights to restorative care and violated their fifth amendment rights to due process of law. The judge ordered the Medicare Federal Administration to cease and desist this illegal interpretation of the law and pay the denied claims and change their practices by informing the providers of this decision. This decision was challenged by the Federal Government and has been ignored for over thirty years depriving the beneficiaries their rights to restorative services in nursing homes. (Read Jerry Rhoads' book "Elderpride" for a complete analysis of this practice that continues in skilled nursing homes today).

Jimmo v Sibelius a decision by the Federal Court in 2012 finding that the Centers of Medicare and Medicaid Services continues to deny Medicare claims for skilled nursing care in nursing homes "if the patient had reached their prior level of functioning or wasn't improving" … neither of these reasons is supported in either the rule of law or the intent of the law thus illegally depriving the beneficiaries of their rightful Medicare coverage. The judge ordered the Federal Government to change their policies and awarded damages to the providers that has yet to be changed or paid. (Read Jerry Rhoads' book "Failing Government Taketh Away" for a complete analysis of this practice that continues in skilled nursing homes).

For over twenty years my wife, son and I battled the erroneous denials of Medicare claims and were able to overturn over 100% of the denials with software documentation system that proved the patients were being covered for medically necessary skilled care and improving so they could be discharged back to the community ... resulting in the Medicare program paying the claims for 43,500 patients and enabling the providers to restore functionality for discharge back to the community. So, make sure your need for nursing and home care is being supported by such documentation. You will save your financial future by doing so.

Number three, be the advocate for your spouse for medical care and prescription drug use. Shari and I are survivors of medical problems (Shari a congenital heart problem and my skin cancer) by managing our own health care program ... exercise, diet, preventive services and using common sense to manage the cost of our aging. We now have physicians and specialists listening to our natural remedies before we ever pop pills or go to ER.

Number four, be aware and savvy about money and internet scams that are predators preying on aging nice people who are needing legitimate advice and services. Join AARP and access aging web sites to educate yourself on what is happening in the world of unaware or dementia prone elderly. Discuss such threats with friends and family so we all are informed of the risks of using technology.

Number five, be aware that social security withdrawals are exceeding the amounts people have put in. And be aware that of the 77 million Baby

"Baby Boomers" born between 1946 and 1964, 10,000 are signing up for Social Security every day. Though this doesn't mean you won't get your current check it is an indicator of how the overall funding depends on healthy taxpayers paying in as much as they eventually take out. Since the start of the new millennium and its recession years where the 401k plans nosedived in value and Americans aging at a high rate, retirement funding became a giant bubble. That will burst sometime in the next twenty years. Therefore, right now, the baby boomers are the culprits because they want to draw early and not have to consider later retirement than 62 or 64 or 65. Plus there are 7,000 per month going on Medicare that is also underfunded.

The solution to these socio-economic geo-political problems of course is to slow down chronic aging and prevent the trends that has taken hold of our future. Avoid chronic diseases and reverse current aging habits using the Rhoads lifestyle habits.

Number six, Social Security and Medicare are not entitlements. They are each American citizen's savings account for their benefits. Entitlement means a "right" not commitment to pay.

Get a financial advisor, CPA tax accountant who is also an attorney

Guy Talk (Jerry):

CPA's are schooled in counting the beans not making them. So, our advice is to consult with someone that has the experience in financing a business and what the tax ramifications are. Even though I'm a CPA doesn't mean I knew how to start or manage a business. I had to learn those skills but the creative side is where my head is. Even more important is planning for retirement ... here Shari and I are depending on our business interests to fund our remaining years ... after selling the nursing homes we are authoring books to fill in the gaps. As it turned out it would have been a benefit to have had a law degree to deal with the regulators who were arbitrary and capricious in there interpretation of quality of life for our patients.

Girl Talk (Shari):

Since I was in junior high, I babysat and earned money, and worked all through school for clothing money. After we were married and started a family, Jerry could afford to pay our bills, and when the children got older,

I worked in our business, had my own bank account and paid my own bills once again. With that transition in our partnership I used my bank account for purchasing groceries, my and the kids' clothes, gifts for holidays and some fun money on vacations. I also bought my own cars, paid my own maintenance bills and auto insurance. As for the rest of the money advice, I will turn you over to Jerry.

Get advice from your banker and or CPA on investing

Guy Talk (Jerry):

Is your banker or CPA qualified to act as your business confidant or is it better to have a partner who can handle the money side for you? In our opinion experience is the best teacher and instructor ... team up with those that can participate in the investment and the return for their contribution. If you're a corporation get them to be your controller or VP of Finance Business is business but profits are necessary for sustaining businesses. We have been fortunate ... for forty years we have successfully utilized our business experience to finance our lifestyle habits. Even though I am a CPA I am not qualified to advise investors on the stock market since I've primarily invested in my own ventures. We had an IRA 401k plan through our business that we used to finance the purchase of our first nursing home ... not the best investment but it allowed us to have a very nice income and lifestyle.

Use money market accounts that pay some interest

Guy Talk (Jerry):

The current money market rate is 1.5% per annum. Economically and strategically it's a terrible investment ... a better choice is to invest in your or other business opportunities ... look to organizations doing research and development of a new health related product ... pay down high interest loans ... pay bonuses to valuable employees ... buy gold or silver or copper for your IRA account.

Save towards your security goals as you age

Guy Talk (Jerry):

Security is a misnomer. It says safe but also sorry if you die too early. Might it be better to have a high value low cost term life insurance policy and set up a tax-free IRA for funding retirement. Then practice our 12 Fountain of You(th) habits to reverse negative aging and have a longer and stronger lifestyle ... you have your improved Real Age and money to enjoy those later happy, healthy and prosperous years. Have your cake and eat it too. Now that we are retired social security is not going to see us through so we are pursuing other opportunities. We did save enough to provide us some leeway for Shari and I to start authoring books.

Invest in your education and ideas

Guy Talk (Jerry):

Someone told me that everything we see and touch started from an idea. In America ideas are money in the bank if you persist to make them happen. My ideas accelerated after college and working for at least ten years. The true usable ideas I got were from having to solve business problems for clients and my own enterprise ventures. The idea of having experience before dollars and cents is why continuing education in your field of specialty pays great royalties. My greatest luck (preparation meeting opportunity) was to be picked by Arthur Andersen & Co. as a recruit for their emerging health care consulting business. That set-in motion the next 55 years as a CPA and expert in Medicare and Medicaid reimbursement leading to our nursing home investments and software development to manage those businesses. Now that persistence will payoff as we venture into a writing career in our seventies and forever after.

Girl Talk (Shari):

I never envisioned a career in health care administration. After the children left the nest Jerry suggested that I get involved in our consulting business so we could advise nurses (99% females) on how to manage the care for billing and documentation. Frankly, I felt inadequate after being "a stay at home mom". Prior to acquiring our own nursing homes, I was the Office

Manager for our accounting firm and never thought I would be involved in the servicing of the nursing homes. So, I enrolled in a Junior College Business Management course and from that point on I learned the nursing home business so I could eventually be the Administrator of our Washington Iowa nursing home. This was the most gratifying experience I've had since raising our four children. I will never forget the faces of our patients who were getting better so they could go home.

Cover calculating risk by planning and persisting in some form of work skills

Guy Talk (Jerry):

Working eight years for Arthur Andersen & Co. taught me to specialize in the health care field of business and from this I became an entrepreneur and a risk taker … before that I was counting the beans not making them. For the last thirty-seven years we have been making them and now count them so we can continue our Rhoads lifestyle. Work skill now becomes the means to an end in itself until we have a literary agent representing us to the traditional publishers that will buy our books for distribution.

Girl Talk (Shari):

We took over three failing nursing homes and turned them into pleasant, sweet smelling, happy experiences for our staff and patients. I took Jerry's model for the culture, the environment and the philosophy that we could restore functioning for everyone coming to our facility. Not everyone will be well enough to leave but we gave them the opportunity to get better so they could. As a result, we discharged 57% of our admissions back to the community. And the rest had a much better quality of care and life by us being there. We feel we have proven that having the owners there every day to solve problems leads to better quality and more efficient and caring staff.

Take a chance and defy the odds

Guy Talk (Jerry):

There are as many bankruptcies per year (600,000 in 2010) as there are startup small businesses per year. The free enterprise concept of the Law of bankruptcy is America's willingness to allow us to fail then rekindle our fire and do what our dreams want us to do … yes, it's 100% mental … everything starts with an idea, a thought and a vision…you can be either the envision(er) or the envision(ee) but the point is you decide. Either way you're allowed to fail then reorganize and succeed … no other economic system in the world allows for this. This is the greatest part of capitalism versus the other isms … we're allowed to freely choose to fail then choose how to succeed … just remember it is all founded on how you think and what you want to be. However, during this period of high tech, bitcoins, foreign investments, and scams the degree of chance is not calculable. No amount of analytics can predict the Fed raising the discount rates, the government raising taxes, the stock market going up or down, or you losing your job. Then you personally cannot control the decisions that control the ebb and flow of another people's money. However, you can decide each day what to do and how to do it until it turns your way … trying is the guarantee and effort is the way to success. In reality free market enterprise is a way t0 bring capitalism and socialism together in a business … capital is needed to get it started and grow and socialism is a way to reward the enterprising Americans for their work ethic.

Start over if you must

Guy Talk (Jerry):

I have lost count on how many times Shari, Kip and I started our businesses over. Last count is seven and now eight. In health care the regulatory system that the politicians encumber businesses with especially nursing homes make it almost impossible to be efficient and effective in delivering services. In our experience, the costs exceed the amount that the government and private insurance companies are willing to spend to do it right. Our approach was to provide quality first and foremost regardless of the cost and then pursue revenues based on our experience in billing Medicare first then Medicaid. But as Congress started to reduce the Medicare payments through denying claims and forcing our patients onto low paying Medicaid our formula was side tracked and we decided it was time to exit that losing proposition.

It got so bad in our three nursing homes that we had to sell to a conglomerate ... and we have the right idea ... get them in, get them better and get them back with their families (who have to be responsible for it to work). If they have to stay until death their quality of life is always pursuing wellness which is happiness being better. Oh well maybe someday! See my Book 'Restore Elder Pride", iUniverse 2012, for our advice on finding the right nursing home if you must but also how to avoid that experience if possible.

Utilize coupons/discounts to maximize your savings

Guy Talk (Jerry):

Shari and I hate coupons because to use them we have to usually buy something we don't need. But now that we are in retirement we are looking closer and have used some. Being an accountant, I want to save as much as possible to use for having fun. We both love, discount sales and Shari is the best at that ... I'm an emotional buyer and that's dangerous if we end up on social security. Fortunately, we didn't have to retire at 65 and purchased three nursing homes at the age of 70 and sold them at 75 ... then retired to authoring books. We have found that working is the best financial plan for retirement ... that I lovingly call re-hirement.

Girl Talk (Shari):

Our philosophy is to spend our time on our own business and not waste time on sorting coupons ... but only if we can afford to do so. Now that we are retired, we look for those that meet our needs.

Buy quality in everything if you want to save in the long run!

Guy Talk (Jerry):

Quality ends up costing less. Have you purchased something because it was on sale and was a good deal ... then didn't wear or use it? I think we all have. The best example I can think of is the purchase of clothing ...

Shari hates knock offs (designer named but not designer made) from foreign manufactures because they don't last or aren't the same after one washing or dry cleaning. Our motto in our nursing home business was "Outcome means Income" ... in other words the better the outcome the better the income and All-American Care, the name of our company, is the best.

If you've heard of W. Edwards Deming, who taught the Japanese to allow their automobile production lines to stop and fix design errors and not let them be disposed of as waste at the end of the line. This allowed the Japanese to produce better cars for less money. His picture is in the board rooms of the Japanese auto manufacturers to this day. This brings to mind that my dad, George, worked in the factory for Firestone in their hay day and was transferred to Quality Control ... there he would throw out the defective tires namely the steel belted ones that didn't meet safety standards ... because of demand there was a loosening of the safety standards and most steel belted tires were passed through as being safe ... but they weren't and Firestone's business had to be sold to the Japanese due to lawsuits by customers injured in accidents caused by defective steel belted tires. Bridgestone, the Japanese company who bought Firestone then reverted back to the safety standards once practiced by Firestone but also utilized Dr. Deeming's quality control system to prevent defective tires .... Moral of story is quality is less costly than wasted tires, insurance claims and ultimately a failed business.

Girl Talk (Shari):

As a young girl my father gave me a choice ... you can buy three items for the cheapest price or one that you really like and will take care of. This taught me the value of quality over quantity. My sister's thinking was to have more not less and usually borrowed my clothes because she liked them better than those she had decided to buy. Of course, I've taught my children the same habit ... less is more if it's quality.

This has been my philosophy since I was in fifth grade and my parents took my sister, brother and I shopping for new clothes and we were each to pick out three things. One of the three dresses I chose was too expensive, and dad said I had to put it back and choose a cheaper one... I said no, I love this one, and was given an ultimatum. "If you choose that one you can only get two." Mom and my sister tried to talk me out of it, but I stayed firm and walked out with my favorite and one other. I was never sorry about my choice, because the hand me downs from my sister seamed new to me anyway.

Therefore, I try to buy quality products such as stylish clothes, not the new and latest fads. If it looks like something the teenagers are wearing, it's a fad. I have always purchased my clothes from four or five designers that are not fad designers, but style designers with quality garments. Jerry gives me lectures on hanging on to all my clothes, because he is not one to keep his old clothes ... his philosophy is for each new piece, an old piece must go. My philosophy is, it just goes to a closet in one of the spare bedrooms. However, we found out when we had to downsize our home from 4,500 square feet to 2,000 that some of my shoes and purses had to be purged, much to my chagrin. But most of my clothes did make the cut.

Good female fashion goes in cycles and trends such as dress lengths, pants styles, shirts, accessories, jewelry and color choices. If a new shirt fashion is introduced and I like it, I will buy a couple and shop in one of the other closets and pull out pieces to wear them with. It always works. I gave some examples in a previous chapter. However, it doesn't work so much with shoes, because they show the wear too much.

Look for the rate of return you can get on a cash investment

Guy Talk (Jerry):

A business loan that costs an interest rate less than the rate of return from a stock or real estate investment minimizes the risk versus taking the investment out of a saving account. Taking it out of the savings account at low interest seems to be the right thing to do .. or ,is it? No, leveraging off borrowed money is better ... you get a tax deduction for the interest paid and if the investment goes bad it is a tax-deductible capital loss not personal loss and you still have your savings for personal needs.

Invest in a home and insurance for long term equity

Guy Talk (Jerry):

Investing in your personal residence is the best investment for the money as you get a piece of the earth's only permanent asset... real estate. Insurance is no assurance for claims being honored. Self-insurance is the better only if you're not tempted to spend the money on something else in a crisis. But you have to have homeowner's insurance to get a mortgage. And life insurance for protection for the family. And health and auto insurance to spread the risk.

Health insurance is the most expensive no matter whether it's Obama Care or Trump Care. There the best is the commercial insurance your company or business offers. As Obama Care is phased out due to unfunded costs and failed promises the government sponsored State insurance exchanges are going to be gone. Most likely universal health care is twenty years away. In the meantime, without bipartisan support, the uninsured or underinsured American will increase until it is recognized that each individual is responsible for their own health care costs and should be funded through personal savings account administered by the private sector. With Federal block grants to the State Medicaid programs for those not employed or the working poor.

Buy long term care insurance too hedge the risk of loss of health and livelihood

Guy Talk (Jerry):

Usually, insurance isn't to provide a return on investment, if you never have to file a claim. The worst deal in insurance is for the people that don't have to file a claim who are paying for bad drivers, unhealthy people, insurance cheaters. In my opinion, it's better to spread your risk in a mutual fund that specializes in technology, real estate, rare earth minerals, gold or silver. And avoid the risk of bit coins and Red Box rental DVD's and the sexiest high technology. Shari and I chose investing in our own businesses that don't carry any hedge but hard work … worth the risk if you enjoy being your own boss. It is also better to hedge your risk on chronic illness and institutional care by staying fit and avoiding chronic aging and diseases. Long-term care insurance (getting old insurance) is not meeting the needs of later years, for unfit seniors, because it is almost impossible to predict in morbidity tables how long we will live when we are fit or unfit and what the cost of long-term care will be. The best model for aging can be found on our web site www.lifestylesforaging.com.

Teach your children to learn from their financial mistakes

Guy Talk (Jerry):

Kimber remembers that they weren't allowed to say the word can't. Because can't never did anything, and that a can did everything. Christie remembers my philosophy (I learned from Earle Nightingale) that 85% of what you are worried about never happens and the other 15% is only half as bad as it seems … so why waste your life away worrying about odds of 7 ½%. Kip remembers he was told that pursuing your dreams makes you happy, while pursuing a job just for money, can be a dead end. And Kelli our risk taker was encouraged to be what she wanted to be, just be good at it … that includes raising a family and starting your own jewelry business that has taken her on a trip to China to get her product manufactured.

EIGHTY-FIVE PERCENT RULE

*Eighty-five percent of worries
Are impure thoughts that never come to pass
Eighty-five percent of threats
Is something our mind begets
And the remaining fifteen percent
Is only half as bad as it gets*

*So why waste away
When only fifteen percent gets in the way
And only half of that
Takes away your other half
Seven- and one-half percent
Won't make a dent in your future
Or your advent*

*Eighty-five percent of fear
Is fear itself and a factor
Eighty-five percent of failure
Is in the purpose not the actor
Eighty-five percent of life is attitude
But only fifteen percent know
How to seek its gratitude*

*Adage
Eighty-five percent of threat
Is something our mind can beget
And the remaining fifteen percent
Is only half as bad as it can get
So clearly 85% of the problems
Our nation faces
Are from 15% of the sins*

*And not real times and places
Leaving 7.5% as the spaces
In the worries of man
Solved by 85%
Who will say we can
And as we age
85 is just another page*

Not a number on the gage

Despite my 85% teaching our children all made the typical mistakes growing up but never forgot those words that Shari and I put into their minds ... and they turned out to be excellent adults and parents. Kim is a commercial artist, Christie is a court reporter owning her own business. Kip is an excellent musician and recording artist using his skills in applying computer technology as his work skills. Kelli is also a commercial artist having her own jewelry line. Interestingly, their children are emulating the same traits, similar skills and pursuits.

They're also investing in IRA's and college funds for their children ... smarter than their father who invested in family businesses not annuities. However, the government loans for higher education made the grade and they are able to service their loans. Being married with two incomes allows them to put money aside whereas Shari and I didn't. We believed that the business was our nest egg for retirement .... and we didn't sell the nursing homes until we were in our mid-seventies and we still deny being in retirement. I call it re-hirement. We are able to do this based on our lifestyle habits and having a purpose (being ASPIRING authors). This purpose makes it Great to Be Alive and avoiding the harsh alternative:

GREAT TO BE ALIVE

Darn it's great to be alive
Fending with what life can contrive
Taking it on the chin
Yet keeping a winning grin

I have spent many years in the work hive
Working out the problems of man and wife
Then it all comes down to retire
While keeping a smoldering fire

Only birds pull up from a dive
While doctors are cutting the life line by knife
In view of birthdays help to survive
Beyond the age of seventy-five

Never fear that I'm now here
Calling it rehired rather than retired
Looking for a new career
Wanting my experience to be vilified

In a waning job market and opportunity
My goal is to find a challenge
Not tranquility nor invisibility
So, this trip will test my courage

I must stand up to disappointment
As I approach those who review my resume
And reject my desire for an appointment
Even though I've paid my dues and made my pay

Yes I'm qualified to be a consultant
As a confidant and problem solver
Companies aren't necessarily solution insistent
On having me as the trigger to their revolver

To cross that line of resistance
For their good and mine we must agree
The cost of hiring me for instance
Depends solely on my value to a company (now a publisher)

Great to be alive in this bee hive
Where I'm now one of the worker bees
As I make the dive
Into re-hirement

With challenge up to my knees

Girl Talk (Shari):

We are very fortunate to have our three girls married to successful husbands who also depend on their earning power. Our son has been a partner in our businesses and is a computer wizard. They all amaze me by being able to balance a business career with birthing and raising our 12 grandchildren successfully. Now the next generation are following our pattern of getting your education so you can pursue your dreams that will lead you to your financial security.

JERRY MET SHARI (get what we got)

We have always gone on a family vacation to an exotic island as get-a-way for everyone and paying it forward with being smart with money … saving hasn't been one of our better habits but we did for retirement which is now! Our strength has been to spend money on family education first and fun and games second. It's funny, money never was our first priority and was a constant worry as we dealt with the economy, taxes and failures ... but always coming out of it smelling like a rose. We did it our way together and all in all it has turned out great.

SELF-EVALUATION

After reading this chapter take the following Self=Health quiz ... update your Real Age calculation, put a checkmark for your answers and come back later to rate yourself for complying with the actions recommended in this chapter:

	Birth Age	Real Age	YES	NO
Beginning Real Age score	_____	_____		
1. Are you thinking rich and healthy?			____	____
2. Do current habits control your money decisions?			____	____
3. Do you now have a habit of saving rather than just spending?			____	____
4. Do you have a plan for implementing those habit changes?			____	____
5. Do you update the real age calculator to measure results?			____	____
6. Later rate your progress ... 1 being low and 10 being the best.			____	____

Your rating and answers are your confession booth for judging for yourself where you are with your commitment to change your unhealthy habits and lifestyle at this point of your journey.

AFFIRMATIONS

No surprise that conservation

Is the first step to money creation

***

You measure a life by good taste

Not by the dollars they waste

***

Progress is the risk you took

And doubt you over look

***

It's not what you think you're worth that counts

It counts more if you prove it with worthiness

***

Work as if you'll live forever

And take tomorrow off

***

How fortunate can a man be

To have the fortune of being free

***

I want to wear the same thread

Of the bountiful bed spread made of love

Marriage Vow/Lifestyle Habit Number Twelve
GET AND STAY GOOD WITH YOUR MATCHMAKER

"To receive the love of his birth
End of life is next to never
Find heaven here on earth
Believe we are to be married forever after"

Jerry Rhoads

GOD OUR MATCH MAKER IS GOOD AND SO ARE YOU AND YOURS

WORDS CAN'T SAY

Words can't say what I think of you

For there are no words that can quite
Explain you and your attraction
It's a feeling not a function of words
Just as where does love come from

Words won't explain my faith
Nor can they draw the proper picture
Of heaven friendship or success
In the human mental fixture

There are no words to explain intuition

Tis a feeling not an enunciation
There is no way to write speak or think
Of an expression that can articulate
Obsession drive determination or desire

There are no words to write say or think

Of the essence of love or the eternal spirit
Which some misconceive
As only being from above
Above and beyond their reach
Above and beyond their attainment
Above and beyond their abilities

But with that steady earnest effort
It is truly found that this select group
This select evangelical court
Can easily be found
Not with words but with thoughts
Not with touch but with feelings
Not with hopes but with actions
Not with wishes but with virtues
Not idle comments but with prayers

With words that can say who cares
To convey the curse of love affairs
Voicing the wedding vows
Into the ears of those that love endows

Its words of the lord's prayer
Poems saying glad you're there
And the Gettysburg address
That words can say it best

Where more is less

Praying for a younger body and mind is a waste of your exercise time. You have a choice to believe or grieve for each habit's transgression … because no person is perfect and your maker isn't the judge, you and yours are. So, make your maker happy by being healthy by pursing our 12 self-health vows (habits).

In this chapter, we emphasize the importance of values and belief in the ten commandments. It is also about how to avoid divorce or reverse the unhealthy life style habits and behaviors that result from a lack of faith-based thinking and activities. Shari and I also believe our love is eternal and we will be together forever thus, the "Living Younger-Stronger-Longer" is the underlying faith to live forever.

Although we are Christians, we are living our faith as the marriage vows and habits required by the 10 commandments. After getting married Shari and I attended the Methodist Church in Indianola and in the Chicago suburbs, then Springfield, Illinois, then Morton, Illinois then Chicago again. As the children left the nest and decided on how they would express their faith we continued being a living example of how we can be spiritual without being experts on the bible. We practice believing positively, you're doing the right thing, is likely an act of the spiritual. Love for others must also be an element of the spiritual. The desire to improve oneself and others also must be a part of it. This leads us to believe there can be heaven on earth, once the state of mind is such that acceptance and help to others is of first importance. To enjoy helping others is to be fulfilled. To feel good about yourself is the attainment of the spiritual that best serves our maker here on earth and hereafter.

To personally demonstrate my faith, I have published five poetry books (listed in my bio) all based on my spiritualty. But that eternal energy is connected to what I call the Wonders of the World ... my physical body (heart and brain), my metaphysical body (mind and soul) and my forever spirit. These are the foundation of my faith in being able to control outcomes by using the brain and mind to direct the heart and soul for a wonderful life.

LIFESTYLE ROOTED IN OUR FAITH AND BELIEFS

Shari and I both believe in a Good God. Godliness and personal values and vows (habits) of faith and belief in a higher power. It goes back to our personal commitment to live happy healthy and prosperous so it can happen. Prayer, in our opinion is pursing positive habits (goals) for living life for the better or worse in sickness and health. So, help us God.

There was a poll that found that over 90% of Americans believe in a God. However, there was no God in my growing up other than me going to church with my friends. My mother and father weren't god fearing or god blessing. They were products of the depression era of living in rural America with hard work and little future. On the other hand, after getting married, and having a different set of values and beliefs, Shari and I attended the Methodist Church in Indianola and in the Chicago suburbs, then Springfield, Illinois, then Morton, Illinois then Chicago again. But we slowly drifted away from Sunday being our only day of spirituality. It is our family values and belief that the ten commandments are our guidance. And we will thrive if we don't violate those principles.

    Shari and I believe in the spiritual values and practice them. In my poetry books, I mention God and the Savior hundreds of times … still believing in a higher power. As we grow older and we are faced with a eulogy our concern is parting not leaving the good earth. It's my belief that our spirits are eternal and represent infinity. Shari believes it doesn't matter because she and I will be together forever thus, we are living this book is our How to Live Forever after.

FOREVER IS NOW

Loving you is like the seven falls of color
Gathering in a quiet pool at the table
Overflowing from the eyes as if unable
Then spilling down your face to a smile

Loving you is like the blowing wind
Coming from the far reaches unknown
Chilling the skin looking for a friend
But warming the minds habits sown

Loving you is like the climbing ivy
Directing its growth skyward
Looking for something to hold me
As it grasps for a feeling in a word

Loving you is like the newborn kitten
Softly looking for the mother's breast
Calling out for something to smitten
Only secure in the embrace confessed

To find the message of our birth
So, end of life is next to never
That love is heaven on earth

With us as the children of forever

In love and happiness
Till forever after is in my heart
And death as our witness
Shall never do us part

Surely no one lives forever
But as the rose dies in the winter
And rises again in the spring
Together with this wedding ring
We vow that forever after our soul and spirit live on
To another dawn

And We Lived Happily Forever After

Even if organized religion isn't necessary as the median for constructing the spiritual element of a person it is necessary to develop a positive state of mind and spirit. Spiritual vitality may merely be a state of mind. The desires and needs and purposes of the other values may be a result of having a healthy, spiritual faith. Christians speak of the Bible as being The Good Book where the trinity is truth. Jesus is the savior and God is the judge. To this I agree. It is one of many Good Books. All books relating to the positive elements of our well-being are good books. Any book which proposes a better mode of conduct, a better mode of activity, and a better mode of living should be called a good book. Anything constructive which develops the state of mind should be called spiritual.

Therefore, it is possible the positive state of mind is a form of spiritual fulfillment. Believing positively, you're doing the right thing, is likely an act of the spiritual as accepting Jesus as your personal savior. While love for others must also be an element of the spiritual. The desire to improve oneself and others also must be a part of it. This leads one to believe there can be heaven on earth, once the state of mind is such that acceptance and help to others is of first importance. To enjoy helping others is to be fulfilled. This is the attainment of the spiritual.

Many organized religions require the participant be dependent upon a code of conduct to attain spiritual fulfillment. It almost becomes an addiction. It's hard to believe this is the most productive form of spiritual activity. The intent of many of the religions is to attain a state of mind which will allow a person to conduct themselves in a positive worthwhile manner; however, in their enactment they compel the participant to submit to a ritual which is neither understood nor believed. Then, for the sake of attaining the spiritual at the time of death, they must conform to the ritual.

On the other hand, an emphasis on the spiritual in the development of a positive value system, exercised by a positive attitude seems to be more productive. This puts the emphasis on the enactment of a good value system, for attaining happiness, and not just a submission to a process that allows for attainment of heaven later; while heaven on earth is readily attainable. Why not develop the state of mind, as the attainment of the spiritual, rather than submission to dogmatic trials and tribulation?

The positive puts the emphasis upon the attainment of a healthy state of mind, and not on the negative fear of not attaining the spiritual fulfillment, if you break the rules. Mental development puts the action in the mind of the person, rather than submission to the soothsayers. Unfortunately, most denominations of Christianity require a conformity to a commitment so one can believe in a process. In other words, you must believe in a process so you can attain eternal happiness after death. Happiness for the living doesn't carry a high priority. This is done without an attempt to define God.

To define God as being a good healthy spiritual state of mind is so simple, it is attractive to the pragmatist. To believe in a healthy state of mind, is to believe in God. There is no need to be concerned about the later existence of heaven or hell for heaven and hell exist on earth today, tomorrow and forever after. It is our belief that Mortals create their own heaven or hell, and the attainment of one or the other depends on their state of mind. Then eternal life is in the mind of the happy, healthy liver, and the attainment of eternal life must be left to a process not to be understood.

The primer for a happy and healthy state of mind is the teachings of the Bible, the Ten Commandments and the look of love. In my opinion my five poetry books establish a framework for teachings which enable the students to formulate a proper state of mind. Those that learn this code of behavior can't fail to be healthy spiritually. Happiness is to recognize positive thoughts are a worthwhile need and a worthwhile value, and must be attained. The person who does this is spiritually healthy forever after.

The person who doesn't do this is spiritually unhealthy and more than likely living in hell here on earth. This is the way it should be. This is life itself. How can we deny the laws of nature which are the closest we'll get to recognizing the supernatural until we move on? Ultimately, the laws of nature and man emanate from the law of cause and effect. The amount of effort, sincerity and quality, you put into the cause will determine the effect. Therefore, the amount of sincerity, effort, and quality you put into the pursuit of a healthy, spiritual state of mind will determine the happiness you will get from your marriage, relationships and mortal lifetime.

Over the ages man has asked man what is truth and what am I worth ... never realizing that worth is determined by one's self not those around us. When we are worthy, we attract more worth until we are wealthy in mind and spirit. But is that truth, as if God's Willing us to do it?

TRUTH

Truth which needs justice
Is only a folly
Our courts do not decide
The truth
Truth which needs proof
Isn't true
Truth isn't right from wrong
Or laws being the proof of
Rational man's need to conform

Justice is only an interpretation
Of a rational civil habit
It's the fortune given by nature
It's the sensitivity of the soul
It's the peace of believing in freedom

It's God
It's belief
For only God is trut
Not the courts of justice
Not mortal proof
Like the judge of poetry is you
Not me in the confession booth
It's how it applies to your stew

That's truth

ETERNAL TRUTH

Is truth absolute
Or is truth resolute
I've studied this question
In my own way
Making my tests scientifically each day

Today I may say I'm happy
And tomorrow I may say
I'm sad
How can the truth of the matter be
Any more than the resolve of me

On the other hand
What about those things
Over which I have no command
For is truth something to understand
Or the quickness of the sand
Or the word of God's command

For example, the mortality of man
Because man is mortal
Misrepresentation may just be the portal
To a fact that's always been
It's better to know the truth than just when
And all we have to do is stop and feel
For the absolute is at the wheel

It guides us it helps us
With the words of Jesus
Eternal truth being in our mind
As the resolution of mankind

Then justice is only our divining rod
That determines those left behind ... by God

Why do we ask others when the answer is typically couched in what the other person thinks of themselves ... if they are unhappy with themselves we typically will not and cannot get any positive feedback from them ... if they are happy with themselves they don't want to make it any easier for you then they had it ... so guess what ... the truth is in the ears of the listener not in the voice of the speaker? You make your own self-worth minute by minute, hour by hour, day by day.

The saying is "mental attitude has more to do with success than mental capacity" ... if you want it bad enough it shall be yours. But most people do look outside themselves for encouragement, fulfillment, love, understanding, support, faith, endearment, etc. etc. Do they find it there? That is the question that we need to answer.

To build our self-net worth we need to invest our self-worth capital in developing knowledge, beliefs, faith, love, loyalty, honesty, commitment, expectations on what is right for others as well as ourselves. The beggar is repulsive and rejected because we see ourselves in them and fear those consequences of bad luck and avoid feeling good about our own good luck. By giving to the beggar we can feel good about our good luck regardless of how the money is used.

True Giving opens the heart not the pocketbook ... if it is about affording a gift it is not a gift it is a sacrifice and that does not build self-worth it erodes self-respect. Can we give enough to feel good about ourselves? Most times the act is for reasons other than being good to others. Americans during this depressed economy are withdrawing into themselves to protect their family, pride and livelihood. This is the time we can reap the most from our giving because there are always those that are worse off...the very act will make our value increase in our heart and leave the payment of bills to our head. We then will have more coming than going by doing good.

This is not just a religious concept it is the Law of Attraction and Reaction at work again ... good attracts good...need generates a use of our talents ... demand for our talents increases our net self-worth. That is what generates dollars and makes human value into capital for our children and grandchildren. All I can mentally perceive of the wonders of the earth is to believe that of the eight billion inhabitants, having their own spirit, features and personalities, but each alike in their bodily functions and physical characteristics, are the true wonders of an evolving universe. The trip we make on the good ship enterprise is from the same port using the same ship going to the same destination at different rates and states of mind.

THE WONDERS OF THE UNIVERSE

The Wonders of Earth:
The sky clouds sun birds land soil earth mountains
streams snow plains meadows flowers sea salt swales

The Wonders of Life:
Sight feeling smelling tasting touching loving DNA cells birth death

The Wonders of Space:
Comets stars sun spots planets sun moon
White holes blackhole atoms
$E=MC^2$ *continuums in reverse*
Tis all wrapped up in one round ball
Hung upon a trespass of the universe
This round ball called Earth so unique
No wonder it boggles the mortal mind if answers you seek

That black cavern we know as the infinite space

Marked by stars set in place
Unique maybe it's a freak of Mother Nature

As God allows seasons to speak
Something had to happen to place us here
Far Far-Far away not so near
The miracles of life oh so dear
Inhabitants of this sphere
Plants insects reptiles mammals birds and human peer

Sundown and sunup mark the celebration
At the wonder of our life… it's a sensation
The very distance of this will
Narrow the human mind to something small
But maybe just maybe the truth
Of this tiny ball called Earth
Is that it's just the core of much more
Likely given birth layers upon layers
Like a diamond onion or tree's girth

If this be true the value of life should occur to you
We then become the center of something much bigger
Not just the bough or the out rigger
Tis the very wonder of life that
Some cosmic atom colliding created
Not to be apart or ever separated
Be it a big bang or a big God

This round ball we plod
Is all we've got
Unless we expand the plot
Destroy the planet's lot
With our collective disregard
For the deck and the card
Holding onto our sabbath's
Like a nun chasing her habits

With the pull of gravity
The White Hole the womb
Opens the door
To much more
The Black Hole the tomb
Closes the door
To evermore

Then we are dealing with the
Expanse of infinity
Merely the trip of humanity
After death to eternity
Believe what you will
Or disbelieve
The Wonders of it all
Makes us all believers

In the unbelievable

If only we had a crystal bible to show us what is coming; but that would require that we live by that glass ball. Are we willing to turn over our freedom to a vision not reality? Maybe the vision is reality. Is belief in a vision the same as reality? Most people would say no because circumstances beat us to the punch for creating our own reality. What if there were no risk and we had just won the lottery? Would life be that different than what we see in the that crystal ball?

We will never know if we aren't willing to take the risk that the ball is right and we must follow it. In my life, the ball is more than a dream it's reality if I believe I can achieve it and am willing to wait till it happens. Thus, it was an idea transformed to an ideology that evolved into a culture called America. We are still striving to perfect what the bible tells us to do before we break the crystal ball into pieces.

THE CRYSTAL BIBLE

Is the Bible our Crystal Ball

Look and ye shall find
Harken to the signs
Raise the shade
And pull the blinds

Open the future
Look between your life lines
Is it more than you can dare
Is destiny really there

Only to those aware and able
Look into my Crystal Bible

God said
To fate we thee wed

From the cradle to the bed
Unto a spirit once thought dead
So, believe you can
So, believe that in time

Sketched on your hand
Is within your life line
The answer's there
With habits and family to revere

Listen to the wings sweep
The spirits call us liable
As mortal's weep
To the crystal bible

What will the Crystal Bible hear
Before you do sleep
Away from the Devil's leer
You will recite prayers to keep

Through the crystal ball
God watches us fall
Then tells Jesus for us to repent
Before Heaven or Hell is sent

To our life line
And our horoscope sign
That heaven on earth we must find
The mortal and immortal must align

With the stars in my Crystal Bible
That are orbiting in my mind
For the brain has more atoms
Than stars in the sky

And they live on when we die

RESEARCH STATISTICS:

God is frequently invoked in American public life. Indeed, there is no shortage of instances of official acknowledgement of the divine, from the appearance of "In God We Trust" on our currency to the phrase "one nation under God" in the Pledge of Allegiance. To be sure, the vast majority of Americans still believe in God. But there are strong signs that many are less certain about this belief than in years past. And a small but growing minority of Americans say they do not believe in God at all. When asked if they believe in "God or a universal spirit" in the Pew Research Center's 2014 Religious Landscape Study, 89% of U.S. adults say yes – down from 92% from the previous religious landscape study in 2007. Nearly one-in-ten (9%) now say they don't believe in God, up from 5% in 2007. The changes have been even more substantial when it comes to certainty of belief in God: 63% of Americans are absolutely certain that God exists, down 8 percentage points from 2007, when 71% said yes without a doubt.

NO OTHER SALVATION

I have no other salvation
Than my own thoughts
When I think of good
I think of family and our relation

It's with this realization
That I prepare each day
With mental exercises
To sustain the creation

The creation of jubilation
Through a state of mind
Which won't know doubt
By believing in elation

That sheds guilt
Quells lies
Exposes truth
Expounds youth
Rewards faith

Dispels thoughts
Of never believing

Of negative feelings
Of never conceiving
Such utterances

But achieving
Respect for my acts
Belief in my facts
Relief from attacks

A savior of what my life lacks

THE DO'S:

1. State your beliefs in some written form so it can be reread and reread for entry into the subconscious.

2. Recite your beliefs daily in prayers, affirmations or absolutions. This is planting the seeds in your habit forming subconscious.

3. Make meditation as a part of your morning and/or evening routine as a priority since it will be there that your good subconscious habits form.

4. Whether it be God, or a variety of symbols of religion, the point is we believe in a higher power to affect our lives. Not always in a positive sort of way. It is the honoring and rewarding of faith that is important.

5. Making plans for a family and a happy life has to include the spiritual because we don't control the circumstances that arise. So, faith and belief that the end result will be positive keeps our habits in line with our need to be healthy, happy and God steering.

6. Pray with your spouse for holding love and trust together forever after.

THE RIGHT TO CHOOSE

Are we born equal or "to be equal"?
8 billion coming from the same place
In a journey going to the same place
At a different pace

When I think of my children
It brings the word Amazing to mind
On the other hand, I had no band of brothers
So, my grandchildren get the label Blossom

And Great Grandchildren Awesome
Making more from a bond of mothers and fathers

To me it's amazing what people do to themselves
While it's just as easy or hard
What people can do for themselves
Such is the enigma of the devil's dish
Or the Savior's wish

Why will anyone choose the devil's dish
Pleasure at the stake of self-respect
Health happiness and life itself
When they can have the Savior's wish
Peace for the sake of self-respect
Health happiness and eternal life to expect

It's amazing we all must choose
for or against ourselves
Some choose to do themselves in with sin
While others forgo habits and urges to fortify
Themselves with a loving family to supply
Amazing Blossoms with Awesome moves
For this is life itself ... to win or lose

We are born with freedom to " be" equal
Just because of the way we choose
And the Vows we don't abuse

THE DON'TS:

1. Don't say never or whatever.

2. Don't assume that everyone believes in a higher power.

3. Don't take anything for granted but faith grants you a way to dream.

4. Don't say can't unless you decide to do what you can't.

5. Don't regret what you haven't tried yet.

6. Don't be an agnostic or an atheist. What more can we say ... conceive, believe and receive blessings? Get good with your beliefs. I believe the spirit in all of us is the seed from Atom(s) and Eve (the eternal spirit).

ATOM AND EVE

Space is so permanent
Time is so fleeting
Space is so vast
Life is so finite

The continuum is so incomprehensible
While death is too sensible to be forever
For even the sky is made by the eyes of life
While our energy (atoms) never dies

(the American constitution establishes that
Americans are born free not to be equal ...
equality is a social liberty not spiritual)

Where do the dead butterflies go?
Who buries the ants and spiders?
Who takes the lives of the mammals?
Where do the dying leaves go?
They don't fly away

Until their atoms redeeming
Are released from their finite beings
Into infinite energy for later arrival
That's death and life incarnated for survival

As Man the atom of God
And Eve the mother of Nature
When it's time to fly
Father time is the sky

And the human spirit is infinity

But if you must, please consider the Wonders of the Universe. I have been doubtful in my younger years but life seems to confirm the higher power. In my five poetry books I use the spirit in all of us to state why the world, universe, cosmos and its inhabitants are Wonders to be believed and achieved in our daily prayers.

A DAILY PRAYER

Today I took life seriously
I looked it in the eye
It said -
"Bend your head and pray
Ask don't tell
Father of your needs"
"Give yourself unto others
And you shall overcome adversity"

So I pray - - -
In God's name I pledge
Respect to my parents
Love to my wife
Attention to my children
Interest to my business
Gratitude to my fellow men and women

Amen

THANK GOD FOREVER

Thank God for
The morning breeze
The rising sun
And kids to squeeze

Thank God for
The life we live
The memories we've had
And the time we give

Thank God for The sun at noon
The warmth it brings
And the rising moon

Thank God for
The love we feel
The friends we have
And things so real

Thank God for
The birds on wing
The eyes to see
And the words to sing

Thank God for
The children we have
The good times to come
And the urge to laugh

Thank God for
The trees and bees
The smallest creature
And the sense it frees

Thank God for
The lives gone by
The still waters
And the tears we cry
Thank God for

Everything
Yesterday today and no end
To what tomorrow will bring
Forever Amen

BELIEF IS

Oh ye of so little faith
Gather your mind together
To withstand the passing of time
Until truth is your tether

Tis like the smoke you smell
But the fire you don't see
Tis like the fog that fell
You see but can't flee

Tis like the mist you feel
But don't smell
Tis the belief which is real
For to have no relief is hell

Since we live in the purgatory
Of ourselves
Challenging with our own story
Belief that delves

To seek and we shall find
The subconscious mystery
Deemed habits of the mind
That become our history

Into the magic kingdom
That will unwind its sanction
The Eternal Secret from
The Law of Attraction

Belief is the fraction of
Good lifestyle habits +
Good health +
Good luck +
Happy wife =
Prosperous life

FOREVER, AMEN

In summation our advice is to practice what we preach which is … GET WHAT WE GOT, with sex, kids and roll-n-roll plus happy work with an active participation in some group activities (church, boy/girl scouts, political campaigns, dance clubs, theater, etc.) brings you happiness by getting good with our maker. Neither Shari or I have ever been drug users but enjoy a glass of wine and believe any chemical habit will turn into an obsession then an addiction preventing true happiness and one with our spirit.

The Rhoads family has been driven by goals, objectives and as soul mates have faith designed by those who are doing it. Self-help books and educational tape cassettes were the backbone of my becoming a believer in how to honor the ten commandments and take personal responsibility to consider what the other individual may be thinking and wanting. It's doing unto others as they would do unto themselves.

Our overall home and family life are belief based. We aren't ardent church goers but have brought practicing the ten commandments into our morals, relationships and life principles and style. Religion is definitely a positive in a world of negatives and must be a partner in our living longer.

Shari and I can agree that God, is our spirit that lives in our DNA (atoms), that never dies but lives eternal, as a partner, in every life form here on earth and hereafter.

GOD IS OUR PARTNER

Descartes Aristotle Socrates and Plato
Found a God through thought
We've read what they've said
And been taught likely than not
That none of us know
If judgment day is friend or foe

If you choose to rain and blow
Deciding on pleasure in spite of shame
Fending for desire of a misspent mind
There is little likelihood of love or fame
Only grief that won't let go
It's the self your foe

If you choose God as your partner
The inner self can come to peace
Proud to be a person not a sinner
Living every hour knowing hope will not cease
Then heaven on earth will bestow

Its-son Jesus
Not Satan its foe

VARIOUS WAYS TO GET GOOD WITH GOD:

Pray for the ideas you birth and the love you have on earth

Guy Talk (Jerry):

Prayer for me is the Lord's prayer and the daily affirmations I recite … my asking for guidance in my new venture and to seek God's blessing on those I love and those in need of my help.

Girl Talk (Shari):

Prayer for me is before I go to sleep and relates to our family more than anything.

Ask not what your life can do for you, ask what your life can do for others ... JFK interpreted

Guy Talk (Jerry):

A phrase from President Kennedy's acceptance Speech, "challenge seems appropriate when doing the right thing in spite of wrong results", pays dividends if your life requires trust and confidence in your abilities. There is a whole lot about Jesus in those trials and tribulations. "Do the Right Thing" was a movie that I always remember and have patterned my response to wrongs that need to be righted ... namely our nursing homes. We must correct our view of aging and how to make our aging healthy rather than chronic and miserable. All are chronicled in this book and my book "Restore Elder Pride", iUniverse 2012.

Girl Talk (Shari):

Jerry and I working together has been the most rewarding part of my life next to our family. It took a lot of faith to do the ventures we have taken on. Most of which emanate from how we lived our lives in general ... dream it do it. Find a path that you can be passionate about and pursue that dream.

Take the road less traveled (navigating life's hard road)

Guy Talk (Jerry):

In the book A Road Less Traveled Scott Pruitt takes us on a journey of decisions that affect our lives later. My take on it is, doing the opposite of those swimming downstream may get you where you want to be upstream. Taking the risk to prove it is courage. Or call it belief or faith or common sense ... regardless you may be alone on that hard road less traveled. I deal with the

Wonders of the World in my five poetry books focusing on belief and faith to navigate life's hard road.

Girl Talk (Shari):

I'm not as deep as Jerry when it comes to dreams, goals and why things happen. I mostly deal with life in more "what's now" terms. But together we make a great team in pursuing those dreams and overcome the what's happening now and it setbacks. And we do believe we will be together forever … love being eternal.

Our Maker will deal with us personally if faith is our belief

Guy Talk (Jerry):

I believe faith is our spirit directing us towards eternal life … what becomes of it is your lifestyle and habits. Try to link those together to have good health, marriage and eternal happiness. Another analogy is practice what you preach. Such as, I believe none of us will see God until we become the loving spirit in our next life. Our incarnate energy will live on forever in the Cosmos (Heaven) … the venue for the Keeper of the Stars (God). Most people professing to be Christians require that Jesus be the center of our life … we consecrate ourselves to him … however, I consecrate myself and my family to Jesus as the result of having loved and a lived by his principles thus life well lived for others. In other words, I live my life by his and God's 10 commandments.

Girl Talk (Shari):

Much of conventional religion seems too speculative to be real. But on the other hand, when I look back on our marriage and family there has to be a God in that formula. Therefore, I feel faith is the same as love … it's God given if you let it into your heart.

Meditation and prayer for relationships not spontaneous gain

Guy Talk (Jerry):

Dream on says Steven Tyler and his band Arrow smith … speak and ye shall be heard says Jesus … meditate and you will be content says Deepak Chopra … think on it pray on it have it says … conceive it believe it achieve it … all sayings to inspire us to get good with our maker. The spirit that lives in our DNA as our genome, our mind, our actions and most importantly in our marriage. Fame and fortune comes from mediation not medication. Shari and I have kept our eye on the goal of helping the elderly restore their functionality and return to their families using a home like environment and a loving culture to restore dignity to aging and the journey back to living not dying.

UNSAID PRAYERS

My wonder is … are my prayers heard
Or are they just my searching word
To ask for the absurd
And defend what has occurred

Truth likely isn't in the prayers we've said
But in the action to which we're wed
Many of these if you please
Aren't our own personal decrees

Many times we're pushed or led
By the prayers unsaid
For usually those things we are willed to do
Emanate from thought prayerfully new

It's those inane things that occur
Without forethought to prayerfully confer
Because actions with the proper power of thought
Shall abide by higher powers sought

But it's those things which seem to be the thing to do
Which is the tendency to sin by the hell in you
With our lack of resistance to temptation
That leads to the downfall of a lost generation

And the tracks merely demonstrate the tread
Of having fallen victim to prayers unsaid
To a forgiving God we've plead
Our fate when we are dead

Girl Talk (Shari):

I have trouble going to sleep. Kip knows that and just bought me a Zenergry by iHome system of 10 white noise music presets and 10 light therapy presets right next to my bed. Now I have my own meditation device pared up with my iPhone to put me to sleep. Thank God for technology.

Believe heaven and hell is right here and now

Guy Talk (Jerry):

Whatever I'm writing in this section is purely my opinion and I approve of the messages. I believe heaven and hell exist right here, right now as we create our own reality. But the transition of our spirit (atomic energy) in the form of atoms leaving our gravesite eternal life exists ... as does my love for Shari. Thus, as we are living together now, so we are living together forever after.

Girl Talk (Shari):

Jerry and I believe about the same when it comes to a distinct heaven and hell. It seems to me that heaven and hell are what we personally create in our lives. Pursuing it is a lifestyle and attaining it is a habit. If it's hell then change it ... if its heaven, enjoy it.

Make a pledge to living forever to please your maker

Guy Talk (Jerry):

This book is our pledge to each other to live forever as if we love eternally in the spirit of our genome that is God. We have the faith that what we have will continue in the inner space of the universe where God manages the atoms of the infinite energy we have in our bodies. We're creations of an atom (an emolliate inception) and an eve (an immaculate conception) that has evolved over a billion years that allows us to determine our own destiny. In my book "Americana 2084" I present a theorem that the Cosmos is the journey between the white holes as the womb through reality to the black holes as the tomb for our atoms in their cyclical trip back to incarnation in another world. Shari doesn't necessarily buy this theorem. Regardless, I believe this will eventually be proven scientifically so we can enjoy the journey to forever after.

Girl Talk (Shari):

I plan to be cremated and Jerry does not ... so I guess we will have to meet up again later. But for sure if it's possible we will either go together or be together forever.

Believe and it will occur if we practice the Laws of Attraction and Reaction

Guy Talk (Jerry):

In the best seller "The Secret" Rhonda Byrne makes the case for the spiritual law of attraction. Her interviews with those that are believers proved to most of her readers, including me, that conceiving an idea, eventually results in achieving and receiving the vision, The law of attraction is proven to me by my seeing Shari standing there in 1953 ... she could not feel me seeing her, I could not touch her ignoring me, but four years later we were having our first kiss at the Des Moines Drive-in and forever began.

Then the Law of Reaction set in when we got married and had to deal with each other's preconceived habits and desires ... having to accommodate the give and take of a partnership. The benefit of just reacting to circumstances and happenstance is there is no risk taking ... just the mundane acceptance of worry, unhappiness, weight gains, depression, chronic illness, divorce, fear, job loss, chemical use and visits to the physician, psychiatrist and finally the coroner. Fortunately, Shari and I are risk takers and seem to attract just the opposite results.

Girl Talk (Shari):

Jerry wears out this story of him seeing me and picking me for his wife when I was in seventh grade and he in eighth. What I remember is my new friend in Junior High pointed Jerry out and it took him forever to ask for a date ... then when he did it wasn't clicking and it took another two years for him to ask again. Give him credit he is persistent and attractive but shy. That's the romanticist in him that I love. Plus he took my hand that Halloween night, October 31 1956, when we were spooked at the haunted house, never to let go till fate do us part.

Include spirituality in our quality of life

Guy Talk (Jerry):

In my poetry books I use the reference to our physical spirit and our mental spirit as being eternal extended by our love. So, quality of life for me is the thoughts and feelings for others that contributes to my quality of relationships with my wife, family and friends.

Girl Talk (Shari):

Jerry is more inclined to have contact with the spiritual aspect of thought through his writings and mine is more about our family and daily obstacles to our security. Then quality is dictated by having a purpose and consistent love for each other.

Say the Lord's Prayer every day or night … it never gets old

Guy and Girl Talk (Jerry and Shari):

The Lord's prayer is said by 2 billion people every day so there is a spiritual belief in our world of doubt. Getting right with our maker (or whatever term your religion uses) is as simple as living by the Lord's Prayer and the Ten Commandments. These are our standards for living, working and staying together forever:

1. You shall have no other gods before Me.
2. You shall make no idols.
3. You shall not take the name of the Lord your God in vain.
4. Keep the Sabbath day holy.
5. Honor your father and your mother.
6. You shall not murder.
7. You shall not commit adultery.
8. You shall not steal.
9. You shall not bear false witness against your neighbor.
10. You shall not covet another more than your, spouse, father or mother.

Girl Talk (Shari):

Besides our twelve self-health wedding vows and lifestyle habits for living longer, the ten commandments have always been my ten rules to live by, no matter your religious affiliation … these ten commandments fit everyone and have certainly served me well. I do find myself silently praying many times either thanking God for something good that happened or asking for something good to happen.

My family went to Methodist church after we moved to Indianola. Before that we lived on a farm and went to a little country church. When we moved to Scranton, Iowa we went to the Methodist church. Iowa farmers are the most dedicated and God fearing due to their profession ... being dependent on weather and crops and the animal world. My dad has always believed in the power of belief in himself and his ability to accomplish anything. He had multiple talents for making children's toys to building a house for us to live in. My mother was a devout church goer in her younger years and had the bubbliest personality ever. She was a maker of dolls for us girls and taught her mothering skills. Her favorite time at the assisted living facility where she lived in after my dad's death was bible study and reading the bible.

Jerry and I grew up in Indianola Iowa that was called God's little Acre since drinking and smoking were banned until the 1950's. Since we were in high school in that era, we are influenced by those standards even today. We don't smoke and only drink a glass of wine with our meals or when we are dancing. Our children and their families have the same standards and self-health habits.

When we moved to Chicago, we attended a variety of Methodist churches in the suburbs we lived in. Mount Prospect, Park Ridge, Addison, Niles and then Springfield, Illinois 1969 to 1973. Then it was Morton, Illinois from 1974 to 1984 and in 1985 we returned to the Chicago area and lived in Hoffman Estates, Schaumburg, Lake Zurich and now Hawthorn Woods. For a 3½ year period (2012 to 2015) we lived in Muscatine, Iowa across from our nursing home.

Jerry and I are writing books together now. He just finished his first novel with my editing. It's about the eternal spirit of humanity being, the infinite spirit forever. Though it's about George Orwell's dystopian world not happening until 2184, most of it is about the evolution and revolution of the human spirit that leads to the cleansing of the Earth of evil only to evolve into another totalitarian government of the Few over the Many. Instead of Orwell's predicted Oceania it is Jerry Rhoads' vision of Americania.in his novel Americana, published by Page Publishing, 2018.

Guy Talk (Jerry):

My parents weren't churchgoers but wanted my sister Kay and I to attend the Baptist Church. After being baptized there I followed the leaders, when all my friends started going to the Methodist Church. Shari was one of them so I too went there. And a few years later we were married there. Though we have been church goers in the past we now have a spiritual family that believes in the sanctity of individual beliefs practiced not preached. Following are those principles and practices.

In 1977, I didn't believe in myself let alone God and the power of belief. But I was forced to hang onto something. My job was gone, my career shattered, my aspirations in pieces before me. I turned to a discipline of thought that are still pulling me up to heights I've never known before. Just one year into depression I reworked my thoughts. The following poem says it best:

IN THE BEGINNING

In the beginning I was born
In the end I will be reborn
Like a new sun
Each morn

Living each day hereafter
Giving hard work
With dedication and laughter
For I shall be free

To be what I want
To be
Free to create
Free to activate

The true pieces of happiness
365 times a year
Made piece by peace
With the past gone forever

Through each new endeavor
Cast with no regrets
Even as life may cease
For the sun never sets

On a spirit incarnated in peace

I'm writing the thoughts I've had at the beginning of each day which carried me through to a Happy Rhoads lifestyle throughout the year. I now believe in myself, in God, in the attainment of all my goals. I'm convinced anyone who can conceive a thought in which they can believe, shall believe in themselves, in God (the personification of belief) and shall achieve their own form of success. For, success is the attainment of what a person can conceive and believe in until it becomes a reality. It's the attainment of peace; peace in knowing you're whole, not pieces of a puzzle with missing pieces.

I believe you can find the same peace by reading some of my daily affirmations at the end of the chapters (which I used as prayers), to rebuild your self-image, your confidence and your belief in values which can't fail. It came to pass that I realized it's up to me to follow the ten commandments and the three acts of God given choices:

- Kindness
- Giving
- Loving

IT CAME TO PASS

Desire can't be
Held in your hand
Like a rose

Intensity isn't
Something you
Find in a field of clover

Humility doesn't
Appear as easily
As a smile

Immortality won't be
Earned without
Desire intensity and humility

For the past is written
And the future is made
As the resting place of
All mortal men and women

This trip is mapped
Not by those that accept
Little and want no more
But by the soul and amore'

Of great men and women that assume
The pathfinder's role

A role of inspired faith to exhume
Leadership leaving us whole

With followers following
The weaker spirits
Who instinctively question
Their own existence

So, it came to pass
With the leaders' insistence
To be the makers of history
And legends in life's mystery

By getting right with our maker
The eternal undertaker

At the end of the book are listed the poetry books that I have written. My first poem was written in eight-grade about the Russian Premier Georgy Malenkov. For a period of twenty years I never wrote another. Then in 1972 I bought a 35-millimeter camera and became obsessed with writing about my favorite photographs. These were mostly on the back of the pictures I enlarged and farmed for our home. Over the years, I would write a poem for my children and wife on their birthdays … never keeping them for publication. It wasn't until 1977, when I started my own CPA firm, that I started to dictate into a hand-held tape recorder, poems, while traveling to our nursing home clients. Then, when returning from the road, I would have my secretary Jane Jenson type them on stationary for keeping in my three ring binders for later publication.

It took about 7 years of traveling about, a half-million miles, by car to accumulate 2,500 type written poems that were to make up the Wonders of the World five book anthem to America and its people. Of course, there are 562 references to God and more to Jesus so I have to confess I'm religious and spiritual to excess (as you may have guessed by the poems in this book). Finally, in 2009 I decided to go through the 12 three ring binders and pick and choose and edit those for my first book The Eighth Wonder of the World, then the ninth, the tenth, the eleventh and finally the twelfth Wonders of the World emerged from this Law of Attraction to our maker.

After some 3,000 pages and 320,000 words, all edited and blessed by Shari, using poetry as the median, I never thought of it as my life's work, but proof of a wife's love and commitment that evolved into this co-biography of "Jerry Met Shari" to live out our eternal life together.

JERRY MET SHARI (get what we got)

We don't always pray together to stay together but to live forever we must make love forever ... it's our life's mission and we have had it sense hello: it's this attraction to each other's body, soul, goals, interests, values, feelings, passions, principles, habits, lifestyle, culminating in the DNA Fountain of Us. That's what we got, that you can get if that's what you want ... God's willing For you to be healthy, happy and prosperous.

CAN IT BE

I first saw her in 1951
When we were in Junior High
She moved away in 1952
And returned in 1953...can it be

I met her on the square in Indianola
When Sam my best friend, stopped
She and Rosie...can it be
Sam slept over that night in '53

With her picture in his wallet
And as he slept I removed it...can it be
She became my soul mate, my heart, my future
My only love in '53...but not for she

In 1955 I asked her out and we didn't click
She wasn't that interested in me
But then in 1957 when I was a senior
And she a junior something happened...was it to be

It was Halloween when Nancy,
Her other best friend and she left the Youth Center with me
To look up a haunted house in and around Pleasantville...
After getting spooked she took my hand and looked at me in a way
That said it's you and me...more than in '53...can it be

It was love for her and me from then on...
1957, graduation then college for me, 1958,
Her graduation, breaking-up for 180 days,
Then with a ring for she and me,
Discovering, in 1959 we were to be we forever after

CAN IT BE

Can it be we are meant to find that one person and have it last forever and we just happened to find it earlier than most? 4 great children, 12 outstanding grandchildren, 4 great grandsons, 60 years of marriage…can it be we were a product of Nancy and the haunted house or was it destined to be…

She is the "M" in me can it be that "M" is for she…can it be we is the sum of the family tree…she me and we…can it be that life finds true love if we let it be … love finds us if we take an I and add U to form I owe U for my being…can it be that divine is in we not me, forever holding us as one, never done…can it be?

Looking back to then is no different as then now…it's just more time to appreciate how we can be in this place after 60+ years of marriage … can it be? Can it be that on November 27, 2019 that you and I get younger every day because we are, we not just me. And I love you more each day…your IOU Jerry Lee … can it be since '51 or '53?

SELF-EVALUATION

After reading this chapter take the following Self=Health quiz:

	Birth Age	Real Age	YES	NO
Beginning Real Age score	____	____	<u>YES</u>	<u>NO</u>
1. Are you thinking more about your spiritual being?			____	____
2. Do you now feel better towards your thinking about God?			____	____
3. Do you feel like letting your beliefs take a different track?			____	____
4. Does your day start with a prayer about habit changes?			____	____
5. Has your real age calculator improved to reflect better habits?			____	____
6. Later rate your progress … 1 being low and 10 being the best.			____	____

Your rating and answers are your confession booth for judging for yourself where you are with your commitment to change your habits and lifestyle at this point of your journey. Can it be that this will result in the new me … it did for me.

AFFIRMATIONS

I hope that you'll pray before you wish for peace
And don't get either

***

Give me belief or give me death
What else is worth my last breath

***

Faith that be with you
Is more than doubt scaring you

***

Give your children roots and wings
Don't wed them to money and things

***

He who waits for a better life to come
Is patience willing himself to become

***

Listen and learn that faith cares
By showing others that love only exists in pairs

***

Life is profound competition
Man versus Himself … while Jesus saves Him from self

Last Chapter and Verse
LOVE NOW AND LIVE FOREVER AFTER

The question we always get is "can you guarantee our needed results"? Our answer is "if you can guarantee you need the results and make the effort you'll eventually see and have the results you truly want; despite resistance to changing your lifestyle habits, since luck is effort meeting opportunity. We can guarantee you that the DNA Fountain of You is there for you to pursue and capture; and if you're lucky to have found it, then and only then will you know if you and your mate can live as one soul together forever after, till fate do you part. Amen.

LIFE IS A GAMBLE

Is lotto a wing
Or a prayer
No matter how I pray
It's better to get my pay

Living in the past
Dwells on regrets
Living in the future
Dwells on mind sets

Living in the now
Dwells on outlets

Living just plain knowing how
Needs to blend all three mind sets

If you're going to be happy
Yes Siree
Give it all your money
For no bets give birth to regrets

And flexible mind sets
With plenty of outlets
Pursed without frets
Is living for whatever life gets

Because winning is placing your bets
And losing is living with past regrets
So gamble as you may lose as you may
But what you'll gamble is what life will pay

As betting is taking a chance
Ignoring circumstance
While exploring happenstance
As the pot at the end of the rain dance

Called romance

RESISTANCE TO CHANGE

We all innately suffer from resisting the very changes that will make life happy, healthy and prosperous ... why because they are habits that are controlled by our subconscious mind at work ... Dr. Phil

Root cause analysis of the proverbial bad habit is psychological and counter intuitive since acknowledging the cause is convenience while change of the cause is inconvenience. There lies the law of reaction ... we react before we act and we act out our habits. The Earlier you become the inconvenient truth the sooner you will learn a better convenient habit. Meditation and Affirmations are the vitamins for habit change. Drugs are an enabler not a cure for destructive habits ... Jerry Rhoads

Science advances one funeral at a time ... Max Planck Conventional wisdom is invariably out of date. Because the time it takes to become conventional wisdom to become what everyone believes to be true the world has moved on. Conventional wisdom is a remnant of the past. Michael Crichton, Next.

Given how often society claims that aging and divorce are neither preventable or reversible Shari and I won't be surprised if our publisher, editors and readers are skeptical of why our personal success will influence others to change their lifestyle habits and successfully live together younger-stronger and longer. Since the proof is in our life how can we be so confident that it will work for others ...

When I wrote my first self-health book "Never Too Old to Live", I was managing three nursing homes full of skeptics who accepted conventional knowledge that age is the determent of longevity of life. As a result, most if not all, suffered from bad life altering habits and ended up in their bad dream, a smelly nursing home. I ask whose fault is that? I'm not talking about someone unfortunate to be a victim of a car wreck or a congenital defect at birth. I'm talking about the prevalent cause of incarceration in a nursing home; chronic diseases brought on by poor habits (given death panels by the very physicians who prescribe pills for cure and living wills for ending a damaged body, brain and spirit) as their epitaph.

All generally caused by the disabling of a body, mind and spirit by and one of the 12 lifestyle vows/habits we've proposed as being the way to prevent or reverse accelerated aging. Take the road less traveled and embrace change ... resist temptation, deprivation, submission to the subconscious violation of our health happiness and longer stronger years. The skeptics of change and depending on conventional knowledge are invariably thinking:

- Marriage is meant to challenge permanence
- Aging is set by circumstances or happenstance
- Habits are an uncontrollable mechanism in our bodies
- You and Shari are different genetically
- You aren't an MD, PhD, therapist or exercise Guru so how do I know it will work
- I've tried most of this and have not improved
- What does a nursing home have to do with me
- All of these folks generally consider aging and marriage as a physical event rather than a mental event.
- "I'm getting old because that is inevitable"
- "I can't function as well anymore"

- "My body is breaking down"
- "My memory is going"
- "My parents died early"
- "My children feel we need to give up driving"
- "Why don't you sell your belongings and move to assisted living"
- "I'm over 55 and a member of AARP and draw social security ... that's old"
- "Aging isn't reversible and chronic disease isn't preventable"
- "Aging can't be slowed down ... it is set by my biorhythm"
- "Divorces aren't usually reversable and most not preventable and never last 60 years anymore"

If you fit this mold you will age at a faster pace than Shari and I have and never stay married for 60 years, without adhering to similar marriage vows and lifestyle habits. Per Dr. Bredesen's author of The End of Alzheimer (The First Program to Prevent and Reverse Cognitive Decline) "society has become more complacent in basic exercise, nutrition and sleep patterns, as a result, most of us now die from chronic, complex illnesses such as cancer, cardiovascular disease, and neurological disorders. Unfortunately, we tried to solve the problem of chronic illness in the same way we solved the problem of acute illness with a single pill or monotherapy. This is like using your checkers strategy in a chess match."

Will our 12 Rhoads self-health vows/habits for aging prevent chronic and/ or acute illnesses. According to Dr. Bredesen's genetic ReCODE multi discipline approach (reversing cognitive decline) 21st century medicine should be treating the cause of the habit not the source of the habit. Confucius says: "do it or die trying" and live longer, stronger and more youthful forever more. Our personal success in the nursing home business as published in my books is as follows:

Proposing a new publishing genre called Self=Health as a Self-science and a new discipline that studies the causes of aging of one's own body and senses and how to slow the process in a happy, healthy and prosperous lifestyle. Shari and I are the empirical evidence with our lifestyle habits being the physical miracle because of our commitment to cleanliness, honesty, selflessness, loyalty, affection for people, sensitivity or those in need covering all of the 12 Rhoads self-health vows/habits for aging longer, stronger and youthful (we personify a proven DNA Fountain of You).

MY FOUNTAIN OF YOU(TH)

Shari
Mother of NATURE
A Fountain of Youth
Where age is an open door
To evermore

Time a lovely example
Of life being ample
For hope in the shrouds
Among the higher clouds
Which stunned the crowds

Flashing a smile
And all the while
Being sweet with hospitality discreet
Helping us all to our feet
Energy burning family yearning
Never concerned about what she's earning

Just working long and hard
Treating hurts before our children scarred
Always there if needed
Nothing ever exceeded
Her ability to cope
Even on a downhill slope

Because she always comes up
Like the Fountain of Youth is to erupt
Upon us all if we heard the same call
Before she can catch our fall
Into an older stage
With little to do with age

But more with attitude
Loving family life with gratitude
In a life where thoughts are things
And happiness is what DNA brings

For Sharon Kay at any age
Is an open door
To much-much more

Then most will ever restore

She's a lovely example
Of youth the fountain of time
With finite life being ample

Thank God this Fountain is mine

In Dr. Bredesen's book he proposes "targeting a symptom that appears after a disease has taken hold, as most conventional methods do, is very different from attacking the root cause of a disease at the cellular level. In other words, we want to get to the cause of decline, fixing any imbalances before it becomes irreversible. That's what we propose. We want to address as many of the 12 self-health habits as possible, not just one at a time, since each of the 12 affect the other 11. Our holistic approach of replacement of harmful habits with our self-health habits impacts the overall reversal of premature aging. We have seen in our lives that as we preserve your physical and mental health, we are preventing destructive illnesses that accelerate and exacerbate advanced aging.

We have chosen the REAL AGE calculation as the analytical method (self-scientific based on current self-health habits) for measuring your personal habit immune system for preserving your health and preventing chronic illness. By taking one chapter at a time then recalculating your REAL AGE gives you the will power to continue with each succeeding chapter. Rereading chapters reinforces your establishing the routine and experiencing the rewards. Craving the success becomes the reason to continue the program.

How and why did we choose only 12 marriage vows and lifestyle habits to build our "real age"? They are really 12 building blocks to our eternal love of life. As we do with the 12 Rhoads self-health habits, Dr. Bredesen maps out the 12 root causes of cognitive decline into end stage Alzheimer's and solutions with his ReCode system. We reiterate as fit for what we got:

1) Diet, 2) nutrition, 3) regular exercise, 4) new sleep patterns, 5) reduce stress-meditation, 6) brain training, 7) Resolve cellular inflammation, 8) healing the gut with biotics, 9) hormonal imbalance, 10) metal homeostasis using supplements, 11) detoxification, 12) food allergies

His amazing success (700 to 800 cases of reversing Alzheimer's) has changed the conventional one pill approach for analyzing and treating other chronic diseases. We recommend you read his book in conjunction with ours if you are having symptoms of cognitive and physical decline.

In Girl Talk she Shari gives advice on the nonphysical ways of thinking young. She is promoting appearance, clothing, makeup, positive self-image, smile, perfume, music tastes, etc. My examples are more mental and physical conditioning that promotes muscularity, endurance, positive thinking, never give up attitude and reinforcement conditioning. Can our success be replicated by following our regimented lifestyle for aging? Yes, if you think you can. Our children are utilizing it to have better lives for themselves and their families. More globally, the proof is in the patients we had in our three nursing homes; they are real examples of reversing chronic disease and restoring their functioning so many could return to their homes or with their families. They suffered from dementia, Alzheimer's, chronic diseases, acute illnesses, and we utilized the 12 Rhoads self-health habits in our Caregiver Management System, for over forty years, restoring functionality and instilling hope in thousands of our patients who were able to slow down the aging processes and reverse some of the damage done by previous habits and lifestyle and return to their families.

Those who could not be discharged improved their quality of life, even though we restored some functionality and slowed down the dying process, they were not able to leave. Using restorative therapy, socialization activities along with family involvement we were able to discharge more than 43,500 cases.

We took on troubled nursing homes as consultants and owners and repaired and replaced disabled facilities and warehouses for the forgotten sector of our aging population and restored their hope and quality of life. This book "Never Too Old to Live" and my others "Remedy Eldercide", "Restore Elderpride", "The Boomers Are Coming", "America in the Rezone", "Never Too Old to Live", "Failing Government Taketh Away", The Monopsony Game" and "Life Styles" present the way we did it in spite of the regulators who wanted us out of their purgatory and Gestapo system.

I rest my case for the skeptics, including noncaring lawmakers, politicians and the traditional medical community that has a different agenda and claim that nursing homes and long-term care can't be set up to restore and discharge their chronically ill patients. We proved otherwise. Not only is this what we need to do for the Baby Boomers so they don't die early and painfully, we need to reduce the cost of aging as Medicare and Medicaid will not be able to treat those 77 million aging all at once.

In our government's current health care programs, there is no mention of health preservation and only lip service to prevention. As we presented in the introduction most self-health books about health and wellness are written by physicians, psychologists, Harvard PhD's, and/or therapists who 1) focus on one cause for one problem, 2) Offer one type of solution, 3) Don't focus on how marriage affects aging 4) Don't fully understand the senior audience. And more importantly, don't have proven results for preserving overall health and preventing chronic diseases … nor do they usually live, as we do, simple doable solutions. Following is our prescription for how to live forever after …

LIVE FOREVER YOUNG

Life has no age
It only has you

Love has no limit
It only has us

Feelings have no time
They only show us the way

Memories have no reason
They only pass us by

Birthdays have no certainty
They just count for today

Habits are our enduring
Legacy for living younger longer and stronger

Surely no one lives forever
But you've just met Jerry and Shari

We Believe our spirit lives on
Together, forever young
For love is eternal

As our Marriage Vows and Lifestyle Habits are its Kernel

SUMMATION OF GIRL TALK (SHARI):

Jerry and I believe we will transcend death and be together forever after. To this we Vow

In love and happiness
Till forever after is in my heart
And death as our witness
Shall never do us part

Surely no one lives forever
But as the rose dies in the winter
And rises again in the spring
Together with this wedding ring

We vow that forever after our soul and spirit live on
To another dawn

I like being with Jerry. We have fun with each other and relish the healthy days we have left. Since high school we have been together almost constantly.

We've been in business together for almost 40 years. Most of it related to aging Americans. Jerry has always had an affinity for older people that needed help. He tells the story about living on 405 West First in Indianola Iowa across the street from an old folk's home run by a neighbor. Every day delivering the Des Moines Register he passed by this house saying hello to the old folks rocking in their designated chairs on the front porch.

It stuck with him that life at that stage should be more than a rocking chair on the porch. Ironically, we got caught in the nursing home business trying to prevent this from being the lifestyle of our parents and eventually the "Baby Boomers". We succeeded in restoring over 43,500 patients in nursing homes back to the community but were never able to make the change stick across America. We still have that goal with this book and Jerry's others pertaining to health care in America. I also have to say fortunately for me, my partner and the love of my life, is a strong, determined, dedicated to me, loving and family oriented man who has given me more than I could have ever imagined. He has always looked ahead with hope and plans for the future. I hope this book will inspire you too and make the most of your health and happiness. Shari.

SUMMATION OF GUY TALK (JERRY):

Shari and I believe we will transcend death and be together forever after. To this we Vow

In love and happiness
Till forever after is in my heart
And death as our witness
Shall never do us part

Surely no one lives forever
But as the rose dies in the winter
And rises again in the spring
Together with this wedding ring

We vow that forever after our soul and spirit live on
To another dawn

Shari is my inspiration to stay as young as possible. Scientists call it transcending the human genome. She comes from great stock as I have pointed out. It is somewhat unbelievable that she can stay the same after all these years. She literally doesn't visually or physically age the way most women do. This is the very essence of the Self-Health program. Kick old bad habits and embrace new good habits. As her husband, we fit together like birds and a feather because I've always been into self-health. From the day, I was exposed to athletics I have been obsessed with being healthy in physical and mental shape. We do have differences but very few, other than gender and personality. The one's that we share and practice daily are the 12 healthy and happy marital vows and lifestyle habits for living and loving each other forever after.

WINNERS VERSUS LOSERS

Does the positive
Make a negative
Into a winning hand
And a successful wedding band

Optimists sometimes lose
Pessimists always lose
Optimists sometimes win
Pessimists never win

Finding a way is winning
Running away is losing
Scaling the obstacles for
Victory is so sweet

Skirting the obstacle is defeat

Take your best shot
Give it all you've got
Cause all you got to lose
Is the failure to choose

Right there and then
Is the time to work till you win
Persistence is the fuel
Of where you've been

Are your grades in school
Where you're going or happenstance
What you're knowing is cool
Experience is from taking a chance

Is fantasy more than romance
Where winners are losers in disguise
And failure is the culture of being wise
While gaining life's first prize

Love happiness health and blue skies

PROFILE OF A GRADUATE OF OUR DNA REAL AGE MAKEOVER

In closing we have quantified and practiced 12 vows/habits for changing life styles as we 300 plus million Americans age. The graduates to a Real Age profile, less than their birth age, will always be thinking, as they age, about increasing longevity by looking and feeling younger than their peers. Feeling that they are in control of their fate. Really feel good about their appearance. Have dreams coming true due to realistic goals and a purpose. Happy about the present and future. Able to let their hair down and have fun. Eat and sleep with satisfaction and healthy results. Exercise is a daily habit that must be done (otherwise guilt sends you to the treadmill). Sociable without a drink or a cigarette. Finding that great sex often, is for older people. Treat giving as a necessary expenditure even when you can't afford what you now owe. Use a daily affirmation or prayer to give thanks for your loved ones, family and future to create a positive subconscious, ageless mind.

Any one of these successes, graduates you to a happier, healthier and more prosperous lifestyle. Shari and I believe this makeover is necessary for most Americans due to stress, financial problems, marital problems, aging process, dementia and other chronic diseases of the body and the mind. We all can practice our own Self-Health agenda at home or at play or at work. (Age is the first three letters in agenda and agenda means life style habits). Modern medicine and the cost of health care and divorce in the US is the biggest cost of living. So, we all must be concerned and involved in our own health and fitness costs. We do believe Self-Health care will shift the paradigm from institutional care to holistic Self-Health care for prevention of chronic health problems and preservation of the human genome to extend life expectancy in a habitual and joyful lifestyle.

Of course, we all, from time to time, continue to have these feelings of inadequacy. Why, because our feelings aren't under our control ... or are they? This is the psychological obstacle to sustaining our marriage and better habits. Ironically, the new profile you have built is nothing more than your current habits planted there in your subconscious by your conditioning. It's now focused on improving your positive thinking which demands rereading certain chapters in this book for retention and always recalculating your Real Age versus your birth age. (I have reread all of my self-help books numerous times to keep positive … we hope you do the same with our book. As our maker tells in the scriptures "to those that find the path to a better self shall be the betterment of their life towards others and your husband or wife".

Success At Last

What is Success
Is it the man who climbs the highest mountain?
Or the woman who swims the widest sea
Or is it the team that somehow wins
Or the person who stands amid fame and fortune
Or is it possible, it's you or me
Let's take a look and see

Are you good at what you do
So you take pride in living
Are you bright instead of blue
And do you get joy from giving

Are you an open book
With passages to be read
Inviting a passerby's look
Even when you're dead

Will you children be proud to say
"That's my mom and dad,
They helped put me on my way
And taught me good from bad"

If you can honestly say, these things
I feel you certainly confess
That what your life brings
Is a bountiful success

At Last

And to Forever Last

We hope, we have been able to assist you and yours to strive for being a better Fountain of living and loving together younger, stronger, longer with happiness as your ageless epitaph. Living Forever After is a long time but so is dying too early.

Signed: Shari and Jerry Rhoads

Together forever and hereafter

Our love and souls are eternal

AUTHORS' BIO AND OTHER TITLES

The authors were born in Iowa have been married 60 years and at the age of 80 now live in Chicago, Illinois. They have four grown and married children, twelve grandchildren and four great grandsons and four step great granddaughters.

Jerry Rhoads has had over 50 years' experience in health care. He is a CPA and a licensed nursing home administrator. He has owned an accounting firm, a consulting business and a software business servicing long term care and skilled nursing homes. He, Shari and their son Kip also have owned three nursing homes and managed four others during his 37 years specializing in nursing home operations and Government regulations concerning Medicare and Medicaid. Shari Rhoads is a trained cosmetologist, nursing home owner. administrator and business partner with Jerry and their son Kip Rhoads a, computer expert, for thirty years.

ARE THE AUTHORS QUALIFIED TO WRITE ABOUT HEALTH, HAPPINESS AND ITS IMPACT ON AGING?

In my first Self=Health book a reviewer questioned my credentials for writing about physical and mental fitness since I'm not a physician, therapist or nutritionist. Well I questioned a reviewer's credibility unless they are physically and mentally fit. Because my credentials are: I'm physically and mentally fit due to the Rhoads lifestyle and exercise program. That is the Self=Health program. Most doctors, therapists, nutritionists and book reviewers can benefit from practicing my experienced results.

Shari and I were both licensed health care administrators of one of our three nursing homes. She is also the editor and coauthor of this book, and we both are the ultimate physical and social example of what's possible following the 12 vows/habits in this book.

OTHER BOOKS WRITTEN BY THE AUTHOR(S)

www.jerryrhoadsauthor.com

All poems in this book were written by Jerry and pictures either taken by Jerry or belong to he and Shari.

- Life Styles (Of the Healthy, Happy and Prosperous) (a self=health book)
- The Boomers Are Coming (a self=health book)
- Never Too Old to Live (a self=health book)
- America in the Red Zone (a self=health book)
- Restore Elder Pride (a self=health book)
- Remedy Eldercide (a self=health book)
- The Monopsony Game (an economic analysis)
- Failing Government Taketh Away (a political analysis)
- American Enterprise Manifesto (a government analysis)
- Basic Accounting and Budgeting for Long Term Care Facilities
- Americana 1984 2084 2184 (a novel remembering George Orwell)
- Mancology (the science of managing human value)
- Cost Accounting for Long term care facilities
- The Eighth Wonder of the World (first Wonders poetry book)
- The Ninth Wonder of the World (second Wonders poetry book)
- The Tenth Wonder of the world (third Wonders poetry book)
- The Eleventh Wonder of the world (fourth Wonders poetry book)
- The Twelfth Wonder of the World (fifth and final of the Wonder series)

Authors' note: If you have read this far hopefully, you're on your way to success with saving your marriage by changing some of your selfish or bad habits to better ones. This may be our last chance to advise you to read it one more time and then another if necessary, to believe that we all live on forever after together … so why not make the trip fun, healthy and continuing to be with your soul mate. Infinity, in my opinion is the human spirit that never dies … it just fades into the next continuum. Shari, on the other hand is still feeling that we seem to be on this trip forever together.

If you need further consultation or coaching, we are available at jerry.l.rhoad@gmail.com or www.lifestylesforaging.com to answer questions or provide tools and advice for making the 12 steps work for you. The only limitation is we aren't marriage counselors, physicians, therapists or ministers. However,

SHARI AND I ARE BEST FRIENDS AND LOVERS

Lovers can be best friends
Can best friends be lovers
I thought when I looked at you
You were my best girlfriend

The more I looked at you
The more courtship came through
Friends and lovers are they two
Or are they just someone I knew

Or can they be the same
And you said yes
When I asked you for your hand
I'd be your lover I guess

But there was no guarantee
You would be my friend
Not till time could tell us
What we mean together until the end

We held each other close
We knew what need could mean
That we needed one another
To us there was no in between

And our infatuation grew stronger
As we stayed together longer and longer
We needed more than each other
For the warmth of our lifetime affair

Affection needed to be much more
Much more than just the sexual pair
We needed to be able to talk and be aware
To walk and be together and really care

And this I guess you'd call friendship
Wanting to be together
But not just for the embrace
That could come in any case

And you needed somebody to talk to
Someone who wasn't impatient
And forgot to caress you
You needed someone to lean on

Someone to confide in
And pick you up when you're down
This is the friendship
That had to be found

If I were to be your last
While time past so fast
Leaving only bits and pieces
Left behind as life ceases

Unless we're friends
As well as lovers
Giving support versus
Just pulling down the covers

Friends must become lovers
Yes we found we could be
Lovers and friends in matrimony
So after 60 years of wiping away

Our fears with our kids on the way
I believe being best friends and married is the best
As our parents, would have guessed
Happy Anniversary

Of Friends and Lovers Forever

AND HEREAFTER

After the sun sets
After the love making
After the job is done
After the prayer is answered
What is Hereafter

Hereafter the sun still sets
There is still a love maker
The work is still never done
The prayer is the setting sun
So what holds hope

Hope is not tomorrow
Why would yesterday matter
Unless todays have meaning
I must have hope for the sun to rise
For my job and life likewise

A lover of you and my work
As prayers get replies
"Be my love that never dies
For now, forever and hereafter"

Goodbye on your journey to happy town

CPSIA information can be obtained
at www.ICGtesting.com
Printed in the USA
BVHW071014100521
606942BV00002B/94